THE FIGHT OF THEIR LIVES

A 21st Century Primer on World War II

ANDY KUTLER

Black Rose Writing | Texas

©2024 by Andy Kutler
All rights reserved. No part of this book may be reproduced, stored in a retrieval system or transmitted in any form or by any means without the prior written permission of the publishers, except by a reviewer who may quote brief passages in a review to be printed in a newspaper, magazine or journal.

The author grants the final approval for this literary material.

First printing

This is a work of fiction. Names, characters, businesses, places, events, and incidents are either the products of the author's imagination or used in a fictitious manner. Any resemblance to actual persons, living or dead, or actual events is purely coincidental.

ISBN: 978-1-68513-424-2 (Paperback); 978-1-68513-479-2 (Hardcover)
LIBRARY OF CONGRESS CONTROL NUMBER: 2024934621
PUBLISHED BY BLACK ROSE WRITING
www.blackrosewriting.com

Printed in the United States of America
Suggested Retail Price (SRP) $24.95 (Paperback); $29.95 (Hardcover)

The Fight of Their Lives is printed in Book Antiqua

*As a planet-friendly publisher, Black Rose Writing does its best to eliminate unnecessary waste to reduce paper usage and energy costs, while never compromising the reading experience. As a result, the final word count vs. page count may not meet common expectations.

A NOTE TO READERS

Sometime around my twelfth birthday, my father, a professor of Constitutional history at the University of Wisconsin, handed me an encyclopedia of the Second World War. For years, I immersed myself in those pages, enthralled by infinite tales of Omaha Beach, the USS *Arizona*, B-17 *Flying Fortresses*, and so much more. The book was a wonderful, alphabetized compilation of virtually every aspect of the war, but left me with little understanding of how all the puzzle pieces fit together. The larger picture came together in my adult years, but to be truthful, it was not until I completed the research for this book that I truly understood the full breadth and depth of the story, from beginning to end.

From my travels and personal experiences, I have learned there are history-minded readers, young and old alike, yearning to learn more about this incredible era. Many are eager to understand key elements—what caused the war, who the major belligerents were, how it unfolded, and why it matters today—but are a bit daunted by some of the more lengthy and exhaustive works out there. With that in mind, I began penning *The Fight of Their Lives*, a concise but still-comprehensive account of the war, employing a style, narrative, and level of detail designed to appeal to the widest possible audience.

Generations after it ended, there is an opportunity to broaden our understanding of this historic clash and apply its lessons to our troubled times today. World War II was a vivid demonstration of our will and capacity to respond to great crises, to rise in defense of humanity and our most sacred values, and to prevail against the darkest evils that lurk among us. Learning from this experience is imperative, as there is little doubt we will be tested again someday.

–Andy Kutler
June 2024

*For Franklin, Winston, Ike,
Rosie, and so many more…*

CONTENTS

Foreword
Introduction: The Enduring Relevance of World War II ... 1

The European Theater
Introduction: The Rise of Fascism ... 9
Poland: The War Begins ... 25
The Fall of France ... 33
Battle of Britain ... 42
Battle of the Atlantic ... 53
The Eastern Front: Operation Barbarossa ... 65
The Eastern Front: Stalingrad and Kursk ... 75
North Africa: A First Test ... 83
Italy ... 93
The Skies Over Germany ... 103
The Final Solution ... 110
The Liberation of France ... 123
The March Toward Germany ... 137
Battle of the Bulge ... 149
The End of the Third Reich ... 159

The War At Home
Introduction: Economic Resurgence and the Struggle for Equality ... 169
Arsenal of Democracy: America's Industrial Might ... 175
Women on the Line ... 186
Segregation in Wartime America ... 197
Wartime Injustice: The Fate of Japanese Americans ... 210
The Manhattan Project ... 219

The Pacific Theater
Introduction: A Gathering Storm in the Far East ... 229
Day of Infamy ... 243
Pacific Retreat ... 255
The Doolittle Raid ... 268
Midway: The Turning Point ... 277
Guadalcanal ... 287
Island Hopping ... 297
The Philippines and Leyte Gulf: MacArthur Returns ... 309
Iwo Jima ... 321
Okinawa ... 329
Meetinghouse and Downfall ... 336
Final Surrender ... 344

Conclusion: The Dawning of a New Era ... 352
A Note About Sources
Acknowledgments

Index

FOREWORD

History may not repeat itself, but it certainly rhymes. World War II remains relevant today because we continue to find ourselves in situations that evoke comparisons to that time in world history. It happens almost daily. We are who we are today because of that generation's sacrifice, determination, and courage. They left us a blueprint for overcoming adversity and recognizing the signs of threats to democracy before they rise to the level of what was witnessed in the 1930s and 1940s. Our lives are intertwined with that period in history, whether we recognize it or not. The arc of World War II is a story that needs to be chronicled from the beginning of the conflict in early September 1939 to its end onboard the USS *Missouri* almost precisely six years later in September 1945. In between, there are battles, stories, and people whose actions changed the world for the better and, often, for the worse. Many are told in this incredible book. History should not forget either side of this global conflict. If we ever do, we may be back where this all started, and we would have learned nothing from a war that saw sixty million lives lost.

    -Tim Gray
    Founder, President, and Filmmaker
    The World War II Foundation

THE FIGHT OF THEIR LIVES

INTRODUCTION
THE ENDURING RELEVANCE
OF WORLD WAR II

"If war was once a chivalrous duel, it is now a dastardly slaughter."
–Artur von Bolfras, Austrian general, 1914

"No other war has so definitely lined up the forces of arbitrary oppression and dictatorship against those of human rights and individual liberty."
–General Dwight D. Eisenhower, 1943

For six years, an epic clash raged around the globe, as military forces of unprecedented size and lethality dueled across continents and oceans. Wielding modern weaponry and machinery that far surpassed the technology of the previous world war, the ensuing scale of death and destruction remains unequaled in human history. When the guns fell silent, at least sixty million souls had perished, the majority innocent civilians, with much of Europe and Asia left in ruins.

The Second World War began on September 1, 1939, when German naval and air forces attacked neighboring Poland. Masses of German soldiers and panzers (tanks) flooded across the shared border, and within days, wide swaths of territory had been captured. Much of it was claimed to have been unjustly stolen in years past. Such grievances, punctuated with lectern-pounding calls to liberate other ethnic Germans from ancestral lands, were common refrains from Adolf Hitler. The Austrian-born political leader had ascended to power in Germany by stoking nationalistic fervor and promoting the most radical brand of cultural and racial purity the world had ever experienced.

From the outset, the Poles were unable to match their opponents, leaving officials in Warsaw pleading for intervention from their Western allies. Satisfying past pledges, France and Britain declared war on Germany shortly after the invasion began, but both were ill-prepared and reluctant to launch major offensives beyond their own borders. The United States also remained a distant observer, with practical reason. While the European powers had at least begun mobilizing for war, America's armed forces in 1939 were in feeble condition. The US Army counted fewer than 200,000 men—even outnumbered by Portugal—with few tanks, and rifles of World War I vintage.

Poland fought on, tenaciously but alone, and when the Soviet Union joined the invasion from the east as part of an earlier secret agreement negotiated with the Germans, the fate of the Poles was sealed. Less than four weeks after it all began, Warsaw fell. A week later, the fight in Poland was over.

The swift takeover owed much to Hitler's rebuilding of the German military. Hitler and his Nazi Party rose to power in 1933, gaining the loyalty of those in uniform by railing against humiliating limitations imposed by Allied victors in the wake of World War I that were intended to pacify Germany for decades to come. Military leaders were swayed by Hitler's pledges to reassemble German forces and reclaim territories yielded by weak-kneed aristocrats who had shamefully frittered away German honor and prestige. In 1935, Germany reinstituted universal military service, swelling the army to half a million men, and formed a new air force. In a few short years, Germany's military power grew exponentially.

Well before the invasion of Poland, Hitler began pressing outside German borders, finding little resistance. In 1938, his forces annexed Austria without spilling a drop of blood, followed by a move to absorb the Sudetenland, a portion of Czechoslovakia where some three million ethnic Germans lived. The maneuvering drew an initial outcry from Britain and France, but civilian leaders, wary of armed conflict, opted to placate Hitler rather than risk war. They negotiated what became known as the Munich Agreement, forfeiting disputed land in exchange for a mere promise that Germany abstain from further aggression. The strategy was an abject failure; within months, an emboldened Hitler annexed the rest of Czechoslovakia.

Even as most in Europe saw war on the horizon, America remained aloof. With the country still recovering from the economic wreckage of the Great Depression, public sentiment was firmly against meddling in overseas disputes. Throughout the rise of the Nazis, which included withering rhetoric vilifying Jews and trumpeting the superiority of the Aryan race, most Americans were mistrustful, if not contemptuous, of Hitler but opposed to military confrontation. He was Europe's problem.

By late 1940, public opinion had shifted in the wake of German forces sweeping across much of the continent in a series of blitzkrieg (lightning war) attacks. One by one, Western and Northern European states fell to the blazing speed and firepower of the Germans after remarkably brief clashes, including France, Belgium, Holland, Denmark, and Norway. Others, like Sweden, Switzerland, and Spain, declared their neutrality, while Italy and its Fascist dictator, Benito Mussolini, sided with the Nazis.

In early 1941, with only Britain and its Commonwealth left to resist Hitler, the United States finally entered the fray. Though not officially at war with Germany, President Franklin D. Roosevelt and Congress moved to arm and equip the British—and later the Soviets after they broke with the Germans—with desperately needed war materiel. A domestic transformation took root, as American factories began producing mountains of weapons, munitions, and other war goods to be shipped overseas.

Europe was not alone in its turmoil. In the early 1930s, an increasingly industrialized Japan, facing severe shortages in raw materials and food supplies for its booming population, sought to broaden its empire. Militant factions within the government and the Imperial Army saw opportunity on the Asian mainland, where Chinese Nationalists and communist insurgents were mired in civil war. Japanese forces took advantage, seizing much of Manchuria, a large province in northeastern China and producer of food and other resources Japan desperately needed to sustain its population and fuel its military expansion. By the end of the decade, Japanese armies had fully invaded China and were at the doorstep of British Malaya, the Dutch East Indies, and other Western colonies with abundant raw materials. The United States, a key trading partner of the Japanese, answered with economic sanctions, and when Roosevelt blocked oil exports to Japan in the summer of 1941, military leaders in Tokyo denounced the act as a provocation of war.

The American public was unfazed by the escalating tension in the Pacific, and dismissive of Japan as a threat to America's shores. Few believed the Japanese would brave the great distance or were capable of battling past American naval forces in their path. Undeterred by either, the Japanese began plotting to strike the United States while it was still unprepared for war.

On December 7, 1941, without warning, Japanese bombers and torpedo planes, launched from six aircraft carriers, raided the US Pacific Fleet anchored at Pearl Harbor, Hawaii. The surprise airstrike killed more than 2,000 Americans while sinking four battleships, damaging numerous other vessels, and decimating Army air forces stationed nearby. On the US mainland, breathless reports filled the radio airwaves, arresting the nation as Americans listened in dismay, grief, and rage.

The day after the attack, the United States formally declared war on Japan. Soon thereafter, Germany and Italy declared war on America.

With the president, Congress, and a vengeful public now in lockstep, America was in the fight. A mass buildup began, one that culminated in the induction of millions into the armed forces, a historic expansion of war manufacturing, and a final conquest over two great military powers. Long-regarded as soft and lacking the fortitude to overcome such powerful adversaries, a shared tenacity and unity of purpose emerged among the American servicemen deployed overseas and the civilians back home, surprising those who misjudged the ability of an untried nation to measure up to all its great promise and potential. In these regards, it proved to be America's finest era.

Other aspects of wartime America had less of a shine. The country was beset with legalized racial segregation, a practice that extended to the military, as African Americans who wished to serve in uniform faced a torrent of abuse and other obstacles, including doubts about their aptitude and courage. Nonetheless, hundreds of thousands of Black men stepped forward to serve, many of them with segregated units that accrued some of the most prolific combat records of the war.

Racial animosity was not confined to the African American population. Shortly after Pearl Harbor, President Roosevelt ordered the forcible relocation of some 120,000 men, women, and children of Japanese ancestry—two-thirds of them American citizens—to remote desert and mountain camps. They subsisted there for three years, locked behind barbed wire fences and under the watchful eye of armed guards, their imprisonment one of the most shameful legacies and injustices of the war...and twentieth-century American history generally.

Beyond the compelling battlefield drama and innumerable tales of individual heroics, World War II offers clear lessons for twenty-first century policymakers. Most apparent was the failed mission of the League of Nations, an institution conceived to promote peace and guarantee security among member states, and its wilting under the international spotlight. The conspicuous lack of military preparedness among Western democracies also invited trouble, leaving the global community powerless to stem the rising tide of authoritarianism, or deter Hitler from invading other sovereign lands and declaring them his own.

Also instructive is perhaps the most extraordinary achievement of the war—the ability of allies and rivals with varying strategic and political interests, governance models, and cultural values, to join in common cause to defeat shared enemies. In assembling the most powerful military coalition in history, and unifying behind a single aim, Americans, Britons, Soviets, Chinese, resisters in occupied France and Eastern Europe, and others all made indelible contributions to the ultimate triumph, a testament to the power and virtue of global partnership and collaboration.

The American home front, for its part, achieved record levels of industrial production, but widespread social inequities and injustices persisted. Beyond its clouded legacy of racial and gender inequality, the United States wrestled with other moral quandaries. That included a balancing act between high-minded ideals long embraced by democratic nations and the realities of modern warfare. One example was the willful causation of civilian casualties and the Allied strategy to diminish industrial output and break the enemy's spirit by bombing population centers across Germany and Japan. The mass air raids achieved their military objectives but produced staggering numbers of civilian deaths. Officials viewed it as an acceptable trade-off then. Would they do so today?

President Roosevelt's early knowledge of Hitler's plotting against European Jews posed another quandary. Was there a moral obligation to disrupt the transporting of prisoners to concentration camps and killing centers by bombing the railway lines? Or were practical constraints a legitimate rationale for inaction, no matter the magnitude of mass murder? Such questions are as difficult to grapple with today as they were in the 1940s.

World War II will be forever remembered for its unfathomable inhumanity, when those yearning for power brutalized, enslaved, and murdered millions of innocents. But it was also a time of great perseverance, when an unshakable resiliency and innumerable acts of selfless courage and sacrifice propelled the Allies to victory—a victory that came with profound costs to the belligerents and humankind.

THE EUROPEAN THEATER

INTRODUCTION
THE RISE OF FASCISM

On the eleventh day of the eleventh month of 1918, a cease-fire brought welcome silence to blood-soaked trenches across stretches of Europe, ending a period of prolonged violence and suffering bred from political and ethnic disputes. The four-year struggle, known as the Great War, was later pronounced the "war to end all wars" by those unable to fathom such folly repeating itself. Yet just two decades later, blood spilled again across the globe, and as the sum of dead and wounded multiplied to record new levels, the "war to end all wars" simply became the First World War.

The origins of the Second World War can be traced to the 1918 armistice, when the warring parties met in Versailles, just outside Paris, to settle on terms for peace. With the fall of empires—including those of Germany, Russia, Austria-Hungary, and the Ottomans—centuries-old boundaries were redrawn and the map of Europe remade. The birth of new nations gave sovereignty to some, while others became subjects of new rulers, often from distant lands. Hopes for future global stability were pinned to a new League of Nations, an international institution chartered to defuse potential disputes and guarantee collective security for member states. It was an idea championed by President Woodrow Wilson, though to his great shame and regret, America would remain an outsider after the United States Senate refused to ratify the treaty. The League would prove a failure, its mission undermined, ironically, by what happened at Versailles, where a peace agreement intended to ensure lasting harmony instead planted seeds of bitterness and antipathy, destined to catapult feuding nations back into bloody conflict.

The discord began in the last months of the First World War, when the German people turned against their monarch, Kaiser (Emperor) Wilhelm II, who led them into the conflict that claimed the lives of some two million of their soldiers. Wilhelm was forced to abdicate power, leading to Germany's transition to a parliamentary system and the fledgling Weimar Republic, named for the city where it was formed. Weimar representatives arrived in Versailles hoping to negotiate a reasonable settlement, but there was no negotiation, as the French and British, still fuming at their own losses in the war, were more interested in vengeance and amends than reconciliation. The final terms imposed on the defeated Germans were punitive, declaring their country solely responsible for starting the war and liable for billions of dollars in reparation payments. Germany was permitted only a skeleton military, and much of its lands and overseas colonies were parceled out to others. After surrendering thirteen percent of its territory, along with ten percent of its population, millions of ethnic Germans were subjected to foreign rule.

The losses and concessions were humiliating, and prideful Germans who venerated their military lineage and cultural achievements were predictably aghast at what emerged from Versailles. Howls of protest echoed across the country, as wrathful mobs began castigating the treaty as a "stab in the back" by treacherous Weimar men, their capitulation a stain on German honor.

In the years that followed, Germany struggled to recover from the war, unable to revive its floundering economy or reverse soaring unemployment. Hyperinflation plummeted the value of the national currency at the same time Versailles reparations bankrupted the treasury. Political unrest followed, as factions ranging from far-left communists to far-right nationalists and fascists stoked rising hostility toward the democratic government. One particularly boisterous coalition arose among jobless workers and aggrieved war veterans, stirred to life by a former soldier and his fist-shaking demands for a spiritual and political awakening across Germany.

His name was Adolf Hitler.

A native Austrian who fought in the German Army during the war, Hitler was a hateful zealot consumed with grotesque theories about the racial supremacy of Aryans—non-Jewish Caucasians with Nordic features—and grandiose fantasies of building and leading an all-powerful, thousand-year German Reich (realm). In the post-Versailles years, Hitler became politically active in Bavaria, his adopted home in southeast Germany, where he began mesmerizing audiences with his fiery rhetoric and strident tone. Tales of the German rebirth he promised, where the people would serve a racially pure state and a rebuilt military would return prized lands and global prominence to the German people, enraptured listeners.

By the early 1920s, Hitler and the National Socialist German Workers' Party he led, known as the Nazi Party, were expanding their influence and galvanizing followers. As Hitler raged against the betrayal at Versailles and vilified those eroding Germany from within, he surrounded himself with brown-shirted toughs who thrived on violence and intimidation. Their formal name was Sturmabteilung, or SA, but they were better known as stormtroopers and operated on the streets as the Nazi Party's thuggish muscle.

Hitler remained a minor figure then, attracting little attention outside Bavaria, but other authoritarians were on the rise outside Germany. That included Italy, where Benito Mussolini, the founder of its Fascist Party, had risen to prime minister. By 1922, he had become a dictator, wielding absolute authority, just as a fellow tyrant but ideological opposite in the East, Joseph Stalin, was taking the helm of the Soviet Communist Party. Stalin had an insatiable thirst for power, and for three decades, he subjected the Soviet people to the most repressive conditions. Millions would die from war and famine, with millions more banished to hard labor camps in the Siberian wilderness.

Compared to Stalin and Mussolini, the 34-year-old Hitler had little stature when 1923 began, but that changed after French forces marched into the Ruhr Valley, Germany's industrial heartland. With the French demanding payment of wartime reparations the penniless country could ill-afford, Hitler saw an opportunity to take advantage of the nationwide indignation over foreign troops on German soil. He led several hundred of his rough-hewn stormtroopers to a Munich beer hall, where they disrupted a gathering of local political and police leaders and attempted to elicit a revolt. The next day, Hitler and 3,000 armed Nazis flooded the city streets in open rebellion, but the amateurish putsch (coup) gained little traction and the army easily quashed it, arresting the ringleaders.

It was during his trial for treason that Hitler rose to national prominence. Though convicted, his searing indictment of those in power drew wide support, particularly among those suffering under Germany's wretched fiscal conditions. Hitler eventually served nine months in prison, where he wrote *Mein Kampf* ("My Struggle"), an autobiographical manifesto of his political and racial beliefs that became a creed for his followers. It also embraced a lesson Hitler had learned from his failed revolt in Munich—future power must be won through legitimate political means and with the army in his corner.

Following his release from prison, Hitler resumed his leadership of the Nazi Party and continued to rally the downtrodden, preying on their hardships while fanning racial and cultural animosities. Presenting himself as a national savior, Hitler began invoking the concept of lebensraum (living space), a code for expanding Germany's borders by pushing into neighboring lands and those to the east, including Eastern Europe and the Soviet Union. Such a move would not only yield vast stores of crops, iron, oil, and other economic resources needed to sustain an enduring Reich, but millions of ethnic Germans would be returned to German rule.

Throughout its rise, the Nazi movement was fueled by a fervent loathing of Jews. The hatred became an obsession for Hitler, who demonized them at every Nazi rally with scathing broadsides and outlandish charges and lies. Antisemitism had existed for centuries in Europe, but Hitler's caustic words rekindled long-simmering antagonism, appealing to likeminded extremists who cheered his portrayal of Jews as monstrous subhumans responsible for Germany's decline. Accusations that Jews were polluting the German race and culture, and masterminding a global conspiracy to subjugate Germany, became the catalyst for future persecution and genocide.

By the end of the 1920s, amid sky-high unemployment and inflation, and widely held perceptions of an inept democratic government incapable of lifting the country out of crisis, the moment had come. With much of the populace yearning to prosper once again and break free from the humiliation of the Versailles debacle and loss of German esteem, the embers of radical political upheaval in Germany began to burn brighter.

PRELUDE TO WAR: A TIMELINE OF EVENTS

1930

SEPTEMBER: The Nazi Party broadens its base of support, winning 107 seats in the Reichstag, the German national parliament. Still a minority, it is a sharp increase from two years earlier, when the Nazis held a mere twelve seats.

1932

JULY: Adolf Hitler campaigns for president and loses the popular vote to the 84-year-old incumbent, Paul von Hindenburg, an iconic military hero of the First World War. The Nazi Party, however, makes substantial gains in the general election, easily winning one-third of the seats in the Reichstag, and the Nazis become the largest bloc in a chamber deeply fragmented among numerous competing parties.

NOVEMBER: With the United States bogged down in the Great Depression and historic unemployment, Franklin D. Roosevelt coasts to electoral victory by pledging to focus on America's domestic plight. Consumed by their economic troubles, few Americans monitor events unfolding in Europe.

1933

JANUARY: Seeking political compromise and a unified government, von Hindenburg appoints Hitler to the post of chancellor—essentially the head of government—expecting him to be mostly a figurehead. Paralleling Hitler's rise is an expansion of the Schutzstaffel, also known as the SS. Formed in the mid-1920s to serve as Hitler's personal bodyguard, by 1933, it is the paramilitary arm of the Nazi Party, numbering over 50,000 members. The fanatical, black-uniformed service is led by Heinrich Himmler, a Hitler enthusiast who rises to become the second most powerful figure in Germany. At its peak, the military wing of the SS grows to one million soldiers.

FEBRUARY: Six days before another national election, a mysterious fire breaks out in the Reichstag. Though a young Dutch communist is arrested, the Nazis themselves are likely complicit in the blaze. The next day, Nazi propaganda decries the arson as the start of a communist uprising, prompting von Hindenburg to approve an order expanding emergency police powers and suspending the rights of German citizens. Freedom of speech and assembly are rescinded, as Germany's young democracy begins to crumble.

MARCH: After the Nazis win forty-three percent of the vote in the general election, a clear plurality, the Reichstag passes the Enabling Act, transferring broad political powers from parliament to Hitler. It marks the beginning of the Third Reich, a dictatorship and successor regime to prior empires that once reigned over German lands. The Nazis commandeer radio stations and newspapers, declare a boycott on Jewish-owned businesses, and open the first concentration camp for political prisoners in an abandoned factory in Dachau, just outside Munich.

JULY: The Nazi Party is designated the official political party of Germany, and all others are abolished. Public assemblies are held across the country to burn books by the tens of thousands, including those considered "un-German" or authored by Jews, part of a concerted campaign to impose state-sponsored censorship and cultural influence.

October: Germany withdraws from the League of Nations.

1934

June: Maneuvering to eliminate rivals within his own party, Hitler orders the arrest and execution of conservative officials and key SA leaders. The bloody purge, carried out by the SS and the Gestapo—Hitler's secret police—becomes known as the Night of the Long Knives.

August: In the wake of von Hindenburg's death, Hitler abolishes the elected office of president and declares himself both chancellor and führer (leader). After commanding German Army leaders to swear an oath of personal loyalty, his power is absolute.

1935

March: In clear defiance of the Versailles terms, Hitler introduces compulsory military service and begins a massive buildup of the armed forces. Applauded by Army leaders, the lavish spending on the production of tanks, aircraft, and other military and public works programs revitalizes the German economy and reduces unemployment, boosting Hitler's popularity.

August: With the American public adamantly opposed to intervening in the brewing cauldron of overseas affairs, the US Congress passes the first in a series of Neutrality Acts. The measure prohibits the sale of arms and munitions to countries engaged in war and is intended to preclude President Roosevelt from actively aiding any belligerent and drawing the United States into a broader conflict.

SEPTEMBER: The Reichstag passes several measures known as the Nuremberg Laws, revoking German citizenship of Jews, prohibiting marriage between Jews and Aryans, and legalizing discrimination.

OCTOBER: Italian dictator Benito Mussolini sends troops into Abyssinia (present-day Ethiopia), seeking to erase the stain of Italy's embarrassing defeat there forty years earlier. Appeals from Abyssinia to the League of Nations go unanswered, and their poorly equipped forces are defeated the following year. The League's failure to intercede is widely seen as institutional weakness and an inability to guarantee the security of member states.

1936

MARCH: Hitler orders troops into the Rhineland, a large swath of German territory adjoining France and Belgium. It is another brazen violation of the Versailles Treaty that requires such border areas to remain demilitarized, but the move proves widely popular across the Rhineland and greater Germany. Though they have superior military forces, the French decline to enforce the treaty terms, unwilling to risk armed conflict.

JULY: Civil war erupts in Spain between right-wing Nationalists, led by General Francisco Franco and the Spanish Army, and supporters of the left-wing government. The Nationalists ultimately prevail, resulting in a dictatorship under Franco, as early fighting distracts much of Europe from Germany's rapidly accelerating mobilization.

AUGUST: Hitler welcomes the Olympic Games to Berlin, where he hopes to showcase the supremacy of the Aryan race. African American track star Jesse Owens spoils his plans, winning four gold medals.

OCTOBER: Germany and Italy sign a secret agreement to coordinate their foreign policies, and Mussolini delivers a speech referencing an "axis" around which likeminded nations may cooperate in the future. The term is later adopted to describe the formal alliance between Germany, Italy, and Japan.

DECEMBER: Enrollment becomes mandatory for millions of German boys and girls in the various branches of the Hitler Youth, an organization that indoctrinates children in Nazi ideology and grooms them for service to the Reich.

1938
MARCH: As prescribed years earlier by Hitler in *Mein Kampf*, German troops move into his native Austria, a neighboring, German-speaking country of seven million people with its own indigenous Nazi movement. There is no resistance from the Austrian government, and Germany annexes the country without firing a single shot.

SEPTEMBER: With Hitler threatening Czechoslovakia over the return of the Sudetenland—territory surrendered at Versailles that included three million ethnic Germans—leaders of Britain and France travel to Munich to negotiate a peaceful settlement. Desperate to avert war, British and French leaders pressure the Czechs to cede the Sudetenland in exchange for a pledge from Hitler to refrain from attacking the rest of the country. It becomes known as the Munich Agreement, but the strategy of appeasing Hitler by trading land for peace fails completely. Six months later, German forces invade Czechoslovakia, and the country surrenders without a fight.

NOVEMBER: A young German Jew murders a German diplomat in Paris, and in reprisal, 7,500 Jewish-owned shops in Germany and Austria are ransacked and looted. Hundreds of synagogues are also destroyed, and tens of thousands of German Jews are sent to concentration camps, where they are held prisoner under abysmal conditions. It becomes known as Kristallnacht (Crystal Night) after countless shop windows are broken in the melee.

1939

MARCH: With Czechoslovakia in his possession, Hitler turns his attention to Poland, a gateway to further conquests in the East. Britain and France abandon their disastrous appeasement strategy, pledging to aid the Poles if their independence is jeopardized.

MAY: Ravensbrück, a concentration camp for women outside Berlin, is opened, supplementing a growing network of detention camps across Germany and its occupied territories where millions of Jews, political dissidents, homosexuals, Roma (then known as Gypsies), and others are imprisoned. That same month, Germany and Italy sign the Pact of Steel, a ten-year military alliance between the two dictatorships.

AUGUST: After years of bitter fighting with Russia in the First World War, and Hitler's ongoing denunciation of communism as an existential threat, the Germans shock much of the world by signing a nonaggression pact with the Soviet Union. Bracketed by the two countries, the accord unnerves Poland, and the country of thirty-five million people hastily prepares for war.

• • • • •

Adolf Hitler

Adolf Hitler (1889-1945) was born in the small Austrian hamlet of Braunau am Inn. After spending his young adult years as an aspiring artist in Vienna, he moved to Munich, Germany in 1913. When the First World War began, Hitler refused to enlist in the Austrian army, repulsed by the religious and cultural diversity tolerated by the Austro-Hungarian Empire. He volunteered instead for a Bavarian infantry unit, separate from the main German Army, and served on the Western Front, mostly as a dispatch runner. After suffering minor wounds on the battlefield, Hitler was awarded two Iron Crosses, Germany's highest military decoration for valor.

When the war ended, Hitler became politically active, marching with other embittered war veterans in the streets of Bavaria to protest the "November criminals"—those accused of betraying the German people at Versailles. He joined a nascent German Workers' Party, and less than two years later was at its helm, reshaping the organization into the Nazi Party. His public speeches electrified his followers, inciting them into action with rage-filled tirades assailing the political elite, Jews, and communists.

In barely over a decade, Hitler completed his rise to power. As Germany's political and military leader during World War II, he presided over a string of early successes before several strategic blunders doomed Germany's chances. His most fatal missteps came in 1941, when he ordered an invasion of the Soviet Union before Britain had been subdued and needlessly declared war on the United States. The damage from opening a two-front war—plunging his armies deep into Soviet territory and inviting a dangerous, new adversary into the European war—proved catastrophic, leading to eventual defeat.

Gestapo

Formed in early 1933, the ruthless and ironfisted Geheime Staatspolizei, known as the Gestapo, rooted out all political opposition to Hitler and the Nazis. With boundless authority, Gestapo agents instilled terror throughout the Third Reich, arresting, interrogating, and torturing whomever they pleased, and enforcing maniacal devotion to Hitler's regime.

Alfons Heck

Born in 1928, Alfons Heck was raised in the small German town of Wittlich, nestled in a wine-producing region twenty-five miles from the French border. Heck was just beginning his schooling when Adolf Hitler came into power. Under a new curriculum imposed by the Nazis, schoolchildren were indoctrinated in German nationalism and instructed to revere Hitler for his restoration of German values and global stature. Heck and his young peers came to worship their führer as a savior—"I would have gladly died for him," Heck later confessed—and devoted themselves entirely to serving the Nazi state.

When Hitler ordered the Wehrmacht (German Army) into the Rhineland in 1936, the wide-eyed Heck was enthralled by the smartly uniformed soldiers garrisoned among the vineyards of his town. Two years later, before his tenth birthday, Heck joined the Jungvolk, the junior branch of the Hitler Youth, a paramilitary organization that immersed boys and girls in Nazi ideology and prepared them for future service to the "Fatherland." Donning special uniforms, they learned to drill and march with precision, took part in war games and tests of courage, and held spirited sporting contests – all free from the watchful eyes of their parents.

When he turned fourteen, Heck joined the senior service of the Hitler Youth, training as a glider pilot and dreaming of flying fighter planes for the Luftwaffe (German Air Force). He became a leader within the youth organization, and by the last year of the war, the 16-year-old was the equivalent of a brigadier general, commanding thousands of other children manning anti-aircraft guns and defensive positions. As rumors swirled about mass atrocities against Jews and others, Heck refused to believe them, certain the Nazis would never resort to such measures. In the last weeks of the war, Heck was finally selected to serve as a Luftwaffe pilot, but a compassionate senior officer saved his life, ordering Heck to return to his hometown on furlough, away from the heaviest fighting. American soldiers occupied the region, and though Heck expected to be arrested or shot, they instead made use of his English skills, employing the teen as a translator.

Heck survived the war, and later immigrated to North America, where he befriended a German-born Holocaust survivor. The pair began speaking publicly together about their wartime experiences, sharing their infinitely different perspectives at over 150 colleges and universities. Guilt-ridden and shamed by his past, Heck authored a book in 1985 chronicling his time in the Hitler Youth, including his seduction by the Nazis. He acknowledged his indifference then toward the treatment of Jews and his unwillingness to shed doubts about the Holocaust until after the war, when he attended the war crimes tribunal in Nuremberg and was finally convinced by the many testimonials he heard. After years of repudiating the Nazis and his own part in the war, Heck died in 2005 at the age of seventy-six.

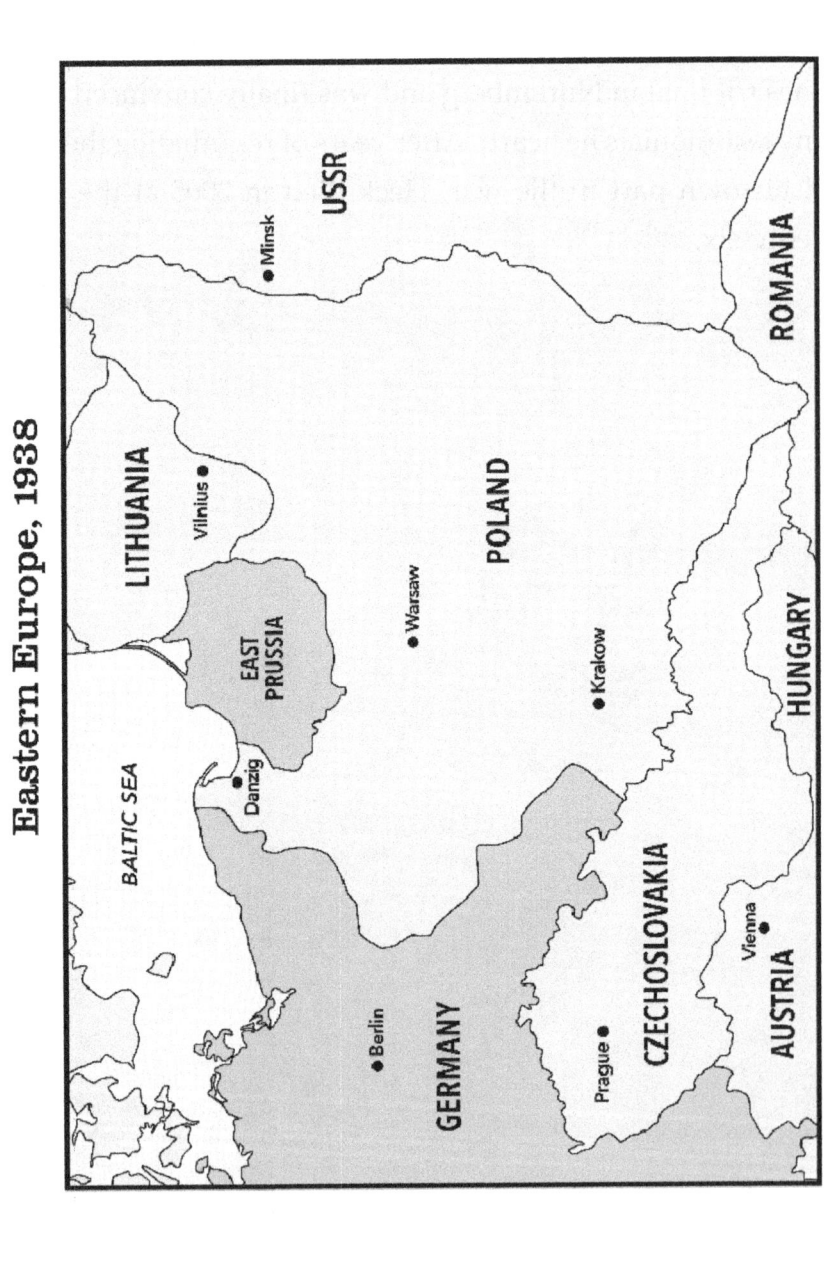

Eastern Europe, 1938

1
POLAND: THE WAR BEGINS
SEPTEMBER 1939

"I believe it is peace for our time."
–British Prime Minister Neville Chamberlain, praising the 1938 Munich Agreement with Hitler

"[W]e have sustained a total and unmitigated defeat...a disaster of the first magnitude."
–Winston Churchill, Member of Parliament, in response

By spring 1939, the Third Reich had fully absorbed Austria and Czechoslovakia, a feat largely attributed to Hitler's skillful maneuvering and relentless browbeating. The conquest also exposed a barefaced reluctance among British and French leaders to risk war, leading Hitler to turn his attention to a long-coveted and far grander prize, the Soviet Union. The trove of economic resources in the East could sustain a Greater Reich for the next millennium, but the path to the Soviet Union went through Poland, a country that brushed off Hitler's predictable threats and bluster, and with good reason. The Poles had a respectable army, promises of support from Western allies, and a steely resolve.

Hitler's ire, as always, was rooted in the Treaty of Versailles and the ceding of German territory to Poland two decades earlier. With the newly independent and landlocked state requiring sea access for trade and commerce, treaty architects had created a "Polish Corridor," a strip of land slicing through German territory and linking Poland to the port city of Danzig and the Baltic Sea. East Prussians were cleaved off from their native Germany, and Danzig and its surroundings—predominantly inhabited by ethnic Germans—were declared a "Free State," to be administered by the League of Nations. Germans seethed over the crafty mapmaking.

Twenty years later, Hitler's saber rattling toward Poland was answered by British Prime Minister Neville Chamberlain, finally discarding his failed strategy of accommodation after the broken promises in Czechoslovakia. He issued a stern public warning that any move against Poland's independence would trigger war with Britain. The French soon followed suit.

While the Poles found some comfort in such assurances, the pledges only infuriated Hitler. He forged his own alliance in the months ahead, furtively negotiating a nonaggression pact with the Soviets he loathed. The pact ensured Moscow would not intervene on behalf of the Poles should Germany invade, and a trade agreement was tacked on to enrich both signees. The accord between the two longtime antagonists became public in late August, sending tremors rippling across Europe, even as its most consequential clause—one that would later doom the Polish state—remained a closely guarded secret.

• • • • •

Throughout its history, a succession of imperial overlords from Moscow to Vienna had drawn and redrawn Poland's boundaries to suit their own political and economic interests. Aware of how fragile and vulnerable their post-Versailles autonomy was, the Poles had amassed an army of more than one million soldiers by 1939, the fifth largest in the world. They invested little in modernization, though, leaving the Polish military with few armored vehicles, an antiquated air force, and regiments of horse cavalry that hearkened back to an earlier era. After several years of mobilization, the Germans not only had far more troops than the Poles, but their powerful armor also portended a significant mismatch. By the eve of war, the German invasion force bulged with 1.5 million soldiers and thousands of tanks, trucks, and armored vehicles.

The Nazis also plotted to blame Polish agitators for the coming hostilities. The German people had enthusiastically cheered Hitler's prior territorial gains, but those had been achieved almost entirely through coercion and intimidation, and without bloodshed. Most Germans were averse to war, and still haunted by memories of the prior one, when so many fathers and sons were sent off to fight on distant battlefields, never to return. To win public backing for the operation in Poland, where substantial casualties were a possibility, the Nazis dressed a dozen concentration camp prisoners in Polish Army uniforms shortly before the invasion began. After poisoning the men, the Nazis dumped their corpses in a wooded area outside the German town of Gleiwitz, just across the Polish border, and sprayed them with bullets.

The following morning, Hitler's propaganda ministry trumpeted the "discovery," using Nazi-controlled newspapers and radio broadcasts to denounce the illusionary Polish attacks. Appearing before the Reichstag, Hitler condemned Poland's aggression and promised to vigorously defend the German people, vowing that "bombs will be repaid with bombs." There were no Polish bombs, of course, but the fuse was lit. On September 1, German salvos began raining down on the Poles, marking the beginning of World War II.

Blitzkrieg

The accelerated German buildup of the late 1930s produced the world's most advanced arsenal — and the most innovative — with an emphasis on speed and mobility. Contemporary military doctrine prescribed masses of infantry spearheading major offensives, with armor and air units in support, but against Poland, the Germans planned to introduce a revolutionary form of warfare. Air power and mechanized armies would be in the forefront, smashing through defensive fortifications and overpowering the enemy with brute firepower.

The blitzkrieg unleashed in Poland was unlike any other military offensive in history. It began with naval forces attacking from the sea, shelling and assaulting the Westerplatte stronghold in Danzig's harbor. The Luftwaffe struck next. Flying state-of-the-art aircraft with powerful engines and modern airframes, the German aviators annihilated their Polish counterparts before raiding ammunition depots, rail hubs, and other essential infrastructure. Population centers were also targeted, sparking terror and panic across the country.

With control of the skies, German ground forces blasted through the Polish defenses, streaming across the border and crossing the frontier mostly unimpeded. Resistance gradually stiffened, as the Poles hoped to stall the German advance long enough for reserves to be mobilized and Britain and France to strike the Germans at home. Two days after the invasion began, the Western powers honored their past pledges, declaring war on Germany. But instead of British bombers walloping Berlin, and French armies crossing into the Rhineland, the Allies mustered only token demonstrations. Neither Britain nor France was ready for war, and with the promised support never materializing, the Poles were on their own.

They fought on, with courage and backbone, but it was not enough to stop the onslaught of tanks and armored vehicles crossing the Vistula River and charging toward the capital of Warsaw. The fatal, shocking blow came on September 17, when the Soviet Union invaded Poland from the east. Hundreds of thousands of Red Army troops flooded into the country after Moscow claimed a collapse of the Polish government had left ethnic Ukrainians and Belarusians in eastern Poland vulnerable to persecution and violence from their Polish neighbors. It was ludicrous, of course, and the flimsiest of pretenses, but the

Germans and Soviets had secretly agreed to the invasion earlier, part of a conspiracy to defeat the Poles, dismember the country, and share equally in the spoils. The pact was of mutual benefit — a two-front war would lessen the pressure on Hitler's forces, while the Soviets would gain eastern Poland as a buffer, hampering future attacks from the west, including by the Germans they mistrusted.

The Soviet invaders faced initial resistance from the Polish troops in their path, but it would not last. Squeezed by two powerful enemies and vastly outgunned, the remaining Polish defenses soon cracked, and on September 27, a besieged Warsaw fell to the Germans. One week later, Poland surrendered.

AFTERMATH

Just five weeks of fighting had claimed the lives of an estimated 70,000 Poles, 15,000 Germans, and an unknown number of Soviets. Territory adjoining Germany's eastern border, as well as the city of Danzig, was absorbed into the Greater Reich, while other parts of western Poland, including Warsaw, were organized under a new General Government, with a Nazi Party official appointed the ruling authority.

More than 900,000 Polish soldiers were taken prisoner. The Nazis ignored existing conventions for their treatment, pressing most of the men into service as forced laborers in Germany. With sharply rising demands on industrial output, and increasingly more German workers pulled into the military, the use of slave labor to compensate for worker shortages became a staple of production in the Third Reich.

The most appalling consequence of the month-long battle was the killing of tens of thousands of civilians, a practice that continued even after Poland's defeat. It was an early precursor of the fate that awaited noncombatants at the hands of German and Soviet invaders. With the Nazis eager to dismantle any semblance of a Polish state, they targeted political figures, scholars, clergy, lawyers, and other intellectual and cultural leaders, all of whom began disappearing from towns and villages across the country, as did Polish Jews. The systemic, murderous campaign continued for years, and by 1945, the number of Polish dead had reached 5.5 million.

The triumph in Poland was a significant milestone for Hitler. In just over a month, his forces had defeated a substantial army and added significant new lands and resources to the German war economy. He had also reached an accord, however tenuous, with his principal rival in the East. As he pondered his next move, the British and French he was now at war with awaited with angst. Under no illusion Hitler would stop in Central and Eastern Europe, they hurriedly mobilized their own forces, certain a showdown with the Nazis loomed on the horizon.

• • • • •

Following their surrender, more than 15,000 Polish military officers captured in the East were murdered at the hands of the NKVD, the Soviet secret police. In early 1943, the Germans discovered 4,500 of the corpses in the Katyn Forest, near the city of Smolensk, Russia. The Germans, bitter foes of the Soviets by that point, shared evidence of the mass graves widely, hoping exposure of the atrocity would fracture the alliance between the Soviet Union and the West.

Einsatzgruppen

As German forces swept across Poland in the opening weeks of the war, they were closely trailed by SS Einsatzgruppen. The security forces were ostensibly responsible for policing captured territory, preventing sabotage, and arresting resisters, but mostly operated as execution units, murdering Jews and Polish elites wherever they could be found. Their role expanded significantly in mid-1941 during the German invasion of the Soviet Union, when they began massacring mass numbers of Jews, Communist Party leaders, government officials, and others the Nazis considered enemies of the Reich. According to a post-war military tribunal, Einsatzgruppen were responsible for the murders of more than two million people in German-occupied territories during the war.

Tanks

Tanks were heavily armored vehicles that used track propellant systems to navigate difficult terrain. Introduced to battlefields in the First World War, early prototypes were rudimentary and produced in limited numbers, but the Germans made significant strides in the 1930s, developing more sophisticated models, including the Panzer IV, first deployed during the operation in Poland. Anchoring its armored forces early in the war, the panzers were the vanguard of Germany's blitzkrieg attacks, and their success prompted the Allies to speed up their own modernization plans. By mid-war, thousands of American Sherman tanks, Soviet T-34s, and German Panthers and Tigers were dueling across the Western and Eastern Fronts.

Invasion of France & Low Countries, 1940

2
THE FALL OF FRANCE
MAY–JUNE 1940

"Strength lies not in defense but in attack."
–**Adolf Hitler,** *Mein Kampf*

"I wonder what I will do with a simple machine gun against armored tanks."
–**French soldier Jules Beaulieux, in a farewell letter to his family**

The thunderous German march through Poland was followed by a quiet, months-long interlude. With opposing armies sequestered behind their respective borders, the period was mocked by many as a "phony war," but both sides were far from idle. As the Germans replenished their losses from the operation in Poland, adding to existing inventories of tanks and aircraft and priming their armies for future conquests, the Allies ramped up their own mobilization efforts, anxiously awaiting Hitler's next move, widely expected to be against France.

Inside the Reich, a bustling industrial base continued to meet rising demands for additional machinery and armaments. Production increases depended on the import of raw materials from abroad, and among the most critical for new tanks, ships, and heavy guns was iron ore, mined in neutral Sweden and hauled to Germany by sea. To reach German ports, cargo ships first had to transit Scandinavian waters, where such shipments could be intercepted by Allied naval forces. To secure that vital pipeline and acquire needed coastal bases for its own naval activities, Germany ended the so-called phony war, invading Norway and Denmark in April 1940.

A mostly defenseless Denmark surrendered within hours, but the Norwegians refused to fold. Vastly overmatched, Norway's meager air force was swept aside by the Luftwaffe with ease, allowing German paratroopers and assault troops to pour into the country. The Allies sent what aid they could, but British and French ground forces arrived ill-equipped to slow the German march. The Allies fared better at sea, where British warships and Norwegian shore batteries hammered the German fleet prowling the coastline, but it made little difference. Barely two months after the fighting began, Hitler's army was in firm control.

By that time, a far more extensive operation was underway across the North Sea. Hitler's grand offensive in Western Europe, including the long-anticipated clash with France, pitted the two most potent armies on the continent against one another. It was Hitler's most audacious ploy to date, designed to topple his most bitter enemies and avenge a stinging defeat from two decades ago. The French were presumed to be ready for such a move, raising hopes across the globe that the Nazi march that began in Central Europe would finally be brought to a halt.

• • • • •

When the war opened, the French-British alliance was an imposing challenge to Germany. The British Royal Navy was the premier fleet in the world, with a reach that extended from the Mediterranean to the Far East, while France fielded the largest army in Europe, armed with quality weapons, and led by accomplished veterans of the First World War.

Like Germany, France had made significant investments in modernization and mechanization, with one key distinction: While the French had dispersed their armor among armies spread across hundreds of miles, the Germans had concentrated their panzers into massive, armored fists, designed to punch through heavily fortified positions. Favoring conquest and sweeping offensives, Hitler had also built his armies for movement and mobility. French leaders, in contrast, had a more defensive mindset, haunted by their experience in the First World War when so many of their countrymen had been slaughtered in futile charges against entrenched enemies. To ensure that experience would not be repeated, the French labored throughout the 1930s to construct a miles-deep network of fortifications along the length of their nearly 300-mile border with Germany. Known as the Maginot Line, it was manned by hundreds of thousands of first-rate troops and layered with concrete bunkers and fortresses, anti-tank and machine-gun emplacements, minefields, and other challenging obstacles.

By 1940, French leaders were confident the Maginot Line was impenetrable. The Germans largely agreed and plotted to skirt it entirely, devising a plan to advance their forces west instead, through Luxembourg, Holland (present-day Netherlands), and Belgium. The German armies would then turn south, crossing into France from Belgium and its relatively unfortified border. The "Low Countries" — so-named because much of their land is below sea level — had not yet formally sided with the Allies and hoped their neutrality would shield them from Hitler's scheming. They were mistaken.

The French and British, fully aware the Germans had marched into France from Belgium during the previous war, anticipated another such move and massed additional armies just across the Belgian border. They deployed to the north, where vast stretches of rolling fields and flat farmland would be favorable to German mechanized forces. There was an alternative path through southern Belgium, a region known as the Ardennes, but it was filled with steep ridges, thick woods, and unpaved roads. The French placed few forces across from it, certain any advance there with tanks and trucks would be painstaking, allowing ample time for reinforcements to be summoned.

It proved to be a fatal miscalculation.

Invasion

The Germans divided their infantry and armored divisions among three large army groups. Army Group B was positioned in the north, across from Holland and northern Belgium, while Army Group A, with most of the German armor, was placed at the edge of the Ardennes. A third force, Army Group C, faced the Maginot Line, its presence mostly a diversion to occupy the attention of the French divisions there.

The offensive began on May 10, 1940, with German columns rolling into tiny Luxembourg unchallenged, and Army Group B launching blitzkrieg-style attacks against Holland and Belgium. With only a modest army, the Dutch turned to their natural defenses, flooding low-lying fields and farms to slow the invasion force. It did little good, as the Germans struck from behind, dropping thousands of paratroopers inland and seizing vital crossings over the country's canal system. Defensive positions were overrun, and with the Luftwaffe threatening to turn Dutch cities into rubble, the country had little choice but to surrender.

The Belgians had a more formidable army and entrenched it behind two natural barriers—the Albert Canal and Meuse River—cutting across the width of the country. Anchoring their lines was Eben-Emael, a modern fortress brimming with heavy guns aimed at key crossing points over the water. To neutralize the stronghold, the Germans launched one of the most daring operations of the war, landing gliders with just eighty-five paratroopers on its roof. They disabled the heavy guns with explosives, allowing German armies to cross the canal in force. The main defensive line was soon shattered, sending the Belgians into wide retreat.

As the Germans romped through the Low Countries, the Allies initiated their long-planned response. Three French armies and nine divisions of the British Expeditionary Force (BEF) rushed into northern Belgium, determined to meet the German invaders head-on and prevent a single enemy tank from reaching French soil. It was a move the Germans had entirely predicted.

As the Allies marched north, forty-five German infantry and panzer divisions of Army Group A swept into southern Belgium through the Ardennes. The rugged terrain slowed the German panzers, but they navigated it far faster than the Allies thought possible and were soon crossing into France. After muscling past French infantry near the town of Sedan, the Germans unveiled another surprise. Rather than continuing south toward Paris, the armor wheeled to the west and charged toward the English Channel. The panzers reached the coastline within days, splitting the Allied army in two before advancing north and capturing two key ports, Boulogne and Calais. Though British-led forces were nearly encircled, hundreds of thousands managed to reach Dunkirk, a port still open near the Franco-Belgian border, and eventually escape to England.

The evacuation was a success, but the sudden withdrawal of so many Allied forces and Belgium's subsequent surrender left France in grave peril. When the Germans turned south for a final drive toward Paris, the French gamely stood their ground, counterattacking with their limited reserves and armor, but more defeats and wrenching losses followed.

On June 14, German columns marched into Paris, and the next day, a French army of 400,000 men surrendered near the Swiss border. With other resistance also collapsing, Paul

Reynaud, the French premier, resigned and was immediately replaced by Marshal Henri Phillipe Pétain, a hero of the First World War. Hoping to spare the country further turmoil, Pétain brokered an armistice with the Germans, and the remaining French armies soon laid down their arms. An exultant Hitler arrived in Paris, eager to return the humiliation of Germany's defeat two decades earlier. After arranging for French officials to surrender in the same railway car where the Germans had conceded in 1918, the fall of France was complete, and a sea of German troops began parading down the Champs-Élysées.

Aftermath

The western offensive of 1940 was a resounding triumph for Germany. The Allies in Holland, Belgium, and France had fought with courage, but they were outmaneuvered from the start and unable to overcome German firepower, planning, and leadership. An estimated 90,000 French soldiers were killed in the fighting, doubling German losses. The British, Belgians, and Dutch also suffered their share of casualties, but the most astounding figure was the number of Allied soldiers taken prisoner—over 1.5 million French alone.

With the surrender came a four-year occupation by German forces in Paris, the northern provinces, and along the Atlantic coast. Southern France, lacking any strategic importance, was permitted a somewhat autonomous government, with an official capital in the resort town of Vichy. Pétain was named head of state, and with the Germans expected to easily prevail against the British, his government fully cooperated with the Nazis, hoping to improve its post-war fortunes. Government ranks filled with French fascists and antisemites, as the Milice, a brutish paramilitary force, battled a budding resistance movement and joined the SS in scouring towns, villages, and the countryside for French Jews.

Much of France was plundered, with domestic production diverted to German war needs and hundreds of thousands of French workers shipped off to labor on Reich farms and factory floors. Throughout the occupation, the Gestapo and SS lurked everywhere, enforcing strict food rationing, curfews, and travel restrictions, and rooting out Jews in hiding. Some French collaborated with the Nazis, betraying their neighbors or associates for political or monetary rewards, while others joined resistance groups, subverting the Nazis and aiding the Allies at great personal risk. Most, however, simply sought to survive the occupation, hoping for future liberation from across the English Channel.

France's swift capitulation was a jarring shock to much of the world. Few could fathom how such a powerful army had been routed in just six weeks, and the downfall caused an immediate stir in the United States. With Hitler's sweep across Europe beginning to untether public opinion from longtime isolationist sentiment, American leaders finally came to life, recognizing how grossly unprepared the country was for what was unfolding beyond its shores. A military buildup would take time, though, and Britain, alone and facing possible invasion, was dangerously short of food, fuel, and war materiel. Many Americans remained opposed to military intervention, but it was plainly evident how precarious the plight across the Atlantic had become. A sense of urgency emerged among President Roosevelt and the US Congress to lend a hand and aid Britain's desperate fight for survival, soon to reach a fever pitch.

· · · · ·

French Resistance

Across defeated France, strong-willed partisans who refused to concede their country to the Germans organized themselves into a loosely confederated network of resistance. Known as the Maquis, they undermined the Nazis in secret, spying on occupation forces and smuggling downed Allied pilots to safety. When the Allies stormed ashore at Normandy in June 1944, the Maquis fought as guerillas from behind German lines, sabotaging rail lines and transportation hubs and pinning down reinforcements needed at the front.

Throughout the occupation, the Gestapo relentlessly pursued Resistance members, and reprisals against the general population were common, including mass executions of innocent civilians. One of the worst atrocities of the war occurred in Oradour-sur-Glane, a rustic farming village in southwestern France. On June 10, 1944, soldiers from the 2nd SS Panzer Division rounded up every villager, and those from the surrounding area, supposedly in retaliation for local Resistance activities. After shooting nearly 200 of the villagers, the SS locked another 450, including children, in a church and set it afire. The Nazis then burned the entire village to the ground. The charred remains of Oradour-sur-Glane have stood untouched since, a testament to the horrors endured by so many in France under the Nazi occupation.

Equally robust Resistance movements fought the Nazis in other occupied countries, including Norway, Denmark, Poland, Czechoslovakia, Belgium, Holland, the Soviet Union, Yugoslavia, and Greece. The courage among these men and women, of all ages and from all levels of society, was immeasurable, and each contributed to the eventual German defeat.

Charles de Gaulle

Throughout the heaviest fighting in France, one notable combatant was 49-year-old Charles de Gaulle, the youngest French general in the field. Commanding a single armored division, de Gaulle led several bold strikes against German panzer forces before escaping to England, where he became a leading and often controversial figure. He organized the Free French movement and future Resistance efforts against the German occupation, but also frequently quarreled with other

Allied leaders. In 1958, de Gaulle was elected president of France.

ⓘ Once retreating Allied soldiers began arriving on the beaches of Dunkirk by the tens of thousands, they lined up in long queues for transport to England, just forty miles away. Dive-bombers strafed and bombed the exposed men, as well as the docks and piers, but British air cover and foul weather eventually drove off the German fliers. As German panzer forces continued rolling up the coastline, a rear guard of British and French troops managed to slow their advance, and when German commanders inexplicably halted the armor just fifteen miles short of Dunkirk, the British took advantage of the pause, orchestrating the largest seaborne evacuation in military history. Amid a shortage of transports to ferry the men home, the British improvised, sending an armada of more than 800 naval and civilian ships across the English Channel, including troopships, fishing boats, tugboats, and other seaworthy vessels capable of making the short journey. Expecting to save just a fraction of the stranded men, the Royal Navy and civilian mariners who pitched in rescued 338,000 British, French, Dutch, and Belgian troops from certain capture. It was a stunning achievement.

3
BATTLE OF BRITAIN
JULY 1940–OCTOBER 1940

"I have nothing to offer but blood, toil, tears, and sweat."
–Winston Churchill addressing British Parliament, May 1940

On the heels of France's collapse, and with the might of the Third Reich looming just across the English Channel, invasion fears swept across Britain. Such anxieties were compounded by swirling doubts about the ability of the British Army to withstand a German landing. Nearly a quarter-million soldiers had been rescued from the beaches of Dunkirk, but most were exhausted and disheartened, and much of their equipment and heavy weaponry had been abandoned in France. Defeatism began surfacing among prominent figures in the British government, with some openly clamoring for a peace agreement with Hitler.

Winston Churchill was not one of them. The new prime minister, a former soldier and naval official, had been a blistering critic of his predecessor's appeasement strategy and refused to be cowed by Hitler and the Nazis. In a stirring public address following the calamity in France, Churchill vowed Britain would fight on, no matter the odds.

> "We shall go on to the end. We shall fight in France, we shall fight on the seas and oceans, we shall fight with growing confidence and growing strength in the air, we

shall defend our Island, whatever the cost may be. We shall fight on the beaches, we shall fight on the landing grounds, we shall fight in the fields and in the streets, we shall fight in the hills; we shall never surrender."

Churchill's inspiring words that day were intended to rally a demoralized Britain while appealing for support from across the Atlantic. They proved prophetic, as there would indeed be a fight over the nation's fate, but not on landing beaches or hillsides. It would come in the skies above England, as the vaunted German Luftwaffe prepared to shatter Britain into pieces and bring the broken country to its knees. Only a spirited but untested corps of Royal Air Force (RAF) pilots stood in its way.

• • • • •

By July 1940, Germany was in firm control of the European continent. An invasion of southern England seemed likely to many, but there was little enthusiasm for such an operation among Hitler's military hierarchy. The Wehrmacht had no training in amphibious landings, nor did the Kriegsmarine (German Navy) possess the means to carry so many troops and tanks across open water. Hitler, rankled by Britain's refusal to concede, brushed aside such practical concerns and ordered his staff to finalize details for toppling his pesky nemesis. The planned invasion was codenamed Sea Lion and projected to begin August 15.

An operation of such scale across the English Channel could not succeed without first neutralizing Britain's naval and air forces. With the Kriegsmarine and Royal Navy already tangling at sea, Britain's air defenses were left to Hermann Göring, chief of the Luftwaffe. A decorated former pilot, Göring was a longtime Nazi, and both a confidante of Hitler and his designated successor. He assured the führer his planes would destroy the RAF in a matter of weeks.

It promised to be a clash in the sky like no other. Thousands of planes would be involved, all far more advanced than the fabric-and-wood biplanes Göring flew in World War I. The 1930s had been a transformative period for aviation after manufacturers began experimenting with new airframes and single-wing designs. By the middle of the decade, factories across Europe, Asia, and North America were wheeling out the first monoplanes made of lightweight aluminum. Fitted with powerful engines and armament, their speed and maneuverability far surpassed that of their predecessors.

For the coming battle, the Luftwaffe assembled 1,600 modern bombers, a force unheard of at the time. They were a mix of twin-engine, high-altitude bombers and single-engine, dive-bombing *Stukas*, and though they lacked the devastating payloads of later four-engine American and British models, the bombers still packed a meaningful punch. They would be protected by more than 900 fighter escorts, including hundreds of Messerschmitt 109Es, considered by many the finest fighter planes in the world.

With far fewer planes available, the British counted on their innovative air defense system to even the odds. Developed in the late 1930s, it was unmatched in the world, integrating ground-to-air communications and new radar technology to support fighter forces dispersed across England. A network of radar stations dotted Britain's southern and eastern coastlines, capable of detecting incoming enemy aircraft from a distance of eighty miles. Though the technology could provide early warning of enemy formations, it could not discern details — a gap the British intended to fill with hundreds of civilian observation posts sprinkled across the countryside. As the German planes passed overhead, volunteers with binoculars in hand would relay pertinent information about the formations, including the size, composition, heading, and altitude, to Fighter Command

Headquarters in North London. Within minutes, fighter squadrons would be scrambled, and intercept courses plotted.

The Germans began the campaign with a clear numerical edge – some 2,600 bombers and fighters against the 700 planes of Fighter Command. Among the RAF's inventory were Hawker *Hurricanes*, sturdy and heavily armed aircraft that were best suited to take on the German bombers. Supermarine *Spitfires*, faster and more agile than the *Hurricanes*, would match up against the Messerschmitts, but early models of the *Spitfire* lacked the firepower and climbing and diving speed of the German planes. Later upgrades would make the *Spitfire* one of the most revered planes of the war, but its limitations in 1940 added to the daunting challenges facing the British airmen.

THE BATTLE AND THE BLITZ

The Germans hoped to end the air battle before the projected invasion date of August 15, but it took considerable time before the Luftwaffe could marshal its full weight. Aircraft lost during battles in France and the Low Countries had to be replaced, and entire squadrons – aircraft, fuel supplies, spare parts, and munitions – moved to newly acquired airfields closer to Britain. Shortening the flight distance was critical for the range limited Messerschmitts; even from France, the German fighters would have just twenty minutes of fuel over England.

The contest began in earnest in July, when the Germans initially targeted port facilities and the two sides sparred early over the English Channel and coastal areas. The Germans soon shifted their focus to RAF airfields and radar stations, but the British fliers held their own, downing far more bombers than Berlin expected. The slow-moving *Stukas* proved such easy targets they had to be withdrawn from the battle entirely, while the high-altitude bombers were routinely abandoned by the fuel starved Messerschmitts before reaching their destinations. Defenseless against the *Hurricanes* and *Spitfires*, heavy losses ensued, but the Germans pressed on, forcing the beleaguered British pilots to fly from dawn to dusk.

With Fighter Command beginning to stagger, the battle took an unexpected turn after several German bombs fell on London. The British retaliated with their own modest strike against Berlin, and though damage was negligible, the attack infuriated Hitler and humiliated Göring, who had long boasted the German capital would never be touched by Allied bombers. A fateful decision followed, with German bombing runs against British air defenses diverted to population and industrial centers instead.

London absorbed a pounding, beginning in early September, when more than 900 German bombers and fighter planes battered the capital in a single raid, killing and injuring an estimated 1,600 people. More bombers returned that evening, the first of fifty-seven consecutive nighttime attacks, a period Londoners came to know as the Blitz.

Unable to operate at night, RAF fighters were absent from the sky, leaving German pilots free to rain their bombs down on power stations, arms factories, ports, dockyards, warehouses, oil refineries, and even residential areas. Damage and civilian losses were substantial, but the Luftwaffe's pivot away from Britain's air defenses was a gift to the RAF. Grounded during the nighttime raids, exhausted *Spitfire* and *Hurricane* pilots gained desperately needed rest after weeks of continuous combat, and ground crews took advantage of the lull to repair damaged planes and restock depleted squadrons. When the Germans eventually resumed their attacks on airfields and radar stations across southern England, hoping to salvage an invasion, a revitalized Fighter Command rose to the occasion.

Göring's failure to obliterate Britain's air defenses as promised led Hitler to postpone Sea Lion indefinitely, but the Luftwaffe's rampage against London continued. For months, city residents came to dread nightfall, when the blare of air raid sirens sent much of the population scrambling into underground rail stations and other shelters, as bomb blasts turned neighborhoods into rubble and ash. On a single evening in May 1941, over 86,000 incendiaries fell on the capital, sparking some 2,100 fires across the city and killing more than 1,400 residents.

It was the most despairing period of the war for Britain. Throughout late 1940 and into 1941, the country endured daily bombings, blackout conditions, and dwindling food and heating fuel. The British people refused to buckle, wearily climbing out of their shelters each morning to douse fires, sift through burning wreckage and debris, and search for fallen family members and neighbors. Led by the steadfast Churchill, their resolve never faltered, and as air raid sirens sounded day and night, soldiers and civilians alike answered the call, manning anti-aircraft guns, fire hoses, and medical stations. Day after day, they readied themselves for the next attack. As Churchill foresaw before the battle began, it came to be Britain's finest hour.

Aftermath

Attrition during the Battle of Britain was costly to both air forces, but it was the Luftwaffe that lost the far greater share of pilots. Among other factors, the battle was fought almost entirely over England, allowing British airmen to set their damaged planes down in friendly farm pastures, or parachute virtually anywhere and return to their airfields within hours. Downed German pilots who survived their landings were marched into prisoner of war (POW) camps, out of the war for good.

Civilian losses were high—at least 43,000 were killed in the Blitz—but the Battle of Britain was a clear setback for Hitler. After dominating the skies over Poland, Scandinavia, and Western Europe, the Luftwaffe never achieved air supremacy over England, dashing Hitler's hopes for a swift conquest that would allow him to reposition and concentrate his armies for a long-planned campaign in the East.

It was a win that belonged to all of Britain. When Churchill declared to Parliament that, "Never in the field of human conflict was so much owed by so many to so few," it was an homage to not only the young, intrepid aviators of Fighter Command—the average RAF pilot was just twenty years old—but others who stepped into the breach as well. That included the tireless ground crews who kept the banged-up planes in the sky, the radar plotters who remained at their posts during the worst of German bombing raids, and the many civilian observers, firefighters, air raid wardens, and others who volunteered for service and contributed in some form to the outcome.

The defeat ended any German aspirations for a seaborne invasion, but it was hardly the only threat Britain faced beyond its shores. Throughout the early months of the war, German surface ships and submarines scavenged in the waters around Britain and beyond, mercilessly hunting Allied cargo ships carrying precious food stores and other supplies the country needed to survive. The fate of the British people was still very much in doubt.

· · · · ·

Winston Churchill

Winston Churchill (1874—1965) began his military career in 1895 as a second lieutenant in the British Army. Taken prisoner during the Boer War in South Africa, he escaped captivity and returned home to begin a meteoric political career, winning his first election to the House of Commons in 1900. A decade later, Churchill was named first lord of the admiralty, a civilian post leading the Royal Navy, and was serving in that position when the First World War began. In 1915, he received scathing criticism for his role in a crushing British defeat at

Gallipoli. Facing demotion, Churchill resigned from government service but refused to leave the war, re-joining the Army as a battalion commander and serving on the Western Front in France.

Churchill later became a widely celebrated author and public speaker. In the late 1930s, he emerged as a leading voice against the spread of fascism, denouncing Hitler's belligerence and the tepid response of Britain and France. When Prime Minister Neville Chamberlain's appeasement strategy gave rise to disaster, emboldening Hitler to invade Poland, Churchill joined Chamberlain's war cabinet, serving again as first lord of the admiralty. Just eight months into the war, Chamberlain resigned, and the 65-year-old Churchill was chosen to be the new prime minister, later appointing himself defense minister as well.

In a 1940 radio address, Churchill exhorted the British people to remain resilient. "Never give in, never, never, never—in nothing, great or small, large or petty—never give in except to convictions of honor and good sense." Leading a coalition government that spanned the political spectrum, the defiant Churchill publicly decried the Third Reich at every turn as he rallied the British people to the fight. In private, he pleaded with President Roosevelt to bring America into the war and help sustain Britain as it battled Hitler's forces. The two leaders forged a close wartime partnership, and though they would later ally themselves with the Soviet Union out of necessity, Churchill remained deeply distrustful of its dictator, Joseph Stalin, whose long-term political aims clearly extended outside Soviet borders.

Churchill was one of the central architects of the Allied strategy for defeating the Nazis, and though his extraordinary leadership guided Britain through the most perilous of times, his term as prime minister came to a shocking end in 1945. Economic and social reforms backed by the opposition party in national elections carried broad appeal that year, winning the day and leading to the ouster of Churchill's party. He became prime minister again in 1951, but declining health compelled the statesman to step down four years later. Churchill continued to serve in Parliament and was later named an honorary United States Citizen by an act of Congress before passing away in 1965 at the age of ninety.

> **British Empire**
> In 1940, the British Empire, then known as the Commonwealth of Nations, encompassed one-quarter of the world population. All shared a common monarch, but governance within the Commonwealth was largely race-based. Member states with predominantly White populations, including Australia, Canada, and New Zealand, were considered dominions, and permitted self-rule, while colonies with majority non-White populations, such as India and Burma (present-day Myanmar), were primarily governed from London.

Commonwealth members were a pillar of the British war effort, contributing to the fight against the Axis powers from virtually every corner of the globe. Canada and Australia devoted substantial ground and naval forces to fighting the Germans and Japanese, while India fielded a volunteer army of over two million men. Industrial output and raw materials from the Commonwealth were equally vital. More than 150 Canadian factories produced weapons and war goods Britain was desperately short of, including some 16,000 aircraft flown by Allied pilots. Trinidad and Tobago supplied the Royal Navy and RAF with oil, Nigeria provided tin for engine parts, and Ceylon (present-day Sri Lanka) supplied the rubber used in boots, tires, and even tanks. Not all participation in the Allied cause was voluntary. As it had throughout its colonial history, Britain obliged many of its Commonwealth subjects to serve in uniform or labor in factories and mines, even against their will, claiming the necessities of war as justification.

Josef Frantisek

Josef Frantisek was among the highest-scoring aces of the Battle of Britain, downing seventeen German planes. A Czechoslovakian who joined the RAF after fleeing the Nazis in Europe, Frantisek was not alone among foreign-born RAF pilots. From across the British Commonwealth, they filled out RAF squadrons, including Australians, Canadians, New Zealanders, South Africans, and Rhodesians (present-day Zimbabwe and Zambia). There were also French, Polish, Dutch, Belgian, and Czechoslovakian pilots like Frantisek who escaped the Nazi occupations of their countries and formed their own squadrons within the RAF.

 Women's Auxiliary Air Force

Among Britain's preparations for war in 1939 was the formation of the Women's Auxiliary Air Force (WAAF). Conceived to fill essential support roles across an expanding RAF, it became widely popular among young women, with tens of thousands volunteering from the outset.

Initially assigned clerical and cooking duties, it was not long before the women began filling far more substantive roles. They quickly showed an aptitude every bit equal to that of their male counterparts as they took on new jobs, from aircraft maintenance and repair to intelligence and cryptography. Unlike later American auxiliaries, most serving in the WAAF were not grouped into all-women units but posted to specific RAF commands. Many attained the rank of officers and were often assigned hazardous duty in radar stations and fighter operations centers as technical and communications specialists. They became the backbone of the air defense system, remaining faithfully at their posts day and night, amid German bombing and strafing attacks. Many were killed or wounded in the line of duty.

The WAAF reached a peak strength of 182,000 in 1943, but it was hardly the only women's auxiliary supplementing the country's defenses. Another 250,000 women performed a wide range of support functions in the Auxiliary Territorial Service, including tens of thousands who served as radar operators or with anti-aircraft gun crews. The Women's Royal Naval Service (WRNS, or "Wrens") filled another void, with some 74,000 women serving in shore-based positions, including as codebreakers and translators.

4
BATTLE OF THE ATLANTIC
SEPTEMBER 1939—MAY 1943

"Every so often you'd hear that undeniable sound off in the distance someplace of a torpedo going off inside a ship. It's a sound you never forgot."
–John Campbell, US Merchant Marine

In the months following the German triumph in Poland, the ground war between the Axis and Allies remained surprisingly quiet, as the two sides continued to mobilize and stock their armies for Hitler's expected offensive in Western Europe. At sea, a far different narrative unfolded, as rivaling navies clashed repeatedly, from the waters of Northern Ireland to the tip of South America.

By mid-1940, the German Army was no longer idle, having swept across much of the European continent. To weaken their lone remaining adversary, the Germans began preying on Britain's ocean commerce, aiming to sever the lifeline of food—two-thirds of its supply was imported—fuel, and other needed war materiel flowing from Commonwealth allies. As the sea battle intensified, the ubiquitous submarines known as U-boats emerged as Germany's most terrorizing weapon, wreaking havoc on Allied freighters and warships alike. Barely a year into the war, they threatened to starve the British people into submission and deliver another crowning victory to Hitler.

• • • • •

In September 1939, shortly after Britain and France declared war on Germany, a U-boat off the coast of Ireland torpedoed the Canada-bound *Athenia*, a British ocean liner, killing 118 civilian passengers. They were among the first casualties at sea in what became an unsparing campaign against shipping traffic in the Atlantic, where both armed and unarmed merchantmen were hunted relentlessly by the German submarine fleet.

It began with much promise for the Kriegsmarine. The naval service lacked the strength and stature of its sister branches in the German military, having been allocated far fewer resources than the Wehrmacht and Luftwaffe during Hitler's pre-war buildup, but its modest submarine force quickly amassed an impressive early record. The U-boats and their small crews sank a British aircraft carrier, a battleship, and dozens of merchant ships and oil tankers.

Their easiest quarry were defenseless cargo ships scattered across the sea. Naval escorts were an effective deterrent, especially nimble destroyers carrying depth charges (explosives dropped into the sea and detonated at pre-selected depths), but few were available for such duty, the Royal Navy thinned by losses from operations off the coasts of Norway and France. New destroyers were ordered, but production was slowed by scarce raw materials and limited shipbuilding capacity in Britain.

As the U-boats continued to victimize Allied shipping, Canada pitched in to fill the void. With a population of less than twelve million people, the country scaled up its forces in a remarkably short time, providing critical naval and air support to British merchant traffic reeling from an onslaught of German torpedoes. The British also turned to a proven tactic from the First World War, herding freighters and tankers into large convoys that could be defended with few escorts. Land-based bombers were employed as well, as U-boats capable of submerging only for limited intervals could often be spotted from the air, prowling along the surface.

The Germans were also adapting. After the conquest of France provided new bases along the continental seaboard, U-boats began probing deep into the Atlantic, beyond the reach of the British Home Fleet and RAF bombers. Lacking radar, the submarines grouped themselves into "wolfpacks" to search for convoys while spread across a great distance. Hunted by these wolfpacks around the clock, the transatlantic crossings became a terrifying journey for Allied sailors and civilian merchantmen. German torpedoes slammed into freighter after freighter, tearing holes in their steel hulls and sending the great ships to the ocean floor.

Relief came that autumn, following the Battle of Britain, when the invasion threat to England dissipated, and much of the Home Fleet was released from close-shore duty. Sent into the Atlantic, they were soon joined by fifty American-built World War I-era destroyers, transferred to Britain in exchange for several bases in the Western Hemisphere. The handover of the surplus ships — obsolete by existing standards but more than capable of protecting slow-moving cargo ships and tankers — was just the start of American aid to come.

1941: THE PIVOTAL YEAR
Popular opinion in the United States had long held that commercial interests and war profiteering had ensnared America in the First World War. To prevent a reoccurrence, the US Congress passed a series of measures in the 1930s barring the sale of arms to other nations at war. Excluded from these Neutrality Acts were non-military goods, such as food and oil, which could be sold on a "cash-and-carry" basis, so long as payment was promptly received, and the goods were transported on non-American ships. When the war opened, President Roosevelt and Congress agreed to aid friendly nations

at war with Germany by expanding cash-and-carry to include arms sales, but early war spending had drained Britain's treasury, leaving the country unable to pay for needed weapons and supplies.

As Britain continued to struggle against the Nazis, Congress passed a landmark bill in early 1941—the Lend-Lease Act—empowering the Roosevelt Administration to loan or lease war materiel to any country at its discretion. The new law sailed through both chambers by wide margins, and factories and industrial plants immediately began ramping up domestic production. Buoyed by the expected surge of goods and weapons across the Atlantic, Churchill hailed Lend-Lease as "Hitler's death warrant," and indeed, by the end of the war, the United States had become a global arsenal, supplying arms and raw materials worth an estimated $49 billion ($760 billion in present-day dollars) to Britain and some forty other countries, most notably China and the Soviet Union.

Another decisive turn that year came in late spring, when civilian cryptanalysts working at Bletchley Park, a country estate outside London and headquarters for British signals intelligence efforts, achieved a momentous breakthrough. The Germans had long encrypted their most sensitive military communications with the Enigma, a device that resembled a typewriter and converted plain text messages into random letters. The recipient, using an Enigma with identical settings, then converted the encrypted message back to the original text. With the aid of captured materials provided by Polish cryptanalysts, teams at Bletchley Park cracked part of the German encryption system, reaping a bonanza of intelligence. For months, the Allies were privy to German naval messages, including communiqués positioning wolfpacks in the Atlantic. Convoys were diverted to safer waters, steering numerous ships from harm's way.

The intelligence paid other dividends as well. In May of that year, the Germans ordered a prized battleship and a newly built

heavy cruiser into the Atlantic to ambush Allied shipping. The *Bismarck* and *Prinz Eugen* were intercepted by a pair of British battleships in the Denmark Strait, and the two sides traded fusillades from across the water. A shell fired by the *Bismarck* exploded near an ammunition magazine on the HMS *Hood*, triggering a massive blast that tore apart one of the Royal Navy's most storied ships, killing all but three members of its 1,400-man crew. Damaged in the exchange, the *Bismarck* steamed to a base on the French coast for repairs. When decrypted intercepts revealed the ship's intended destination, British naval forces avenged the *Hood*, converging on the *Bismarck* and sinking it with nearly 2,000 crew members aboard.

Operation Drumbeat

The year 1941 had been a grueling one for the Kriegsmarine, but the pendulum in the Atlantic would soon swing back in Germany's favor. In early 1942, shortly after the United States entered the war, U-boats were dispatched to Western Hemisphere waters to disrupt Allied shipping there. British warnings about the planned operation, codenamed Drumbeat, went unheeded by their American counterparts, nor were convoys organized despite scarce naval and air support. Authorities also neglected to enforce nighttime blackouts along the East Coast, leaving freighters offshore silhouetted against the glow of city lights and easy targets for U-boats lurking nearby. A drubbing ensued, and by August, the U-boats had torpedoed hundreds of ships off America's shores.

Allied losses tapered off once convoys were finally employed, even more so as the convoys became increasingly ringed by newly built destroyers and long-range bombers armed with advanced radar and sonar systems and improved anti-submarine weapons. The arrival of new escort aircraft carriers in mid-1943 added to the protective brawn. Smaller and slower than the "fleet" carriers sent to the Pacific, the escort carriers had little problem keeping up with the freighters and oilers and closed a critical gap during the transatlantic voyages, providing close-in air support against U-boats over stretches of ocean unreachable by land-based bombers.

The battle eventually became one-sided. The Germans lost three times as many submarines in the second half of 1942 as they did in the first half, and though they sank over 600 merchant ships in late 1942, they tallied just a quarter of that number in the same period one year later. In May 1943 alone, forty-one U-boats were lost, and barely a dent was made in the Allied merchant fleet. The Battle of the Atlantic would continue for two more years, but the German Navy was no longer a viable threat to the Allied war effort.

AFTERMATH

Steep wartime losses in the Atlantic on both sides reflected a tenuous struggle that teetered back and forth until Allied advantages in shipbuilding, long-range air support, technology, and intelligence swayed the outcome. The German submarine fleet was nearly wiped out by the end of the war, with the loss of 781 boats. Of the roughly 40,000 German sailors who served in the submarine service, an estimated 30,000 went down with their "iron coffins." The Allies suffered as well, with nearly 3,000 merchant and escort ships sunk, and tens of thousands of crew members lost at sea. No one had it worse than merchant mariners—one out of every twenty-six was killed during the war, a higher casualty rate than any of the military services.

• • • • •

 In August 1941, Winston Churchill made a perilous sea journey to Canada to meet with President Roosevelt in

Placentia Bay, Newfoundland. Notwithstanding America's official neutrality, it was little secret the US Government was supporting Britain in its struggle against Germany, and at Placentia Bay, the two leaders signed a Joint Declaration of Principles, all but publicly declaring themselves allies. What came to be known as the Atlantic Charter defined the post-war aims of the two countries, including an agreement not to seek new territories — a failed legacy of the Treaty of Versailles — and a mutual embrace of collective security. The Charter further laid down a series of foundational principles, such as the right of nations to choose their own government and to be free from fear and want, that eventually became the basis for the establishment of the United Nations.

Allied Codebreakers

With the introduction of communications technology in the early twentieth century, and the ease of intercepting messages transmitted across the radio airwaves, came the rise of cryptography — the study of coding and cipher systems. In the 1920s, the German Army acquired a commercially produced system of cipher machines, modified by the Wehrmacht to encrypt their most secret military communications. Users of these "Enigma" machines typed out a plain text message on a standard keyboard, and a set of rotors with prescribed settings produced random letters. Once the enciphered message was received, another Enigma machine with identical settings was used to convert it back into plain text. Widely employed throughout World War II, the Germans considered the Enigma machines impenetrable.

They were wrong. In the 1930s, Polish cryptanalysts created a replica Enigma machine and successfully deciphered German message traffic without tipping off Berlin. The Poles shared their findings with the British in 1939, but to little avail, as the Germans had begun adjusting their machine settings every twenty-four hours, leaving too little time to crack the Enigma ciphers. Tackling this challenge was a team of civilian mathematicians, engineers, and other specialists laboring at Bletchley Park, some forty miles outside London. Among them was Alan Turing, a gifted, 28-year-old mathematician who invented a revolutionary electromechanical machine called a "bombe." Capable of sifting through millions of possible Enigma settings, Turing's bombe, and the capture of enciphering tables and other key materials, led to the eventual unlocking of the German naval codes. The intelligence had a substantial impact in the Battle of the Atlantic, allowing the Allies to safely re-route convoys away from the wolfpacks and thwart German efforts to refuel and replenish the U-boats at sea.

By the end of the war, the workforce at Bletchley Park had expanded to more than 10,000 men and women, including musicians, chess champions, linguists, and others whose unique skills were essential to the historic codebreaking enterprise. Barred by the Official Secrets Act from discussing their wartime function, the work at Bletchley Park remained concealed until the 1970s, when much of it was finally declassified, and the public learned of its pivotal role in the Allied war effort.

 **Franklin Delano Roosevelt**
Franklin Delano Roosevelt (1882—1945) was a native of Hyde Park, New York, and later attended Harvard and

Columbia Universities. He began his career practicing law, and in 1910, was elected to the New York State Senate. Roosevelt became active in Democratic Party circles, and three years after his first election, President Woodrow Wilson appointed the ambitious and charismatic 31-year-old to serve as assistant secretary of the US Navy. When war spilled across Europe in 1914, Roosevelt became immersed in military administration—experience that became indispensable a quarter-century later.

In 1921, decades before a vaccine had been developed, Roosevelt was stricken with polio, an infectious disease that causes paralysis, and lost the use of his legs. Roosevelt was resilient, though, and his political ascendency continued in 1928 when he was elected governor of New York. Four years later, with the American economy shattered by the Great Depression, Roosevelt became the Democratic nominee for president. Throughout the election season, he sounded notes of optimism and determination, vowing to use every instrument of government to end the worst fiscal crisis in American history. Voters swept Roosevelt into the White House in an electoral college landslide, winning 472-59 and gaining large Democratic majorities in Congress.

He inherited an economy in shambles. By the end of 1932, one out of every three workers were jobless, and farm foreclosures and bank failures were spiraling out of control. Factories remained shuttered, and endless lines of hungry, homeless families awaited their turn at soup kitchens from coast to coast. Roosevelt fulfilled his campaign pledge, championing a flurry of government initiatives coined a "New Deal" for impoverished Americans. Hundreds of thousands of unemployed Americans found work with the new Civilian

Conservation Corps; the Agricultural Adjustment Administration stabilized farm and commodity prices; and the Social Security Act guaranteed income security to workers and retirees. Such measures were an early success, providing needed relief, but they were far from a panacea. It would take a war economy and a nationwide industrialization years later to finally reverse America's longtime decline.

During the war, Roosevelt surrounded himself with accomplished and respected advisors from across the political spectrum. Guided by their experience, he presided over a historic mobilization, forged critical international alliances, and immersed himself in strategy and policy deliberations. With his popular "fireside chats" over the radio airwaves, he reached and comforted millions of Americans, boosting their morale during the darkest days of the war.

Roosevelt has been faulted for shortcomings as well, including his administration's wartime imprisonment of Japanese Americans—most of them US citizens—and its inadequate, limited response to the extermination of European Jews. He failed to advance civil rights for African Americans, and, reluctant to risk alienating Southern Democrats in Congress, rarely spoke out against the racial violence and discrimination that pervaded America.

Though clearly imperfect, Roosevelt was an accomplished, popular president, undaunted by the two great crises gripping the country during his tenure in office. He rallied Americans through the Depression and war, winning re-election three times, and remains the only US President ever to serve more than two terms. It is a record likely to remain unmatched unless the 22nd Amendment to the Constitution—ratified in 1951 and limiting presidents to two terms in office—is repealed.

On April 12, 1945, shortly after beginning his fourth term in office, Roosevelt suffered a cerebral hemorrhage while visiting Warm Springs, Georgia. The death of the 63-year-old was widely mourned across the United States.

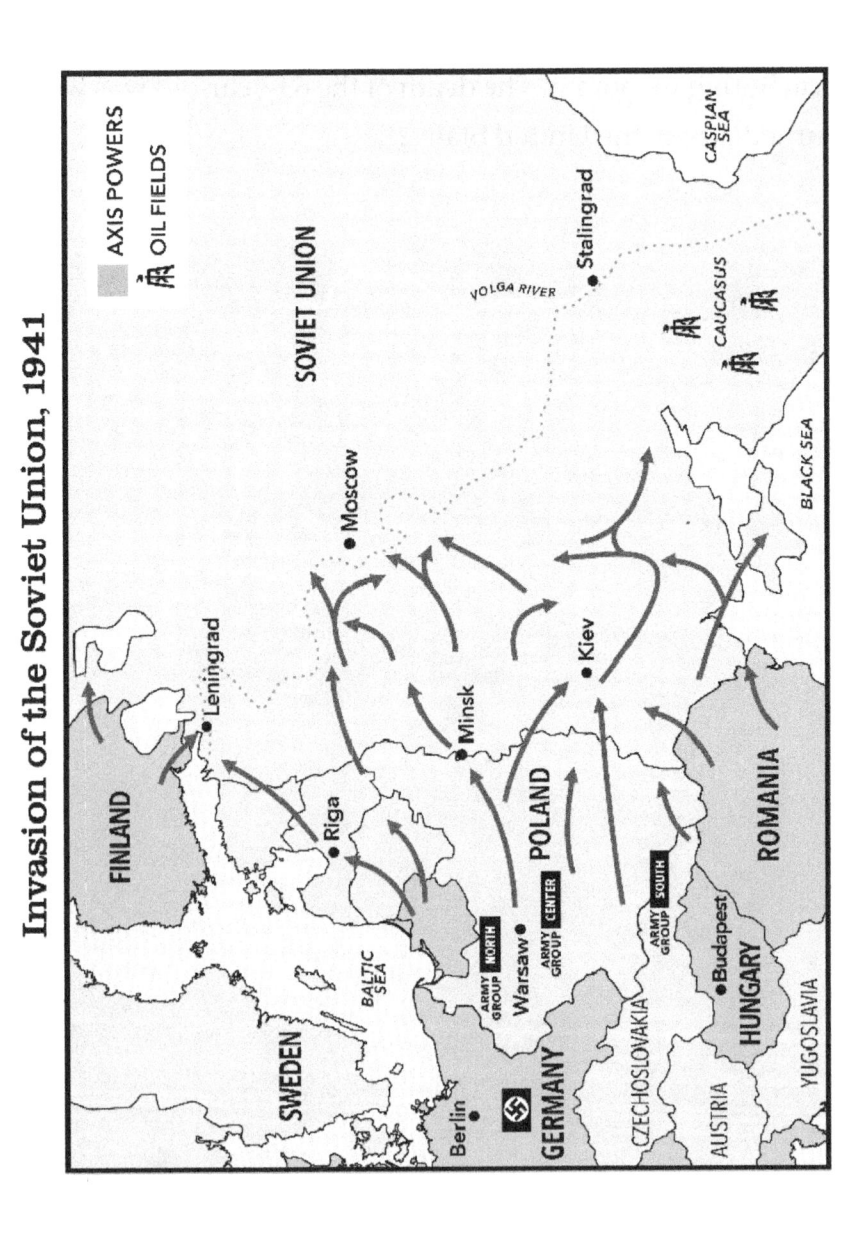

5
THE EASTERN FRONT: OPERATION BARBAROSSA
JUNE 1941–DECEMBER 1941

"The external security of a people is largely determined by the size of its territory."
–**Adolf Hitler, Mein Kampf**

In early 1917, amid statewide hunger and soaring numbers of Russian dead in trenches across Eastern and Central Europe, mass protests erupted in the Imperial Russian capital of Petrograd. Tsar Nicholas II abdicated his throne, the monarchy fell, and months later, the Bolsheviks—a faction of far-left revolutionaries led by Vladimir Lenin—seized control. In 1922, they formed the Union of Soviet Socialist Republics (USSR), and Joseph Stalin, a 43-year-old former editor of the Bolshevik newspaper, became general secretary of the Soviet Communist Party.

It was a powerful political perch, allowing the upstart Stalin to cultivate a loyal core of supporters. When Lenin died two years later, Stalin stepped into the void, eliminating potential rivals by ordering arrests, sham trials, and executions. Instead of a promised utopia of political and economic equality, Stalin's iron fist molded the Soviet Union into a repressive dictatorship. The state controlled virtually every aspect of Soviet life, enforcing political conformity at gunpoint. Public criticism was forbidden, and those who voiced dissent were jailed or exiled to forced labor camps in Siberia called gulags. By the 1930s, the Stalin regime was rooting out all possible opposition, real or imagined, in what became known as the Great Terror, when hundreds of thousands of Communist Party members were purged for alleged anti-Stalin sentiment. Millions of others were banished to the gulags, and as executions became increasingly common, not even the military was immune to the upheaval. Some 30,000 officers—more than one-third of the Soviet officer corps—were tarred with accusations of subversion and treason, and a fractured Red Army began the Second World War far more brittle than it appeared.

Adolf Hitler took notice. Though he had conspired with Stalin in August 1939 to dismember Poland, the German leader plotted to betray his counterpart and capitalize on what he perceived as fragility within the Soviet political system and military ranks. "We only have to kick in the door," he crowed to his inner circle, "and the entire rotten structure will come crashing down." In June 1941, the Germans kicked in the door.

• • • • •

The Soviet-German Nonaggression Pact of 1939 was one of the most consequential bilateral agreements of the twentieth century. It freed the Germans to invade Poland without worry of Soviet interference, while providing Stalin with similar latitude to expand his own sphere in Eastern Europe. It also produced a trade agreement that sent German-manufactured goods and machinery to the Soviet Union in return for raw materials, such as oil, rubber, and lumber.

Following the demise of Poland, an emboldened Stalin bullied his way into the Baltics, strong-arming Estonia, Latvia, and Lithuania into allowing Soviet bases on their soil in exchange for continued independence. When he then demanded territorial concessions from Finland, his northern neighbor flatly refused — defiance the Soviet leader was unaccustomed to.

In late 1939, the Red Army followed the Nazi script in Poland, manufacturing a provocation with the Finns before barreling across their shared border. It was a clumsy beginning, with hundreds of thousands of Soviet troops crossing into unfamiliar terrain with little planning or preparation. The Finnish troops who greeted them were substantially outnumbered and ill-equipped, but well-trained for winter warfare. In sub-freezing temperatures and heavy snow, the hard-nosed Finns bloodied the invaders in a series of early skirmishes, fighting them to a standstill until a flood of Soviet reinforcements arrived. The tide was reversed, and by March 1940, the brief war was over. The two sides signed a peace accord ceding nearly one-tenth of Finland to the Soviets, but with the Red Army's early struggles, international observers were hardly impressed.

That included Hitler. His long-sought lebensraum and eternal Reich depended on copious resources harvested from Soviet lands, including vast oil deposits in the Caucasus (present-day Georgia, Armenia, and Azerbaijan) and bounties of Ukrainian crops and coal. Under the 1939 trade agreement, trainloads of Soviet goods flowed into Germany, but it was far from enough for Hitler. He also wanted the land, which he intended to resettle with the sons and daughters of Germany once existing Jewish, Slavic, and other occupants were disposed of. As Hitler and his staff concocted their plan to invade the Soviet Union, Operation Barbarossa had all the hallmarks of a race war — one the führer had been pining for since *Mein Kampf* first rolled off the printing presses.

Fresh off decisive victories in Greece and Yugoslavia, the Germans marshaled an invasion force of unprecedented size and power. Hitler planned to send more than three million soldiers and 3,400 tanks into Soviet territory, advancing his forces along a front as wide as Chicago to Los Angeles. Logistical challenges loomed large, as the farther Axis forces plunged into the geographical sprawl of the Soviet Union, the farther it would stretch supply lines needed to feed and fuel the men and tanks. Hitler was unconcerned, confident his armies would march into Moscow long before supply problems materialized.

Germany's brisk buildup in the East in early 1941 drew considerable attention in diplomatic and intelligence circles, inundating the Kremlin—the seat of Soviet power and authority—with invasion warnings. Stalin dismissed them all, unwilling to fully mobilize his forces for war—a move he feared would antagonize and provoke Hitler, and end their accord. Stalin also placed great faith in the masses of Soviet ground and air forces posted along his western borders, ignoring the warning signs from the Finland operation, where poor training and equipment and a dearth of capable officers in the wake of the purges had greatly diminished the fighting capacity of the Red Army. With senior ranks filled by those who feared the Kremlin more than any foreign invader, few along the border were willing to question Stalin's judgment and ready their forces for a potential invasion. The lack of preparation sealed their fate.

Invasion

Barbarossa began on June 22, 1941. Some 180 Axis divisions, including half-a-million revenge-minded Finns, as well as troops from Romania, Italy, Hungary, and Slovakia, streamed into the Soviet Union behind a firestorm of air strikes and artillery barrages. The Luftwaffe quickly gained control of the skies, destroying over 1,000 Soviet aircraft on the ground, and as panzer armies charged into Soviet lines and defenses unimpeded, resistance among Soviet ground forces became chaotic and confused. Some units bravely stood their ground as others simply melted away.

There was some thought in Berlin that a Soviet population suffering under Stalin's repressive edicts might welcome the Germans as liberators, but that possibility evaporated after SS Einsatzgruppen trailing the invasion forces began massacring Soviet civilians on a horrific scale. They were utterly barbaric, gunning down Jews and suspected Bolsheviks by the thousands each day, while packing three million other Slavs into railcars like cattle. They would be transported to the Reich for use as slave labor.

At the front, lead elements had little difficulty overrunning the Red Army. German tanks and aircraft dominated the early action against inferior Soviet models, with the speed of the German armor unexpected. Panzer armies drove across the Soviet frontier, encircling entire regiments and divisions, and by late summer, Axis forces had closed in on three prizes: Leningrad (present-day St. Petersburg), an industrial city and transportation hub in the north; the resource-rich Ukraine and Caucasus in the south; and in the center, Moscow. The capital drew the largest German army group, as Hitler's generals were convinced toppling it would shatter any further Soviet resistance. At a pivotal moment, though, an impatient Hitler intervened, delaying the drive on Moscow to divert more panzer forces to the north and south. The pause was a misstep, enabling weary Russian forces defending the capital to bolster their ranks and refortify their lines.

October came, and with it, German failures to capture Leningrad or reach the Caucasus. The assault on Moscow finally resumed, led by some 2,000 tanks, but the Soviets mounted a furious defense, and both sides suffered devastating casualties. By early December, the panzers had battled to the outskirts of the city, but they would get no closer, as a new adversary brought a sudden halt to operations across the Eastern Front. Russia's notorious winter weather had arrived.

Weather issues had first confounded the Germans in autumn, when heavy rains produced rivers of mud, making roads and fields nearly impassable and hindering advances everywhere. The invasion plan had presumed the Soviets would succumb long before winter set in, but as the first snow fell, every German army group remained locked into battle. Few of the invaders had winter clothing and greatcoats—the German High Command had deemed shipments of ammunition and other supplies higher priorities—and as temperatures plunged below zero, oil and other lubricants froze solid. Tanks and airplanes became inoperable, and even machine guns and rifles refused to function properly. Supply lines faltered, and food stores ran low.

The Soviets, meanwhile, grew stronger. Fresh divisions arrived from the east, and hundreds of tank, aircraft, and munitions factories that had been moved from western Russia to prevent their capture had been reassembled inside Soviet-held territory. A manufacturing push began delivering mass quantities of new aircraft, artillery pieces, and other weapons to frontline forces, including modern T-34 tanks that became the mainstay of Soviet armored forces, rivaling the best German panzers. Reinvigorated, the Soviets launched a counteroffensive in December. The exhausted and supply-thin Germans were driven back from Moscow, ending the imminent threat to the Soviet capital.

Aftermath

The final months of 1941 were just the beginning of what became a prolonged and bloody clash in the East. Though stopped short of Moscow and Leningrad, the Germans made substantial gains elsewhere, capturing three million Red Army prisoners that autumn alone. Most would not survive the brutal treatment they endured from their captors.

Despite enormous Soviet losses, and substantial Ukrainian land in German hands, the early phases of the German invasion were badly mismanaged. In addition to their failure to anticipate and plan for supply challenges and the winter weather, Hitler and his generals severely underestimated the Red Army as they marched deeper into Soviet territory. Threatened with demotion, arrest, or worse for battlefield defeats, Soviet generals and field commanders pushed their troops to hold firm, no matter the likely bloodshed. Soldiers were ordered to fight to the death, and those who retreated or cowered from the enemy were shot on sight. Even family members of those accused of shirking their duties were condemned to death.

Yet it was not fear alone that toughened the Soviets. Stalin was as cunning as he was cruel, framing the struggle against the Nazis as a "Great Patriotic War" to preserve "Mother Russia." Such battle cries stirred deeply rooted cultural and ethnic pride among those in the Soviet ranks, a resolve that stiffened further after news spread of German pillaging and mass murder and rape of civilians. The atrocities fanned seething animosity toward the invaders, birthing a guerrilla movement across occupied Soviet lands that would bedevil the Germans for years to come.

Hitler's miscalculations would cost him dearly, as would his puzzling decision to declare war on the United States just days after the Japanese attack on Pearl Harbor. The Soviets became the newest beneficiaries of Lend-Lease giveaways, as American-made tanks, aircraft, and trucks, as well as millions of tons of food and other resources, began arriving in Soviet ports. In the months ahead, a Red Army withered by Hitler's early blitzkrieg was reconstituted from reserves of manpower and newly assembled armored and air forces.

They would all be needed. The Soviets had stopped the Germans outside Moscow and inflicted more than 900,000 casualties among the invaders, but Hitler still wielded a massive army on Soviet soil and was far from through with his campaign in the East.

. . . . .

Joseph Stalin

The son of a cobbler, Iosif (Joseph) Vissarionovich Djugashvili (1879–1953) was born in a small village in Georgia, then a province of Imperial Russia, and later adopted the name Stalin from the Russian word for steel. In 1901, the onetime seminary student joined the Social Democratic Labor Party and its protestations against the Russian monarch, known as the tsar. Influenced by the writings of Karl Marx, a German philosopher and socialist, the revolutionaries sought an end to an imperial system that catered to wealthy aristocrats and landowners and longed for a classless state governed by the people, where wealth and property were collectively shared.

Stalin later aligned himself with the Bolsheviks, a militant faction that rose to power in 1917, and when the USSR was formed in 1922, he was chosen to lead the Soviet Communist Party. Two years later, he became the Soviet premier, beginning a three-decade reign of terror that brought prolonged economic hardship and political persecution to the Soviet people. Throughout it all, Stalin exhibited a callous disregard for human life that extended far beyond his notorious purges. In 1932, after Ukrainian farmers resisted state-centric agricultural reforms imposed by the Kremlin, the Soviet leader orchestrated a punitive food shortage that became known as the Holodomor, a Ukrainian word meaning death by hunger. Millions of Ukrainians starved to death in the ensuing famine, a prime example of Stalin's wanton butchery.

For nearly thirty years, Stalin ruled with impunity. His power and authority were absolute, and the systemic crackdowns, arrests, and slayings of political opponents never internally challenged. He industrialized the Soviet Union, and late in his tenure transformed it into a global and nuclear superpower, protected by communist buffer states he established in Eastern Europe. But political expression and individual freedoms remained forbidden in Stalin's regime, and many millions of Soviets died or languished in prison and forced-labor camps at his direction. History accurately records Stalin as a wartime victor and a central figure in the defeat of Hitler and the Nazis, but he also stands, unequivocally, as one of the great mass murderers and war criminals in modern history.

A fatal stroke ended Stalin's life in 1953, and though Soviet leaders repudiated much of his despotic reign after his death, his legacy continued, with the USSR remaining a closed, repressive society for decades.

Commissars

Commissars were political officers and Communist Party agents embedded in both frontline and headquarters units throughout the Red Army. Though they typically lacked military experience, the Kremlin empowered commissars to enforce loyalty and devotion to the state, promote communist and Stalinist propaganda, and punish any political dissenters. The German High Command, convinced such officers poisoned the minds of Red Army soldiers with Bolshevik ideals and easily swayed impressionable Soviet troops, issued a pre-invasion order declaring that captured commissars would not be afforded recognition as POWs. Many were instead executed on the spot.

ⓘ Horses

Notwithstanding substantial investments in motorized vehicles, horses remained the Wehrmacht's primary means of towing artillery and transporting supplies throughout the war. For Operation Barbarossa alone, more than 600,000 horses accompanied German invasion forces into the Soviet Union. The shortage of motorized vehicles and the lack of mobility among Hitler's armies became a significant disadvantage for the Germans later in the war.

6
THE EASTERN FRONT: STALINGRAD AND KURSK
JUNE 1942–AUGUST 1943

"Panic makers and cowards must be liquidated on the spot. Not one step backward without orders from higher headquarters! Commanders...who abandon a position without an order from higher headquarters are traitors to the Motherland."
–Joseph Stalin, Order No. 227

As a winter thaw settled over Russia in early 1942, Hitler stewed over the failures of Operation Barbarossa. His forces were largely stalled across the East, and though they had clawed their way within miles of Moscow, the Red Army had held. Heavily fortified since, the capital was now hopelessly out of reach.

Hitler was undeterred, blaming the German stumbles on the frigid elements rather than crediting his Slavic foes. His armies had accomplished much, overrunning territory encompassing nearly half the Soviet population, including Ukraine, and capturing millions of Soviet soldiers, but had also fallen short of crucial objectives. A new summer offensive was ordered, this one aimed at winning possession of oil fields in the Caucasus. Soviet oil production had long been the centerpiece of Hitler's aspirations for a Greater Reich, with the capacity to fuel the German military and industrial base for generations to come.

The push to the Caucasus, nestled between the Black and Caspian Seas in the south, began in late June. Supplemented with Italian, Romanian, and Hungarian divisions, the Axis army began its march with much promise, capturing great swaths of land mostly abandoned by a fast-retreating Red Army. Edging closer to the prized oil fields, an opportunity arose to gain control of the Volga River, Europe's longest waterway and a major artery in the Soviet supply network. Hitler ordered the German Sixth Army, under General Friedrich Paulus, to wheel away from the main Axis drive and take Stalingrad (present-day Volgograd), an important industrial center perched on the Volga's west bank. As the Sixth Army began clashing with Soviet forces outside the city, Stalin issued his notorious "Not One Step Back" decree, setting the stage for one of the great struggles in military history.

• • • • •

A sprawling, oblong-shaped city, Stalingrad stretched for fifteen miles along the banks of the Volga. A trio of large factories dominated one end, producing substantial quantities of munitions and tanks for the Red Army.

The operation to take the city began in early September. The Luftwaffe rained incendiaries down on Stalingrad, engulfing virtually every neighborhood in flames. Subsequent bombardments leveled the smoldering remains, leaving an apocalyptic landscape littered with piles of rubble, charred debris, and burned-out hulks of buildings on the brink of collapse.

Though Stalingrad was mostly destroyed, it still had to be pried loose from Soviet forces. Ruins filled the streets, blocking panzers and armored vehicles from maneuvering, and forcing German infantry to advance on foot without tank support. They brawled with the Soviets in the city streets, fighting with rifles, pistols, hand grenades, and even their bare hands, transforming Stalingrad into a ghastly, urban abyss.

By late October, the Germans controlled most of the city, leaving the Soviets clinging to a small foothold on the riverbank, where reinforcements could still be ferried from across the Volga. Outside Stalingrad, the Soviets prepared to turn the tables, having quietly amassed a force of more than one million men and hundreds of tanks. In mid-November, they unleashed it all in a massive counterassault against the weakly defended flanks of the Sixth Army. The ill-equipped and inexperienced Romanian divisions defending the periphery were easily overpowered, leaving Paulus and over 250,000 of his men trapped in a pocket twenty-eight miles long and thirty-seven miles wide. Cut off from reinforcement and re-supply, the Germans were battered every day by Soviet tanks, artillery, and bombers, in what was aptly referred to as "the cauldron."

As the pocket slowly crumpled, Paulus wanted to fight his way out, but Hitler rejected any notion of surrendering ground. He had been assured by his Luftwaffe chief, Hermann Göring, that adequate food, fuel, and ammunition could still be airlifted in. Göring's hollow promises—the Luftwaffe lacked sufficient transport planes and could only deliver a fraction of the needed supplies—doomed the surrounded men. In December, another German army fought to open a supply corridor, battling to within thirty miles, but Paulus refused to attempt any breakout, lacking fuel for his tanks and reluctant to defy Hitler's orders.

As temperatures plummeted, the number of sick and wounded climbed sharply. Food, medicine, and other supplies quickly ran out after German-held airstrips fell to the Soviets, ending the meager airlift and reducing re-supply efforts to the few necessities that could be parachuted in. With his remaining men exhausted, starved, and frostbitten, Paulus stopped issuing rations to the wounded, conserving the little food—mostly horsemeat—for those who could still shoulder a weapon.

Hitler promoted Paulus to field marshal, hoping Paulus would not allow himself to be the first German of that rank ever to surrender to an enemy army, but with 147,000 Germans and Romanians already dead, surrender became the only option. In early February, the remaining 91,000 men were taken prisoner and marched to Siberia. Severely malnourished and resembling scarecrows, only a small fraction would survive their captivity, Paulus among them. The Soviets suffered as well, with casualties numbering in the hundreds of thousands, but Stalin cared little about the losses. His namesake city had held.

Kursk

In the wake of Stalingrad, the two sides continued to battle across Soviet lands in early 1943, with neither tallying a decisive win. Losing his entire Sixth Army had been a stinging blow, but Hitler was unwilling to let go of his obsession with the East and ordered yet another summer offensive. The battleground this time shifted north to an area near the town of Kursk, just 300 miles from Moscow, where the Red Army had driven a 100-mile-long wedge into the German lines. The advance had created a bulge-like salient that left Soviet forces within it exposed on three sides. To annihilate those inside, the Germans had assembled more than 400,000 men and 3,000 panzers.

Aware of their vulnerability, the Soviets readied their defenses. They had ample time, as Hitler had intervened once again, ordering the start of the offensive postponed until large numbers of Panther and Tiger tanks—newer models built with substantially more armor and firepower than the Soviet T-34s—could be delivered. The Soviets took advantage of the delay, fortifying their lines and trenches, and burying hundreds of thousands of anti-tank and anti-personnel mines. By June, the salient was a stronghold, with an estimated one million troops dug in across the rolling hillsides and backed by more than 3,300 tanks and armored vehicles. A reserve army of 450,000 men and hundreds of additional T-34s also idled in the distance.

The Germans finally attacked in early July. As the two armies collided across battlefields that stretched for miles, many in Berlin expected swift victory, akin to past blitzkriegs when motorized German armies steamrolled past awestruck foes knocked senseless by waves of panzers and dive-bombers. But these were not the Poles of 1939 or the Soviets of 1941. After two years of war, the Soviets at Kursk were seasoned fighters, well-equipped and supported by tanks and planes no longer outmatched by their German counterparts. Hitler's new Tigers and Panthers underperformed, and his once-indomitable panzer armies faltered as they lumbered into deadly minefields and walls of T-34s. The Luftwaffe also struggled, unable to win control of the skies after finding the skill among Soviet aviators and the quality of the planes they piloted significantly improved.

The largest tank duel in history became a bloodbath for both sides, leaving corpses and destroyed vehicles blanketing the terrain for miles in all directions. Despite steep German losses and few gains, Hitler's top field commander still believed a nominal victory at Kursk could be salvaged, but the führer was no longer listening. He had turned his attention to the West, where Anglo-American armies had landed on Italian soil. When Hitler transferred several divisions to defend Southern Europe, ending his Eastern offensive, the Soviets smelled blood. They threw their reserves into a massive counteroffensive, and for weeks and months, pushed the embattled Germans back all along the Eastern Front. From that point on, the East became a purely defensive struggle for Hitler, marking the start of the long Soviet march to Berlin.

Aftermath

In the summer of 1941, Hitler embarked on his great crusade in the East, determined to win his sacred lebensraum, seize control of the economic resources needed to sustain his thousand-year Reich, and eradicate Jews, Slavs, and others he considered a threat to his so-called "master race." Just two years later, his military operations in the East ended in spectacular failure. Of the vast sums of German tanks, aircraft, and troops Hitler devoted to his fantasies of conquest, only a fraction ever made it out of the Soviet Union. From the opening stanza of Barbarossa to August 1943, over 2.5 million Germans were killed or wounded on the Eastern Front.

The failures in the East can be traced to a handful of missteps, beginning with the march of an invasion force over 1,000 miles from Germany without adequate logistical support. The boom in Soviet manufacturing and surge of American aid to the Soviets also weighed heavily, outpacing Germany's industrial production and erasing Hitler's ground and air advantages. Soviet manpower also proved too much for the Germans to overcome, as no matter how badly the Soviet ranks were decimated, newly formed divisions continued to arrive at the front, a feat the Germans could not possibly match.

And decimated they were. Millions and millions of Soviet lives were lost during these years—numbers that would have jarred any Western leader but left Stalin unfazed. His coldhearted indifference toward the suffering of his own people, and willingness to trade infinite Soviet lives for however many numbers of Germans were on Soviet soil, proved one of the most decisive factors in the war. His armies suffered more casualties than those of any other nation—twice as many as their German foes—but for Stalin, no sacrifice was too great. The ends always justified the means, no matter the consequences for those he reigned over.

The Soviets, of course, had one other advantage. They faced a single invading force along a lone axis, while Hitler's fateful decision to invade the Soviet Union before the British had been defeated burdened the Germans with multiple fronts and adversaries in the years to come. Indeed, months before Hitler's armies first crossed into Soviet territory, another fracas erupted on another continent—one that would eclipse more than two years and draw in some of the most legendary figures of the war. It also ultimately welcomed a new participant to the struggle against the Axis powers. It was America's turn to face the German panzer armies.

· · · · ·

Soviet Deaths

Approximately 1.1 million American servicemembers were killed and wounded during the Second World War. The Soviets suffered an estimated 750,000 casualties during the Battle of Kursk alone.

Night Witches

Flying its first combat mission in 1942, the 588th Night Bomber Aviation Regiment was one of the most storied units in the Soviet Red Air Force. Composed entirely of female combat pilots, ground crew, and maintenance personnel, they were led by Major Marina Raskova, considered the Russian version of Amelia Earhart, the famed American aviation pioneer. The pilots were young, with most in their teens or twenties, and though Stalin had agreed to form all-women combat units out of necessity, scarce quantities of planes and equipment among the male squadrons left the women with older biplanes made of plywood and canvas. The planes were exceedingly slow, and because the weight of the bombs kept the planes at low altitudes, incoming raids were easily detectable by the Germans. To reduce their visibility, the women operated at night and silenced their approach by cutting their engines as they neared a target. Gliding in toward their targets caused the whipping wind between their wings to produce a whooshing noise, like the sound of a sweeping broom, prompting the Germans to refer to the pilots as "Nachthexen" – Night Witches. It was a moniker the pilots proudly embraced as they terrorized the Germans across the Eastern Front.

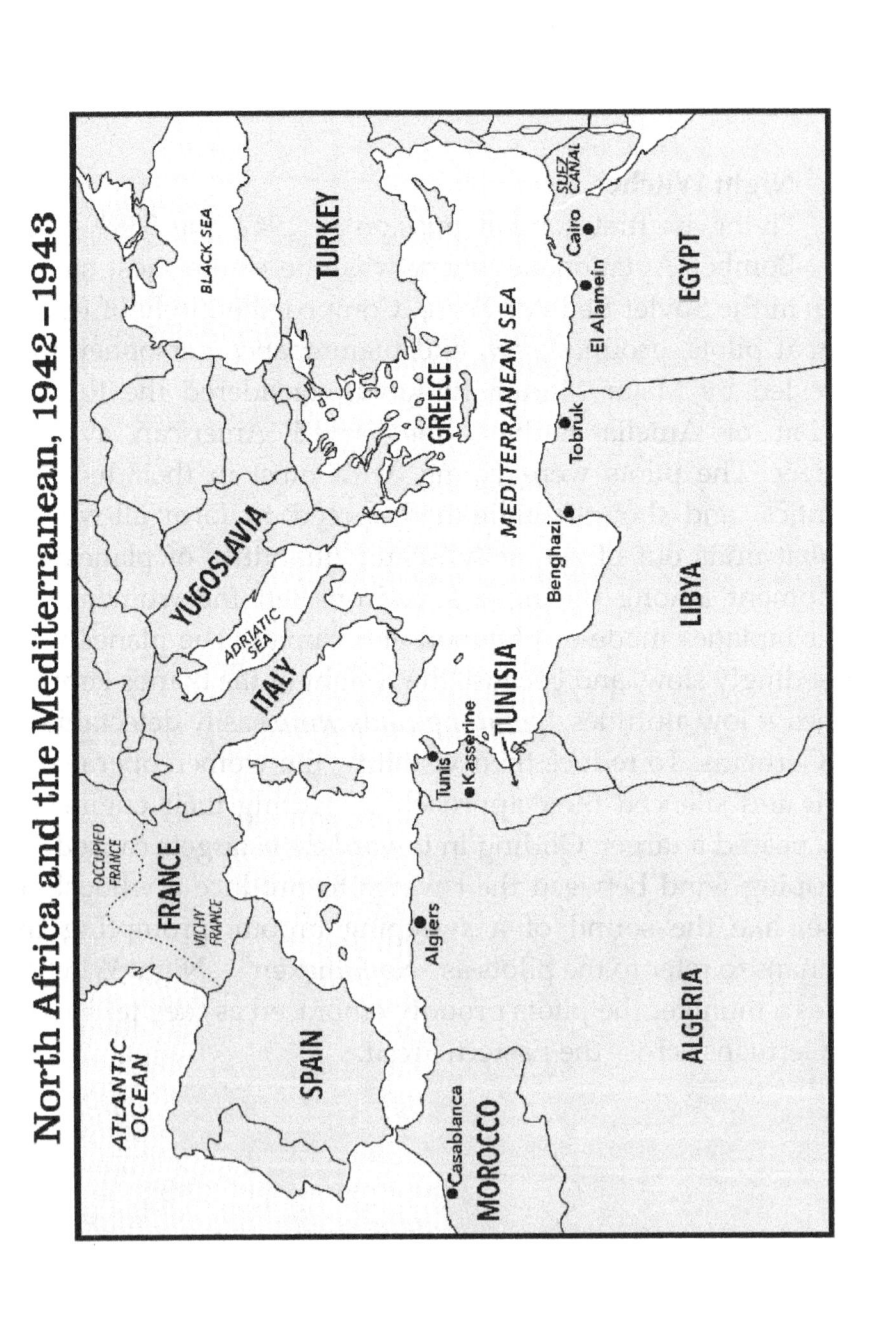

7
NORTH AFRICA: A FIRST TEST
FEBRUARY 1941–MAY 1943

"I want to impose on everyone that the bad times are over, they are finished! Our mandate from the Prime Minister is to destroy the Axis forces in North Africa...It can be done, and it will be done!"
–General Bernard Law Montgomery, August 1942

Early in the war, as the Luftwaffe and RAF skirmished in the skies above England, a new flash point emerged far to the south, in Egypt. The Suez Canal, an artificial waterway, was a longtime gateway to the Mediterranean, linking Britain to Commonwealth allies Australia and India. It was also a shipping artery for freighters and tankers delivering oil, food, and other desperately needed goods to Britain from the Persian Gulf and South Asia.

To protect this vital link to its global empire, Britain had long maintained an armed presence in Egypt. It was not alone, as other European powers with their own colonies and strategic interests had also deployed military contingents throughout North Africa. Following Hitler's conquests in Western Europe, tensions rose sharply among those neighboring forces, with Vichy French troops in Morocco, Algeria, and Tunisia breaking off friendly relations with the British, and Italian forces in Libya continuing their buildup of troops and tanks across the border from Egypt. Aligned with Germany since the invasion of France,

Italy had not yet been a factor in the war. That would soon change.

In September 1940, dictator Benito Mussolini ordered an invasion of Egypt. His army made early gains, but British-led Commonwealth forces rallied, driving the invaders back to Libya while capturing over 130,000 prisoners. Obligated to support his ally, Hitler ordered Major General Erwin Rommel to the continent in February 1941. A hero of the Battle of France and one of Germany's most celebrated military leaders, Rommel took charge of Axis armored forces in North Africa, and for two years, his storied Afrika Korps battled the Allies across the unforgiving landscape. It became a grueling back-and-forth affair, with the fate of the entire Mediterranean in the balance.

• • • • •

Among Rommel's early objectives was recapturing Tobruk, a coveted, deep-water port on the Libyan coast where fuel and other supplies could be ferried from German bases across the Mediterranean Sea. A series of assaults failed to dislodge the plucky, Australian-led garrison, and when Nazi propaganda dismissed them as rats caught in a trap, the besieged defenders proudly referred to themselves as the "Rats of Tobruk." Short of food and water, they held out for eight months, fending off repeated attacks while plagued by disease, dust storms, and infinite flies. Rommel's inability to capture the port led to dwindling fuel and provisions—shortages that worsened after British codebreakers gained access to planned shipping routes. With Allied naval and air forces continuously harassing Axis convoys, ongoing scarcities and supply challenges haunted Rommel for the duration of the campaign.

The two sides continued to trade punches until June 1942, when Rommel achieved one of his greatest triumphs. He outmaneuvered the British, capturing Tobruk and 30,000 Allied prisoners, along with caches of precious fuel and other stores. A jubilant Hitler promoted Rommel to field marshal, a rare honor in the German Army, though Rommel later quipped he wished Hitler had given him another division instead. The fight was far from finished.

With Commonwealth forces reeling, Winston Churchill voyaged across the Atlantic to meet with President Roosevelt at the White House and discuss future collaboration between the two powers. When Churchill requested immediate aid from Roosevelt, as well as longer-term intervention by US forces, the president agreed to fast-track American-built tanks and planes to North Africa, overruling his senior military advisors, who hoped to conserve such resources for an invasion of occupied France.

In Egypt, the retreating British formed a defensive line near the coastal town of El Alamein, where a newcomer, Lieutenant General Bernard Law Montgomery, had arrived to take command of a badly diminished and demoralized Commonwealth army. A cautious leader and meticulous planner, Montgomery was a sharp contrast to the more impulsive and risk-taking Rommel. Always insisting on thorough preparation and organization before battle, "Monty," as he was known, continually strived to outnumber and outgun his enemies in the field, a practice that endeared him to those in the British Eighth Army he led.

Others outside the Eighth Army were less enamored. Though Montgomery became the most acclaimed British military leader of the war, he was widely disliked among his fellow senior commanders, irking American and British peers alike with his abrasive and arrogant manner and overly deliberate pace of operations. He still often delivered, proving an imperfect but effective combat leader in the Mediterranean, where he earned early accolades and notoriety the vain general clearly enjoyed basking in. "In defeat, unbeatable," Churchill once said of him. "In victory, unbearable."

At El Alamein, Montgomery kept Rommel at bay for weeks as he strengthened his hand, restoring the fighting spirit of his army and welcoming hundreds of new tanks and planes from American factories. He led a counteroffensive in October 1942, throwing a revived Eighth Army against an undersupplied Afrika Korps that suddenly found itself on the defensive and without Rommel, away in Germany receiving medical treatment. The field marshal returned and attempted to hold the British off, but with limited reserves and fuel, Rommel eventually retreated from Egypt, saving his remaining tanks and men.

The stunning reversal at El Alamein marked a turning point in North Africa. The British pushed back into Libya, and by November were in control of Tobruk once again. Rommel withdrew to the friendlier terrain of Tunisia, intending to reconstitute his Afrika Korps, but Montgomery and the British were no longer his only adversaries on the continent. A new threat had arrived in the west.

Operation Torch

Hitler's declaration of war against the United States in December 1941 brought relief to those in London and Moscow eager to see America's industrial power and fighting potential added to the struggle against the Nazis. It would not happen overnight, though, as the United States needed time to scale up an undersized military neglected for years by a government weighed down with fiscal crisis.

Efforts to expand America's fighting forces began in 1940. With war on the horizon, Congress authorized the first peacetime draft in American history, boosting the number of uniformed personnel from 269,000 to 1.5 million in a single year. More enlistees swamped induction centers following the attack on Pearl Harbor, straining available training and equipment and lengthening the process for deploying combat-ready divisions to Europe and the Pacific. Even with Roosevelt prioritizing the defeat of Germany before Japan, it would take some time for sufficient men and equipment to be available for Operation Torch, the combined Anglo-American amphibious operation in North Africa.

British and American officials agreed it would be led by Lieutenant General Dwight D. Eisenhower, an obscure figure among those in the upper echelon of the US Army. Eisenhower was intelligent and incisive, and though he had never commanded men in combat, his even temperament and exceptional planning skills were considered a match for an operation of such complexity. Challenges loomed for Eisenhower; chief among them, most of the officers and enlisted men sailing across the Atlantic were new to military service. Some senior American commanders had fought the Germans in the First World War, but none had practical experience with mechanized warfare or the use of modern air power. The Germans and British had become adept at both.

Torch began on November 8, 1942, with naval transports off-loading the first American and British assault troops along the coasts of Morocco and Algeria. There was some hope the Vichy French defenders might defy their Nazi masters and throw down their weapons, but the French fought back, tenaciously in some pockets. They were widely outnumbered, though, and with tens of thousands of Allied troops flooding into the coastal regions, capturing key towns, ports, and roads, French officials agreed to a cease-fire. The Americans celebrated their early success, but Eisenhower was not among them, aware the French lacked heavy weapons and fought half-heartedly against their former allies. A much greater test awaited hundreds of miles away in Tunisia, where Rommel was gathering strength among his German and Italian forces for an opening bout against his newest foe.

KASSERINE PASS

By the end of November, over a quarter-million Allied troops had landed in North Africa. With Rommel bracketed between Anglo-American forces to the west and the British Eighth Army in the east, Hitler funneled more reinforcements to Tunisia, boosting Axis forces there, but supply problems persisted. New tanks and troops required fuel and food, and safe transport across the Mediterranean remained elusive.

In early 1943, Rommel led his forces toward the Kasserine Pass, a corridor in the western Dorsal Mountains of Tunisia defended by part of the US Army's II Corps. Major General Lloyd Fredendall commanded the corps, and though he was highly regarded in the pre-war Army, Fredendall clashed with subordinates and fellow senior officials in North Africa, including his British colleagues. Many of his troops at Kasserine Pass were combat engineers with limited infantry training, and as they dug into the hard ground, their collective inexperience was glaring. Guns were poorly sited, anti-tank defenses were sparse, and coordination between air and ground elements was almost non-existent.

The two sides first clashed in mid-February, with the Afrika Korps dominating early, destroying 183 American tanks at the cost of just twenty of its own. Panicked American troops fled the battlefield, and when it was over, more than 6,000 Americans were dead, wounded, or missing. News of the humiliating defeat drew angry rebukes in Washington and outright mockery in Berlin. With shame reverberating across the US Army, Eisenhower relieved Fredendall and elevated Major General George S. Patton Jr. to take his place.

The iron-willed Patton, a former World War I tanker, was aggressive, flamboyant—he carried ivory-handled revolvers on his hips—and every bit as vain as Montgomery. Itching for redemption against Rommel, he quickly went to work restoring discipline across II Corps. Eisenhower also moved to address the communications failures plaguing the Allied command, devising a centralized, integrated structure to coordinate air, ground, and naval activities and manage the growing array of multinational forces deploying in North Africa. It became a model for future cooperation.

With the debacle at Kasserine Pass behind them, the Allies regrouped and began doggedly pursuing the Germans and Italians across Tunisia. Air and naval attacks continued to stanch the flow of supplies from across the Mediterranean, starving the Axis forces of fuel and other necessities. Setbacks followed, and with Rommel facing certain defeat, Hitler ordered his favorite field marshal to evacuate. For the remaining Germans and Italians in North Africa, the end came in May 1943 when more than 250,000 men surrendered, matching the losses at Stalingrad just three months earlier.

Much of the Mediterranean remained contested, but the success in North Africa was a needed boost of confidence for the Allies. It also left the armies of Patton and Montgomery, as well as substantial air and naval support, just across the sea from Southern Europe. By July, the Allies were poised to take their first significant step toward reclaiming the European continent and liberating tens of millions still suffering in Axis-occupied territories.

· · · · ·

Erwin Rommel
Erwin Rommel (1891–1944) was a highly decorated infantry officer in the First World War, where he exhibited the daring and initiative that became his trademark a

quarter century later. An early supporter of Hitler and the Nazis, Rommel commanded Hitler's personal security in the 1930s and was later awarded a plum command of a panzer division during the 1940 campaign in France. He amassed an extraordinary record, even fighting alongside his infantry battalions on the ground.

His success continued in North Africa, where Rommel earned the nickname "Desert Fox" for his early battlefield wizardry. Promoted to field marshal, his popularity soared at home after Nazi propaganda widely touted his exploits, but Rommel's success waned once he began facing more skilled Allied commanders in North Africa. His beloved and once-mighty Afrika Korps was eventually left to wither from heavy losses and lack of supplies.

Rommel returned to Europe in 1943, later commanding German defenses in France, along the Normandy coast. When he urged Hitler to negotiate peace with the Americans and British so Germany could concentrate its war effort against the Soviets, the proposition infuriated Hitler, who considered such talk defeatism. There was little he could do to punish Rommel, though, given his public standing.

Six weeks after the Allied invasion, British planes strafed Rommel's staff car, hospitalizing him with severe head injuries. Days later, conspirators detonated a bomb inside an East Prussian command bunker where Hitler and his staff were conferring. Hitler survived the blast, and a vengeful Gestapo went on a rampage, interrogating and executing anyone in the German military and government with suspected involvement. Though disillusioned with Hitler's war strategy and likely sympathetic to the aims of the conspirators, Rommel never involved himself directly in the plot. He was aware of it, however, and eventually implicated. Rommel's stature compelled Hitler to avoid a trial and offer the popular field marshal a deal instead, sparing his reputation and family if Rommel took his own life. Rommel did so, poisoning himself on October 14, 1944.

> **Vichy France**
> After the fall of France in 1940, Germany allowed much of the country to remain unoccupied and governed by French authorities in Vichy. One condition of the arrangement was that French forces throughout their colonies would stand with the Nazis against enemies of the Reich. During Operation Torch, French defenders in Morocco and Algeria resisted the Allies at first, but many joined their cause once a peace agreement was brokered. A wrathful Hitler lashed out against Vichy France, stripping local authorities of their powers and replacing the French paramilitary police with German troops. From that point on, German occupation forces firmly ruled all of France.

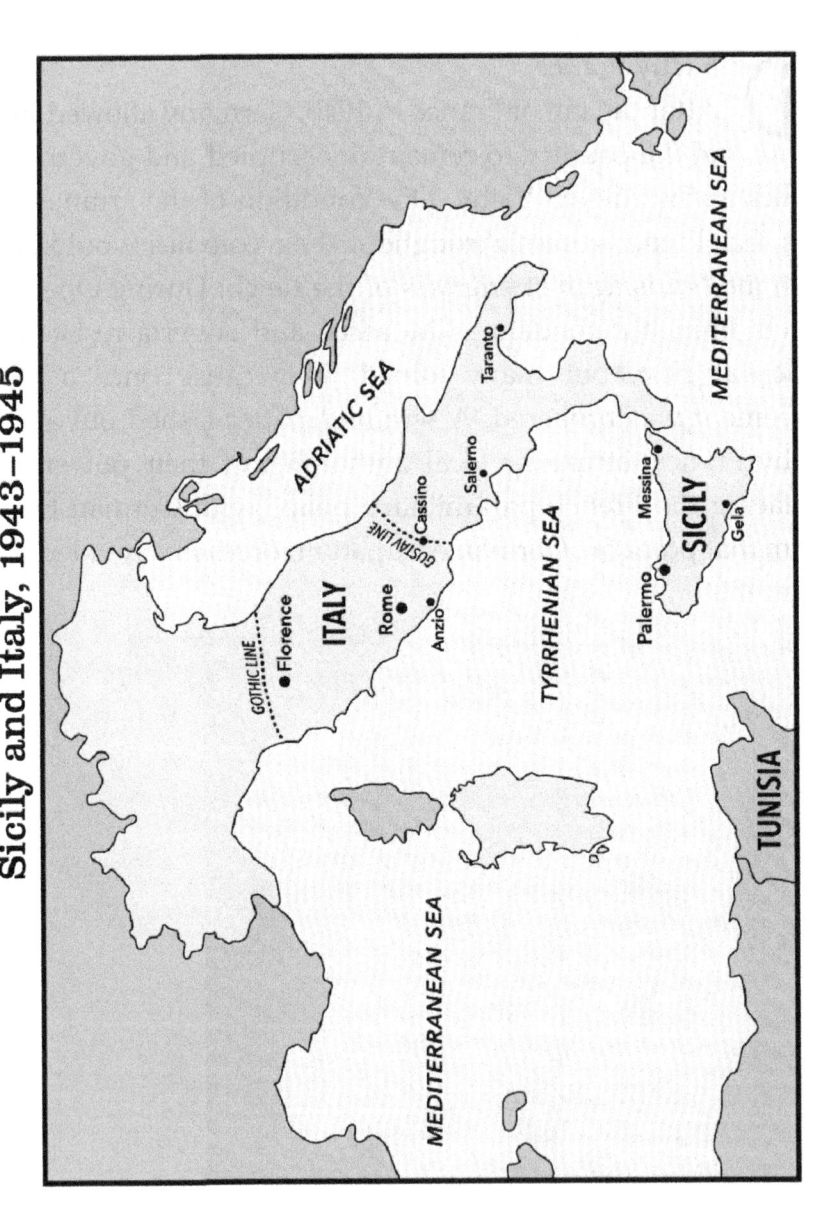

8
ITALY
JULY 1943—APRIL 1945

"I doubt if there are any other troops in the world who would have stood up to it [the Allied bombing and shelling] *and then gone on fighting with the ferocity they have."*
–British General Harold Alexander, on German resistance in Italy

Months before the Allied conquest in North Africa was complete, Roosevelt and Churchill huddled with their senior aides in the French Moroccan city of Casablanca, hammering out a strategy for the next phases of the war. When the pair agreed how it should end—refusing to accept anything short of total and unconditional surrender from each Axis power—the declaration was criticized by some who thought such terms might stiffen the resolve of those unwilling to admit defeat. Their decision was welcomed, though, by the Soviets, who had long fretted the West might negotiate a separate peace with Hitler.

There was less consensus among the Allies about where to strike when operations in North Africa were completed. American military chiefs favored an invasion of France, followed by a direct thrust toward Nazi Germany, but the British insisted on a continued push through the Mediterranean, where critical sea lanes remained under threat. They also pointed to instability in Italy, where popular support for Benito Mussolini and his fascist government was fading fast. Indeed, Italy—one of the three principal Axis powers—seemed close to bowing out of the war.

Though Roosevelt considered an invasion of France inevitable, he knew American forces were not yet prepared for the enormity of such a venture. The Soviets were also demanding a more aggressive press against Hitler on a second front, and with the weight of Anglo-American armies and logistical support already in the Mediterranean, Roosevelt agreed to continue the Allied drive there. As British and American officials deliberated precisely where their next campaign would begin, they eventually settled on the island of Sicily, an Axis base of operations just off the coast of Italy, where an opportunity to splinter the German-Italian alliance awaited.

• • • • •

Just two miles of water separated the Italian mainland from Sicily, a rocky, triangular-shaped island the size of Massachusetts. The city of Messina in the north, from where Allied forces could easily cross over to Italy, was the principal objective, but the most suitable beaches for an amphibious landing were in the south, requiring the Allies to traverse the length of the island. Sicily was defended by an estimated 200,000 Italian troops, all with limited training, second-rate weapons and equipment, and little enthusiasm for Mussolini. Allied strategists were far more wary of the two German divisions on the island, sure to be reinforced from the mainland.

Eisenhower was again selected to lead Allied operations, with British General Harold Alexander serving as his deputy. Alexander was responsible for managing the ground operation, including the invasion force, split between Patton's US Seventh Army and Montgomery's British Eighth Army. Each of the two larger-than-life field commanders lobbied to spearhead the drive to Messina, chafing at the notion of sharing the spotlight. When Alexander chose Montgomery, assigning Messina to his Eighth Army with the Americans in a supporting role, Patton and his staff seethed over the perceived slight. Competitive tensions flared and feuding between the British and American camps persisted for months.

The operation began on July 10, 1943, with British-led forces landing in the southeast of Sicily and the Americans coming ashore to the west, at Gela. The landings were mostly uncontested, a credit to Operation Mincemeat, a ploy to deceive the German High Command about Allied intentions. Months earlier, a corpse in a British officer's uniform had been floated ashore in neutral Spain, where Nazi sympathizers in the Spanish government quickly shared news of the discovery with the Germans. Bogus documents found on the corpse suggested the Allied buildup for Sicily was a feint designed to draw German defenses from other Allied objectives, namely Greece and Sardinia. The ruse worked, convincing the Germans to shift forces elsewhere that could have been employed on Sicily.

After securing their respective beachheads, the two Allied armies began their parallel march to Messina, with the Americans protecting Montgomery's left flank. They made early progress until the Germans shuttled additional troops and tanks to Sicily from the Italian mainland, stalling Montgomery's advance. With British armor also struggling to maneuver in the mountainous terrain, Alexander shifted Montgomery's line of advance farther inland and onto roads that had been earmarked for Patton's army. The change eased Montgomery's path but infuriated Patton, who interpreted the move as further relegating American forces to a secondary role.

The impetuous Patton took matters into his own hands. He marched his army north, occupying Palermo, Sicily's capital and largest city, and capturing 53,000 Italian prisoners. With Montgomery still delayed in the south, Eisenhower approved

Patton's request to begin his own push toward Messina. In stifling summer temperatures, the Seventh Army battled along the northern coast, navigating steep ridges and ravines, demolished bridges, and roads cluttered with mines. Desperate to beat Montgomery, Patton was relentless, relieving any officers who dallied and driving his men and armor through the German defenses. They captured Messina on August 17, shortly before the first British tanks rolled into town.

Though the Allied conquest of Sicily had taken just thirty-eight days, delays in reaching Messina allowed the Germans to evacuate some 60,000 troops and 10,000 vehicles, adding to their mainland defenses. It was still a clear defeat, and the repercussions extended far beyond the Mediterranean. With the German stranglehold on the European continent in jeopardy, Hitler began recalling troops and armor from the East, reducing German strength in the Soviet Union and ending his summer offensive there. There were political consequences as well. As anti-war sentiment rippled across the Italian mainland, Mussolini was ousted from power, and Marshal Pietro Badoglio, a former military leader, was appointed his successor. Badoglio pledged to defend Italy against further invasion, even as he began secretly negotiating a peace agreement with the Allies.

Allied headquarters became equally mired in turmoil after disturbing reports about Patton were brought to Eisenhower's attention. While visiting wounded soldiers in Sicily, the no-nonsense general had slapped two soldiers resting in field hospitals—one suffering from malaria and the other from psychological trauma—and accused each of cowardice. Eisenhower ordered Patton to apologize to the men, but other provocations by his longtime friend, including a series of inflammatory public comments that rankled American and British officials alike, left Eisenhower little choice but to sideline his most proven ground commander. Barely a month after prevailing on Sicily, Patton was exiled to Britain to train

American troops there. His absence in the coming campaign was felt for months to come.

ITALY — THE TOUGH OLD GUT

The Allies moved quickly after Sicily, invading the Italian Peninsula in early September. The vanguard of Montgomery's forces crossed the Straits of Messina, and days later, a multinational army led by American Lieutenant General Mark Clark waded ashore at Salerno as British paratroopers seized the southern port of Taranto. The Italian Army offered no resistance, the result of an armistice quietly brokered with the government in Rome on the eve of the invasion. Incensed by the betrayal, the Germans occupied the entire peninsula in force, disarming hundreds of thousands of Italian troops at gunpoint. Most were transported to Germany or occupied territories for use as forced laborers.

Having anticipated a landing at Salerno, the Germans launched a vigorous counterattack, pinning down Clark's troops for days on the beaches and nearly pushing the Allied army back into the sea. Supporting air strikes, naval gunfire, and the eleventh-hour arrival of the elite US 82nd Airborne Division drove the Germans off, narrowly averting an early disaster.

It was no victory, though, as the Germans had only withdrawn to more favorable ground. In command of their forces in Italy was Field Marshal Albert Kesselring of the Luftwaffe, who served in the German Army during the First World War. Consistently outnumbered in Italy, the resourceful and imaginative Kesselring proved one of the most skillful ground commanders of the war. He became an expert at fusing his defenses and pockets of resistance with the mountainous landscape, creating impenetrable lines that stalled the Allied advance time and time again.

The first defensive belt, stretching across the waist of Italy and layered with fortifications several miles deep, clogged the

Allied advance for weeks, aided by constant downpours that muddied the terrain and immobilized vehicles. When the Allies finally battled past those defenses, they ran into more of Kesselring's handiwork just 100 miles from Rome. Known as the Gustav Line, it was another network of interlocking defenses, with concrete bunkers, anti-tank obstacles, and minefields spread across the mountains of central Italy. Winter arrived, and with it, misery for Allied soldiers lacking protection from the snowstorms and icy temperatures. Thousands were incapacitated by illness or trench foot—the painful, debilitating fungal infections caused by days and weeks of damp footwear.

In January 1944, the Allies attempted a bold flanking maneuver, landing 36,000 troops near the seaside town of Anzio, eighty miles behind the German lines. The amphibious operation surprised the Germans, and had it been led by the opportunistic Patton, the Allies likely would have swept past the sparse troops in the vicinity and taken Rome, just thirty-five miles away. Instead, amid fears of possible German counterattacks against the beachhead, such as those at Salerno that nearly wiped out Clark's invasion force, the Anglo-American force was ordered to dig in and defend its perimeter. "I had hoped we were hurling a wildcat onto the shore," a mystified Churchill later remarked, "but all we got was a stranded whale." The Allied troops were eventually ordered forward, but the delay allowed the Germans to rush reserves into the area, penning in the men around Anzio. The stalemate continued for four months, costing the Allies valuable time and thousands of casualties.

With the operation at Anzio floundering, more attempts were made to crack the Gustav Line. Anchoring the German defenses was the town of Cassino and the mountain that overlooked it, topped by a 1,400-year-old monastery. Early Allied assaults by troops from India and New Zealand could not dislodge the Germans from Monte Cassino, but in May, Polish troops finally wrestled away the blood-soaked high ground. The Allied breakthrough forced the Germans to withdraw again, freeing the Allied forces at Anzio.

What followed was one of the more consequential blunders of the war. Kesselring's army was in full retreat, and though the Allies were in position to give chase, Clark chose instead to liberate Rome, a headline-grabbing feat that posed little challenge given the few Germans in his path. His forces occupied the undefended capital on June 4, celebrating with the civilian population as it rejoiced in the streets, while Kesselring shrewdly consolidated his remaining forces outside Florence, behind yet another stout defensive labyrinth called the Gothic Line.

Hundreds of miles away, Allied armies invading France were struggling to advance beyond their Normandy beachheads. To relieve the pressure, Eisenhower ordered Clark to continue pressing the Germans from the south, and a series of clashes along the Gothic Line sent casualties spiraling once again. The operation in France was at a boiling point, leaving few Allied reinforcements available to Clark, and his army too battered and fatigued to crack the German lines. The bloody skirmishing across northern Italy continued until the very end of the war.

AFTERMATH

By April 1945, the two sides had battled in Italy for nineteen months, and the shocking casualty figures reflected the bitter fighting across the peninsula. More than 300,000 Allied soldiers had been killed or wounded, and German losses topped a half-million. Earlier claims by Churchill and others that Southern Europe would be an easily exploitable "soft underbelly" proved otherwise, as the nightmarish terrain, poor weather conditions, and extraordinary resiliency by the German defenders combined to form what Clark referred to instead as a "tough old gut."

Though the Allies paid a steep price for the ground won, the fighting in Italy had a profound impact on the strategic landscape in both the West and East. Besides knocking Hitler's principal ally out of the war, the campaign tied down significant German armies, preventing their use in other theaters. Importantly, the Allies also gained control of several new air bases, from which heavy bombers could reach Germany and its still-occupied territories.

The Mediterranean campaign paid one other notable dividend—Allied planners had gained substantial experience designing and managing extraordinarily complex amphibious operations. The lessons learned in the early months of fighting in Sicily and Italy became instrumental to later preparations for one of the most daunting endeavors of the war—the long-awaited invasion of occupied France.

. . . . .

Dwight D. Eisenhower

Dwight D. Eisenhower (1890–1969) was a Kansas native and West Point graduate. In the early years of his military career, he served as a junior aide to two of the most revered figures in the US Army—General John Pershing, the iconic former commander of American expeditionary forces in World War I, and Douglas MacArthur, the onetime Army chief of staff who later commanded forces in the Philippines.

As his career progressed, Eisenhower became a respected planner, and in late 1942, he was picked to helm Operation Torch, the Allied amphibious landing in North Africa. After commanding later operations in Sicily and Italy, Eisenhower was appointed supreme commander for the invasion of France in 1944 and continued leading Allied forces in Europe for the duration of the war.

Though he endured his share of early stumbles in the Mediterranean, Eisenhower proved a superior strategist during the Normandy campaign and late-war operations in Belgium and Germany. His greatest attribute may have been his amiable demeanor and ability to navigate competing perspectives and personalities within the Anglo-American alliance, including the incessant squabbling among his American and British underlings. He was, above all else, a humble man, as seen in the public statement he penned prior to the Normandy landings, accepting full responsibility had the operation ended in disaster. "If any blame or fault attaches to the attempt," Eisenhower wrote, "it is mine alone."

Eisenhower was not without his critics. Many British were disdainful of his inexperience, and fellow Americans, such as Patton, often chided "Ike" for being too cozy with the British and allowing diplomatic niceties to slow battlefield progress. Anglo-American relations were hardly Eisenhower's only challenge; he also had to manage an increasingly strained partnership with Stalin as well. The United States needed the Soviets to weigh in against the Japanese, but Stalin's designs for post-war Germany and Eastern Europe were at odds with American democratic values and long-term strategic objectives. Tensions throughout those final months often ran high.

After the war, Eisenhower remained in Europe to oversee the occupation of Germany before returning to Washington to serve as the new Army chief of staff. He retired from the Army, becoming president of Columbia University, but when war erupted on the Korean Peninsula in 1950, Eisenhower donned a uniform once more, leading North American Treaty Organization (NATO) forces in Europe. Politics came calling two years later, and Eisenhower became the Republican presidential nominee, winning the White House in 1952 in an Electoral

College landslide. He served two terms in office before retiring to his farm in Pennsylvania, passing away in 1969 after several heart attacks.

ⓘ In September 1943, a daring and brilliantly executed raid by German commandos freed deposed dictator Benito Mussolini from a mountaintop hotel where Italian authorities were holding him. Mussolini eventually returned to northern Italy to lead a fascist puppet state on Hitler's behalf, but in April 1945, local partisans stopped his motorcade outside Milan. Mussolini, his mistress, and others in their party were all gunned down, their corpses left hanging upside down for public viewing.

9
THE SKIES OVER GERMANY
1942–1945

"The Nazis entered this war under the rather childish delusion that they were going to bomb everybody else and nobody was going to bomb them. They sowed the wind and now they are going to reap the whirlwind."
–Sir Arthur Harris, RAF Bomber Command, June 1942

On the evening of May 30, 1942, masses of British bombers filling a blackened sky closed in on Cologne, the third largest city in Germany. With the RAF scraping together more than 1,000 planes from every operational and training squadron in Britain, it was the largest bombing mission ever assembled.

Over 1,500 tons of explosives fell on Cologne that evening. The blasts lit up the nighttime sky, destroying or damaging chemical plants, machine tool factories, and other military and industrial targets. With just forty-one bombers failing to return to England, officials deemed the losses acceptable and ordered additional thousand-bomber raids against other industrial cities. Those fared less well, with German air defenses over Essen and Bremen downing a far greater proportion of the bombers, and targeted facilities sustaining little long-term damage.

Such uneven results reflected early Allied struggles with bombing raids in the German interior. The Luftwaffe was the greatest menace, whittling down the bomber groups the deeper they penetrated German airspace, but in time, the bombers chipped away at the Nazi war machine. The campaign ultimately proved a success, diminishing production across the Reich and accelerating the German collapse, but it came at significant cost to the air crews, as the skies above Germany became one of the deadliest battlegrounds in the entire war.

• • • • •

Three years into the conflict, Hitler's forces were stretched across Europe, the Mediterranean, and the Soviet Union, straining available manpower and materiel as the Allies gained momentum and ground on both the Western and Eastern Fronts. German losses mounted, but industries across the Reich continued to answer the bell, restocking frontline forces with volumes of new panzers, fighter planes, and U-boats. To siphon off those resources, Allied leaders turned to their growing inventories of heavy bombers.

Strategic bombing was first introduced during the previous world war, when such capabilities were still relatively primitive. By the early 1940s, the range, payloads, and accuracy of modern bombers had vastly improved, and several Allied officials became vociferous advocates, convinced the powerful air groups could shorten the war. One of those enthusiasts was Air Marshal Sir Arthur Harris, head of RAF Bomber Command, who insisted his air fleet could dismantle the Third Reich, brick by brick.

After early raids produced mixed results and heavy losses among the bomber groups, Harris shifted operations to nighttime, when most Luftwaffe fighters could not fly. With his bombardiers struggling to pinpoint targets in darkness 25,000 feet below, Harris ordered the planes to saturate large geographical areas, the broader destruction increasing the likelihood of hitting their marks. Bombs invariably fell on adjoining communities, killing and injuring civilians by the thousands, but Harris was indifferent about the suffering.

Londoners had endured similar losses during the Blitz, and if the raids were taking a heavy toll on German industrial workers, Harris considered that an added benefit.

By 1943, newer, four-engine *Lancaster* and *Halifax* bombers had become the mainstays of the British campaign, delivering far greater payloads than their twin-engine predecessors, and from longer distances. In early sorties over the Ruhr Valley, Germany's industrial heartland, they raided steel and iron works feeding production lines for panzers and U-boats, and demolished dams and other infrastructure providing needed hydroelectric power. The bombers also terrorized a number of industrial cities, most notably Hamburg, Germany's second-largest population center. In July, a major strike was ordered against the shipbuilding enclave, home to an estimated two million people.

The British operation, codenamed Gomorrah after the biblical community destroyed by God with fire, lived up to its billing. On the second night of raids, Hamburg was showered with incendiary bombs, and the entire metropolis, filled with lumberyards, shipyards, factories, and oil refineries, erupted in flames. A firestorm with thousand-degree temperatures swept through densely populated areas, incinerating or asphyxiating over 40,000 people and burning thousands of structures and homes to ash. Smoldering debris littered the scorched landscape as news of the devastation and grisly carnage sped across the Reich, stunning German officials. The Allies were far from through with Hamburg, though, bombing the luckless city seventy more times during the war.

The United States also began adding its considerable weight to the bombing campaign. By 1943, the Eighth Air Force, based in England, swelled with more than 2,000 bombers, 1,000 fighter planes, and 200,000 pilots, crew members, and support personnel. Along with the smaller Fifteenth Air Force, based in Italy, the American bomber groups began raiding military and industrial facilities across Germany and occupied territories in

Southern and Eastern Europe. Their four-engine B-17 *Flying Fortresses* and B-24 *Liberators* were formidable planes. Each carried several tons of bombs and substantial defensive armament, and by mid-year, the heavy bombers were arriving in Europe in droves, with US factories producing a whopping 31,000 of them during the war.

The Americans diverged from the British in tactics, convinced precision bombing was more effective and humane than bombing general areas. To maximize visibility and accuracy, the American bombers flew in daylight, easing the pressure on newly trained bombardiers and navigators, but also exposing the planes to the teeth of German air defenses. The daylight raids were indeed more accurate, but also far more hazardous, with the Luftwaffe downing up to one-quarter of the B-17s and B-24s on every mission. The Germans proved remarkably efficient in rebuilding damaged facilities and restoring production lines, and with losses of Allied bombers and aircrews fast becoming unsustainable, the entire campaign was on the brink of failure.

THE TURNING POINT

The steep losses among the bombers were mostly attributable to the lack of adequate fighter protection. Existing single- and twin-engine fighter planes had limited fuel capacity and could only shield the long-range bombers part of the way to Germany. Once the escorts turned back, Luftwaffe fighters pounced, chewing up the lumbering B-17s and B-24s with their powerful machine guns and cannons.

That began to change in late 1943 with the arrival of P-51 *Mustangs*, powerfully built fighters and the most versatile aircraft of the war. The planes were often armed with rockets and small bombs for use against enemy airfields, railroads, and other ground targets, but their most important innovation was the ability to carry auxiliary fuel tanks, allowing the P-51s to escort the bombers deep into Germany and back.

As new *Mustangs* filled the skies, their firepower and maneuverability were more than a match for a Luftwaffe fighter force beginning to diminish from heavy losses of veteran aviators. German factories continued to turn out respectable numbers of new fighter planes, but few skilled pilots remained. New trainees were pressed early into combat and pitted against those with significantly more time in the cockpit, and as the duels became increasingly one-sided, the Luftwaffe gradually vanished from the sky.

The emerging dominance of Allied air power was catastrophic for German cities and industries. Production levels tumbled, and Hitler's armies soon felt the impact, with losses of oil refineries crippling panzer operations and scaling back mobility on all fronts. That included Normandy, where the scarcity of fuel and Allied bombings of railways, bridges, and other transportation hubs across occupied France became a decisive factor during the 1944 invasion.

But it was Germany itself that suffered the most. From January 1944 to January 1945, civilian casualties soared as the bombers hammered population and industrial centers from the air. Dresden, a wooden, medieval city, became the next Hamburg following a succession of raids in February 1945 by hundreds of British and American bombers. As scores of high-explosive and incendiary bombs fell on military targets across the city, high winds triggered another horrifying firestorm, leaving Dresden ablaze for weeks. An estimated 25,000-35,000 civilians were killed in the inferno.

Aftermath

The strategic bombing of Germany and its occupied territories was a key pillar of the Allied strategy to end the war, severely degrading Hitler's industrial base and wrecking internal transportation systems. Though wartime manufacturing was never halted—German industry proved extraordinarily resilient—the campaign prevented production from reaching levels needed to sustain a frayed military battling for survival across multiple fronts.

The American and British air forces paid a steep price for their success. Losses among the bombing squadrons were staggering, and the men who buckled into the cockpits and fuselages of the heavy planes braved some of the most harrowing conditions of the war. Of the 110,000 British airmen who served in Bomber Command, roughly half would not return from their missions. The US Eighth and Fifteenth Air Forces lost a combined 7,000 bombers, with casualties among the pilots and crew members of the Eighth alone accounting for nearly half of all casualties sustained by the entire US Army Air Forces during the war. Fewer than one-quarter of American bomber crewmen completed a single tour of duty in Europe — twenty-five missions — without getting killed, wounded, or captured.

No one suffered more than the civilians on the ground. In addition to many thousands of French, Belgian, Italian, Dutch, and other victims — all forced by their captors to work in German factories and live nearby — an estimated 650,000 Germans were killed in the raids. The victims were predominantly women, children, and the elderly, but there was little sympathy among the Allies, particularly given the degree of death and suffering meted out for years by Hitler across Europe and the Soviet Union. That included a campaign of sickening depravity and murder, conducted in secret by the Nazis, as they pursued their twisted fantasies of racial supremacy and an eternal Reich.

• • • • •

Jet Aircraft

The Messerschmitt Me262 was the first operational turbojet aircraft. The German creation was a design and engineering marvel, reaching speeds up to 540 miles per hour and outperforming all conventional planes, including the P-51

Mustang. Hitler expected their late-war introduction to swing the conflict in his favor, but only a few hundred were used in combat, as shortages of fuel, trained pilots, and spare parts kept most of the 1,400 planes grounded. Those that flew downed their share of American and British heavy bombers, but they were too small in number to make a meaningful difference, and Allied raids destroyed most of the jets while still on the ground.

ⓘ The 26,000 pilots and crew members of the "Mighty Eighth" who lost their lives in the skies above Europe exceeded the death toll for all US Marines during the Second World War.

10
THE FINAL SOLUTION
1941–1945

"In respect of the Jewish question, the Führer has decided to make a clean sweep. The world war is here, the annihilation of the Jews must be the necessary result."
–Joseph Goebbels, Nazi Minister of Propaganda, December 1941

At the time an ascendent Hitler was coming into power, more than nine million Jews lived in Europe. Years of Nazi vitriol toward German Jews was initially regarded as just the latest iteration of the noxious antisemitism that had pervaded the continent for generations. European Jews, often belittled and ostracized for their religious customs and cultural traditions, were accustomed to such antipathy, and routinely scapegoated for the failings or hardships of others. Such enmity, however, rarely erupted into organized violence.

A notable exception came in the late nineteenth and early twentieth centuries with the notorious pogroms in Imperial Russia and Eastern Europe, when wrathful mobs stormed through Jewish communities, murdering and looting with impunity. Such rampages, condoned and even led by local authorities, were a contrast to the experience of other Jews in Western and Central Europe, where relations had been more tranquil. That included Germany, where Jews lived among non-Jews, operating businesses and farms, worshipping freely, and serving in public office, the police, and the military. They were respected figures and valued contributors to German industry, science, academia, medicine, and the arts.

In the aftermath of the First World War, a nascent Nazi Party began stirring unrest in Germany, exploiting the bitterness and resentment festering among those still livid over the terms of Versailles. Throughout the 1920s, Hitler tapped into such sentiments among his followers, pointing to Jews as the source of Germany's plummeting international stature and failing economy. He accused them of poisoning and corrupting German culture and posing an existential threat to the Aryan "master race." The scathing rhetoric inflamed existing prejudice and gained traction among despairing listeners.

Once in power, the Nazis slowly unleashed their wrath, orchestrating a vicious campaign of coordinated persecution against the Jews they claimed were undermining a German resurgence. Driving Jews out of state positions and depriving them of citizenship were first steps toward Hitler's quest for racial purity — one that would eventually extend across the full reach of the Third Reich. For more than a decade, millions of Jews and others across Europe perished at the hands of the Nazis and their allies, and millions more suffered immeasurably.

It became known as the Holocaust.

• • • • •

In 1933, there were 520,000 Jews in Germany, comprising less than one percent of the general population. Though the number of German Jews was small, the newly empowered Nazis wasted little time imposing a series of measures to diminish their standing and shun them from public life. Jews were removed from the civil service, prohibited from owning property, and targeted for nationwide boycotts of their businesses. By 1935, new citizenship and race laws were in place, rescinding German citizenship for anyone with at least three Jewish grandparents, making Jews outcasts in their own country, stripped of their legal, political, and civil rights.

There were few objections among fellow Germans. Many were already leery of Jews and became openly disdainful once Nazi propaganda began filling state-controlled newspapers and airwaves with antisemitic missives and tropes. Branded a treacherous and deceitful people, Jews were wholly dehumanized, likened to rats and other vermin infesting Germany and targeted for street beatings and public humiliations from Nazi thugs. It all reached a crescendo in November 1938, when Nazi stormtroopers and Hitler Youth, whipped into a frenzy, joined in a night of violent rioting across Germany and Austria, killing, assaulting, and raping Jews of all ages. Their synagogues, shops, and homes were vandalized and burned down, and the Kristallnacht (Night of Broken Glass) ended with tens of thousands of Jews arrested, most shipped off to labor camps.

Throughout the upheaval of the 1930s, Jews were still permitted to emigrate from Germany, and many sought to escape the antagonism enveloping the country. Over half fled, with the most fortunate journeying to the United States and Britain, though the two countries placed strict caps on the number of Jewish refugees accepted. Others resettled in other parts of Europe, but their relief was short-lived, as much of the continent would soon be subsumed by the Nazis.

The exodus continued until October 1941, when Hitler closed the borders, aiming to exert greater control over the Jewish population in the expanding Reich. Armed Nazis fanned across German-occupied Poland, Czechoslovakia, the Baltic states, and the Soviet Union, rounding up Jews by the hundreds of thousands and locking them into more than 1,100 cordoned-off districts and neighborhoods known as ghettos. Sealed off from the outside world by ten-foot walls and barbed wire fences, the ghettos were densely populated pockets of misery and poverty, teeming with rats, lice, and disease. In the Polish city of Lodz, 165,000 Jews were squeezed into an area little more than a square mile, while in Warsaw, 400,000 Jews—one-third of the city's population—were forced to live in just two percent of its living space. Those inside the ghettos attempted to maintain some semblance of community, but severe food shortages led to widespread hunger, and with living areas so condensed, deadly diseases such as typhus spread rapidly.

By the end of 1941, the death toll among Jews in Hitler's grasp was climbing precipitously. Starvation and disease were claiming thousands of victims in the ghettos, while German military and security forces, led by SS Einsatzgruppen, continued their massacres across Poland and—following Operation Barbarossa—in Soviet territory. Most European Jews remained alive, but conditions were worsening, both inside the ghettos and across an extensive network of secret camps, where hundreds of thousands of prisoners experienced unspeakable cruelties and the most heinous atrocities ever conceived.

THE CONCENTRATION CAMPS

In early 1933, the Nazis moved quickly to crack down on all dissent, arresting and removing from German society those considered enemies of the Reich. Most were political opponents of the Nazi regime—communists, liberals, trade unionists, and those who dared to speak out—but others perceived as threats to German culture, such as Roman Catholic priests, Jehovah's Witnesses, and suspected homosexuals, were also targeted. The Nazis held the prisoners inside an abandoned factory in Dachau, a town just outside Munich, in what became Germany's first concentration camp. None of the inmates had been formally prosecuted—their detention was indefinite, and at the sole whim of the Gestapo and other security authorities.

Within a few years, such camps had proliferated across the Third Reich. Increasingly filled with German Jews after 1938, many were built near population centers with large Jewish communities, such as Buchenwald, near Weimar, and Sachsenhausen and Ravensbrück, both outside Berlin, the latter exclusively for women. Over the years, it evolved into an elaborate system, eventually encompassing two dozen main camps and thousands of sub-camps operating across Germany, Poland, Austria, the Baltics, and other occupied territories. Though prisoners were predominantly Jewish, there was no shortage of others the Nazis abhorred, including Roma, a once-nomadic people often referred to contemptuously as Gypsies, who came to Europe centuries earlier from northern India.

Some avoided deportation to the camps, hiding where they could or living under assumed identities. Aided by friends, neighbors, and even strangers, they eluded security authorities for months and sometimes years. It was an extraordinary risk for their accomplices, as the Gestapo searched relentlessly for those in hiding, interrogating whomever they pleased and shooting or hanging anyone even suspected of guilt. Some eagerly collaborated with the Nazis, reporting on neighbors and turning in those they knew to be in hiding. Their motives varied; many were vehement antisemites and Nazi sympathizers, while others sought personal or monetary gain. Foreign governments such as Vichy France also cooperated with the Nazis, directing their police forces to hand over any Jews found within their borders.

It often meant a death sentence. The camps were hellish, barbaric places, where prisoners were routinely starved, beaten, raped, and tortured. Administered by the ironfisted Waffen-SS, the military wing of the SS, the guards were drawn primarily from the Death's Head Division, known for its killing sprees in the East. Among new arrivals, belongings were seized, including wedding rings, family heirlooms, and other valuables. Much of it was looted by the SS, its ranks filled with thieves and profiteers, including high-ranking officials who leased out Jews in their custody as slave laborers to German war industries. Both inside and outside the camps, prisoners labored for long hours in factories and workshops, assembling German war goods from artillery shell casings to uniforms.

Discipline was severe, and conditions in the camps were beyond deplorable. After their heads were shaved, prisoners were issued threadbare uniforms that became tattered, lice-infested rags. Barracks and living spaces were overcrowded, with as many as five people to a bed, and the scraps of food provided were barely enough to keep prisoners alive and working. Medical care was nonexistent, as the only camp physicians were sadistic Nazi zealots who used the facilities as laboratories for human experimentation. They routinely tested deranged theories about racial differences in human anatomy on prisoners, and forced sterilizations, castrations, and other mutilations were common. Any interaction with Nazi doctors and scientists came with fatal consequences.

The Killing Centers

The millions of Jews languishing in ghettos and concentration camps became so wilted by hunger and sickness, the Nazis no longer considered them productive workers. Many in the SS hierarchy viewed their meager food rations as a waste, and the disease-ridden camps and ghettos a health and security threat to the Reich.

In January 1942, a cross-section of senior German government officials met at a villa in Wannsee, a suburb of Berlin, to deliberate "the Final Solution to the Jewish Problem" — a euphemism for the genocide of European Jews. Their principal focus was to improve efficiencies among various government functions involved with the ongoing mass murder in occupied territories. In the East alone, the SS was slaughtering thousands of Jews each week, gunning down large groups as they stood over mass graves. One example came in September 1941, after German forces occupied the Ukrainian capital of Kiev. The city's Jews were taken by SS Einsatzgruppen to a nearby ravine called Babi Yar, where the Nazis shot more than 33,000 men, women, and children in just two days.

With the Nazis intending to expand the scale of murder from thousands to millions, such mass shootings were deemed impractical. The weapons and ammunition were needed on the Eastern Front, and witnesses and evidence would invariably be left behind. There was even concern for those pulling the triggers, with Nazi leaders fretting about the psychological effect on the SS men. They turned to poison gas, a method already tested on Soviet POWs and as part of a "euthanasia" program, when the Nazis murdered tens of thousands of children and adults with mental and physical disabilities.

Using compounds such as Zyklon-B, a highly toxic pesticide, the Nazis planned to administer gassings in newly built, specialized facilities that could accommodate such large-scale slaughter. Sometimes referred to as death camps, each of these killing centers was remotely located in occupied Poland, where most Jews were held and where rail lines could support large-scale transport. The first to open was Chelmno, less than forty miles from Lodz in central Poland, but others would soon follow. After emptying the ghettos and concentration camps of Jews and other prisoners, the Nazis loaded them into railcars designed to hold livestock. Packed shoulder to shoulder, the prisoners were forced to stand for hours and days during the long journeys, often in withering heat. Denied food, water, and access to toilets or medical care, many died in transit.

The trains eventually arrived at what resembled labor camps, but none were built for long-term confinement. Prisoners were prodded off the trains at gunpoint, their luggage and possessions taken and sorted into piles for future plundering by the SS. Ordered to shed their clothes, adults and children alike were handed a towel and bar of soap and led into what appeared to be large shower rooms. Once the doors were sealed behind them, gaseous fumes were released, killing all inside after several excruciating minutes. When it was over, other Jews were ordered to haul the bodies to burn pits or crematoriums, where they were incinerated into ash. The SS also employed large, mobile vans, packing over fifty people into each. Told the vans were for transport to labor sites, prisoners inside were asphyxiated by exhaust fumes during the brief drive, their corpses later dumped into mass graves.

The most notorious facility in the entire system was Auschwitz, an enormous complex some forty miles west of Kraków. Originally built as a work camp, a sign at the entrance greeted new arrivals with the declaration "Arbeit Macht Frei" (Work Makes You Free). The Nazis then separated prisoners based on age and physical condition. The able-bodied, their wrists tattooed with identification numbers, were kept alive to toil in nearby coal mines and factories. Those deemed incapable of work—children, the elderly, and the sickly—were taken to Birkenau, a nearby killing center, and led directly into the gas chambers. Before its liberation in 1945, the SS slaughtered over one million Jews at Auschwitz-Birkenau.

Other killing centers tallied equally horrifying numbers. Treblinka, less than fifty miles from Warsaw, came close to matching the slaughter at Auschwitz-Birkenau; the SS there murdered an estimated 925,000 Jews. Another 434,000 were killed at Belzec; at least 172,000 at Chelmno; and 167,000 at Sobibor. Most were Poles and Soviets, but few European countries under Hitler's thumb were able to shield their Jews from harm. Hungary, an Axis partner, was among them, until early 1944 when its support for continuing the war began to wane. German occupation forces moved in, and 437,000 Hungarian Jews were deported to Auschwitz. Though some became laborers, more than 300,000 others were gassed, all within a matter of weeks.

By the time the Holocaust finally ended, over six million Jews had been murdered. Others—communists, homosexuals, the disabled, intellectuals, petty criminals, and so many more—suffered as well, perhaps none more so than the Roma community. A precise number of those killed in the Holocaust is unknown, but estimates are in the hundreds of thousands, decimating a population that numbered roughly one million before the slayings began.

Aftermath

Genocide, the systematic elimination of non-combatants belonging to a particular ethnic or political group, was not unknown before the 1930s, nor was the Holocaust the last time the world would experience the mass slaughter of innocents. But in expanding their state-sponsored killing machinery across the broadest possible territory, sweeping in as many victims as could be found, the Nazis imposed the most radical incarnation of genocide ever known. What distinguished the Holocaust was not just the scale of the Nazi enterprise—camps, rail networks, a vast administrative arm, the death of millions—but the intent. Other mass murders of select populations were connected to efforts to expand political or economic power, such as Stalin's orchestration of famine among Ukrainians in the early 1930s. In contrast, the Nazi desire to "liquidate" Jews was moved by simple, visceral hatred. In plotting to slaughter every European Jew, the Nazis introduced the world to the darkest, most depraved chapter in human history.

As the Germans began retreating from occupied lands, pushed back by Soviet forces across the East, the SS rushed to dismantle the camps and the killing centers. Any traces of their existence were destroyed; barracks, administrative offices, and crematoriums were razed; and incriminating documents burned. After surviving prisoners were forced to exhume and incinerate decomposed bodies left in mass graves, grounds were plowed over, and crops planted in their place.

Of the remaining prisoners, those unfit for labor were put to death, and the rest moved westward to camps in Germany. Rail transport was limited by then, so most had to cross hundreds of miles on foot. Already weakened, their bodies skeletal, many succumbed to illness, exposure, or starvation on the backbreaking death marches. Those who collapsed or could not keep pace were shot by guards.

The glut of camps and killing centers was impossible to conceal. Those in nearby communities put the puzzle pieces together—trains passing through, fully loaded with human cargo but returning entirely empty; skies darkened with ash from the around-the-clock use of crematoriums; and worst of all, the revolting, ongoing stench of burning flesh. Escapees were few, but they, too, had spread word of the camps, and their stories began reaching the highest levels of Allied governments. Arguments persist to this day whether Allied leaders should have intervened where they could, perhaps by bombing the rail system used for deportations when this became possible in mid-1944. They declined to do so, maintaining that their most effective and expedient means for ending the atrocities was to win the war. Any diversion of resources away from that objective, it was argued, would only prolong the suffering.

Even with the eyewitness accounts, the full measure of the Nazi genocide was not truly understood until advancing Allied soldiers began discovering campsites, many partially intact. The first came in July 1944, when Soviet armies moving into central Poland found remnants of the Majdanek camp, including gas chambers. The Allies began documenting the atrocities, using survivor accounts, newsreels, and photographs of the camps, determined to hold all those involved accountable. In late 1945, a post-war International Military Tribunal was convened in

Nuremberg, Germany, where some two dozen defendants from the Nazi elite, including senior political, military, and industry leaders, were charged with war crimes. With Adolf Hitler and Heinrich Himmler already dead, Hermann Göring was the highest-ranking Nazi official to stand trial. Nineteen of the defendants were found guilty, and twelve sentenced to death. Göring took his own life in his jail cell, while the others were hanged and then, fittingly, cremated at Dachau.

In subsequent months and years, American-led military tribunals and German denazification courts similarly prosecuted other prominent Nazis, from high-level government officials to camp commandants, physicians, guards, and other SS personnel. Not all who were complicit faced consequences. Among them, police officers, judges, government officials, other civil servants, industrialists, financiers, doctors, lawyers, and so many others who willingly facilitated and implemented the Nazi policies that spawned a decade of terror.

They were not alone. Millions of other Germans who were indifferent or harbored genuine misgivings about the early violence and persecution had refused to act or speak out, fearful of retribution from the Nazi regime. The acceptance and tolerance of such appalling evil, and passivity among so many, were elemental to the Holocaust and among its most shameful legacies. From the silence to the savagery, it all remains an indelible and eternal stain on humanity.

• • • • •

Anne Frank

In 1933, four-year-old Anne Frank and her family of German Jews emigrated to Amsterdam. When German occupation forces began arresting Dutch Jews in July 1942, the Franks went into hiding, avoiding detection for several years as Anne diligently recorded her experiences in a diary. The family was arrested by the Gestapo in August 1944, and Anne and her sister were eventually sent to Bergen-Belsen, a concentration camp near Hanover, Germany. Anne died there, likely of typhus, one month before the British liberated the camp. Anne's father survived the camps, and after the war, discovered Anne's diary. It was published in 1947 and quickly became an international bestseller, with millions of copies sold.

> **Warsaw Ghetto Uprising**
> In mid-1942, the SS began deporting more than 300,000 Jews from the Warsaw Ghetto, sending most directly into the gas chambers at Treblinka. When the SS returned to remove the last 70,000 occupants, hundreds of Jews banded together and fought back. With only a small number of pistols and even fewer automatic weapons, the insurgents held off over 2,000 SS troops armed with machine guns and backed by artillery and tanks. The skirmishing lasted four weeks, until the SS set fire to the ghetto and then leveled it with shelling and explosives. Thousands of Jews were killed, and the survivors deported to the gas chambers.

France, 1944

OPERATION OVERLORD

11
THE LIBERATION OF FRANCE
JUNE 1944—AUGUST 1944

"Soldiers, sailors, and airmen of the Allied Expeditionary Force. You are about to embark upon the great crusade toward which we have striven these many months. The eyes of the world are upon you...I have full confidence in your courage, devotion to duty, and skill in battle."
–General Dwight D. Eisenhower

"There are two kinds of people who are staying on this beach — those who are dead, and those who are going to die. Now let's get the hell out of here!"
–Colonel George Taylor, US Army, at Omaha Beach

In November 1943, the leaders of the United States, Britain, and the Soviet Union — known as the Big Three — gathered in Tehran, Iran to plot their combined strategy for ending the war. For more than two years, the Soviets had faced the preponderance of Hitler's armies, with Red Army casualties reaching into the millions. At Tehran, an increasingly piqued Stalin insisted his American and British allies widen their campaign against the Nazis, then limited to just Italy, to relieve pressure in the East. Roosevelt and Churchill agreed, and plans began forming for a long-anticipated invasion of northwestern France.

Codenamed Overlord, it would be the most expansive Allied undertaking of the war. Preparations stretched for months as Eisenhower, reassigned from Italy and appointed Supreme

Allied Commander for the invasion, presided over a historic buildup of forces for both the initial amphibious landing and broader push into the French interior. From offices just outside London, Eisenhower and his Supreme Headquarters Allied Expeditionary Forces (SHAEF) culled together some two million men, along with thousands of supporting ships, tanks, armored vehicles, trucks, fighter planes, and bombers, and countless tons of equipment, supplies, and munitions.

To optimize moonlight and tidal conditions for the airborne and seaborne assaults, an invasion date was set for early June. As "D-Day" approached, Allied leaders became consumed with anxiety, aware their venture to hasten the end of the war was fraught with risks. Momentum was firmly in their favor, with clear edges in manpower, resources, and morale, but the Germans were far from whipped. Immense armies remained dispersed across occupied France, led by Hitler's most venerated combat commander, shaping Overlord into one of the highest-stake enterprises of the war.

• • • • •

With the German High Command finally conceding an invasion of the continent was inevitable, Field Marshal Erwin Rommel was called on once again. Summoned to take charge of coastal defenses spanning from northern France to Holland, the Army Group B he inherited in early 1944 was a mix of veteran units recuperating from the savage fighting in the East, and more motley divisions filled with teenagers, conscripts, and even Soviet POWs volunteering to fight for the Germans. Aware of substantial Allied advantages in armor and air power, Rommel concluded an invasion force had to be defeated on the beaches, before a foothold could be won and reinforcements poured in.

He began with a defensive buildup along Hitler's "Atlantic Wall." For months, German engineers used an army of forced laborers to fortify beaches and overlooks along a 2,000-mile length of coastline. They built bunkers, concrete blockhouses ("pillboxes"), heavy gun emplacements, antitank contraptions, and myriad other obstacles. Rommel did what he could to hurry the construction along, but it was far from enough, as many of the planned additions remained unfinished when summer arrived, nor was there adequate manpower to defend it all.

Adding to Rommel's challenges was the mystery of where the Allies might land. SHAEF had sowed much confusion about that destination, using an elaborate ruse to convince the Germans it was the Pas-de-Calais region, where the English Channel narrowed to a width of just twenty miles. False reports were openly circulated of Patton—widely regarded by the Germans as Eisenhower's most capable subordinate—arriving in England to take command of a fictitious First United States Army Group, based just across the water from Calais. Allied engineers whipped up a phantom army for him, using plywood, canvas, and inflatable rubber to fashion dummy tanks, artillery pieces, barracks, and more, all plainly visible to prying eyes in southeast England, friendly and otherwise. Periodic bombing missions over Calais and a drumbeat of phony radio transmissions fitting the Calais narrative—with the Germans eavesdropping—completed the illusion.

The ploy worked beyond expectations, even duping Rommel. He left his forces divided, keeping the nineteen armored and infantry divisions of his Fifteenth Army in Calais, and dispersing his weaker Seventh Army, mostly infantry, across the coastal provinces of Normandy and Brittany. A reserve force of nine panzer divisions was also nearby, but Rommel and his superiors quarreled over how to employ it. It was Hitler who settled the dispute, allotting just a portion of the armor to Rommel and leaving the majority under his own personal control. It proved yet another misstep by the German dictator.

D-Day

The details of Overlord were perhaps the best-kept secret of the war. The true landing site was some 200 miles south of Calais, on a 50-mile stretch of sand in Normandy. Hours before dawn, 23,000 American and British paratroopers and glider-borne infantry would descend in the dark, landing miles behind the enemy defenses, east and west of the landing beaches. Their mission was to seize control of bridges, roads, and causeways, blocking any potential German counterattacks and protecting the flanks of the Allied invasion army. At daybreak, naval and aerial bombardments would soften the German coastal defenses for the waves of assault troops coming by sea. The US First Army would land on beaches codenamed Utah and Omaha, while farther east, the British Second Army would land in zones designated Gold, Juno, and Sword. The Allies would then push inland, with the Americans wheeling toward the Cotentin Peninsula and driving toward the deep-water port of Cherbourg — critical for supplying the invasion force with fuel and ammunition — and British and Canadian forces converging on the town of Caen, a key gateway on the road to Paris.

D-Day was originally scheduled for the morning of June 5, but heavy rains and high winds forced a postponement. The weather improved only marginally, and with the window narrowing for favorable tides and moonlight, Eisenhower made the wrenching decision to proceed the next day, gambling that his assault forces could overcome the stormy conditions. In the early morning darkness of June 6, the first transport planes and towed gliders lifted off from airfields across Britain, and Overlord was underway.

In the American drop zone, heavy cloud cover and flak from German anti-aircraft batteries sent several transports off course, scattering paratroopers from the US 82nd and 101st Airborne Divisions across the French countryside. Some landed in enemy hands and others in open fields flooded earlier by the Germans, but the paratroopers were well trained, and many managed to reach their objectives. At German headquarters, bleary-eyed staff were awakened with panicked reports of airborne landings across Normandy, but there was little alarm among senior leaders, as few thought the drops or earlier bombing raids were precursors to an invasion. The activities were believed to be a feint, designed to draw attention and resources away from Calais, where Patton was still expected to land.

Along the Atlantic Wall, German defenders also had no inkling 5,000 ships had crossed the English Channel that morning, as the Luftwaffe and Kriegsmarine had long been chased from the area. Just before dawn, the mass of Allied battleships, cruisers, and destroyers let loose with their heavy guns, aiming their thunderous barrages at the minefields, bunkers, and machine-gun emplacements lining the Normandy coastline. When the shelling finally tapered off, hundreds of landing craft packed with assault troops began their treks toward the beaches.

The Germans scrambled to their defenses, but most senior commanders were away from their posts on leave, having assumed the ongoing miserable weather would preclude any large-scale Allied action. That included Rommel, who was visiting his family in Germany. Coastal fortifications remained severely undermanned, and with the Seventh Army stretched thin across Normandy and lacking transport, the German regiments defending the beaches that morning were on their own.

At Utah Beach, the US 4th Infantry Division met little resistance, suffering fewer than 200 casualties. Though the British 50th and 3rd Infantry Divisions had similar success, occupying Gold and Sword Beaches with relative ease, the Canadian 3rd Infantry Division was less fortunate. Several landing vessels struck mines off Juno Beach, and those that made it to the shoreline were raked with blistering machine-gun fire. Casualties were high, but the Canadians eventually fought past the German defenses, linking up with their British brethren and beginning a coordinated push toward Caen.

A far worse reception was in store for the Americans closing in on Omaha Beach. As their landing craft churned toward the shoreline, the assault troops could glimpse the imposing bluffs visible just past the beach. They were well-fortified heights, defended by Rommel's most battle-hardened veterans, and as the Germans crouched behind their concrete walls and mounds of sandbags, patiently awaiting the boats plowing through the surf, each was eager to make the Americans pay for every inch.

OMAHA BEACH

The assault forces assigned to Omaha Beach belonged to the 1st Infantry Division, veterans of North Africa and Sicily, and the less experienced 29th Infantry Division. For both divisions, the operation was a disaster from the start.

It began with transport ships off-loading the smaller Higgins boats miles from the landing zone. Each 36-foot-long landing craft held up to three dozen men, and as the small boats motored toward the coastline, they were tossed by heavy swells, soaking and sickening the men aboard. Fierce winds and currents also pushed boats away from their designated landing sites, putting many of the men ashore in front of enemy strongpoints unscathed by earlier bombardments. Other boats were grounded by sandbars, forcing those aboard to scramble over the sides and into the water. Some drowned, pulled to the bottom by the weight of waterlogged field packs and other equipment strapped to their bodies, while others were cut down by machine guns and small arms as they waded through chest-deep waters and a powerful undertow.

Those boats that made it to the beach lowered their front ramps, spilling the nauseous men onto dry land, where they were greeted with a cacophony of noise and exploding mines. The pre-invasion aerial and naval bombardments were expected to silence the German guns on the heights above the beaches, but hailstorms of bullets and shrapnel filled the air. Those who were not hit stumbled past the wounded and dead soldiers strewn across the beach, desperate to find cover, as artillery and mortar rounds tore into their ranks and machine-gun bursts riddled entire squads. The first waves also lacked fire support on the beach, as much of the heavy armor expected to be floated ashore had capsized or foundered in the rough sea. Nor had any air support materialized, the planes grounded by the poor weather.

Adding to their misfortune, Omaha Beach was defended by veterans of the Eastern Front. Perched on the bluffs above, the Germans mercilessly swept the exposed men sprinkled across the beach with deadly crossfire. Survivors attempted to crawl forward, but the only available cover was a short seawall and shingle embankment that ran along the base of the beach. They huddled there, or behind German beach obstacles in the surf, pinned down by the heavy guns high above. Handfuls managed to advance, scaling the heights under intensive fire until they reached the German fortifications. Demolitions and flamethrowers were brought up to clear the bunkers, and by afternoon, the landing zone was finally secured.

An estimated 2,000 Americans were killed or wounded that fateful morning on Omaha Beach, accounting for nearly half the Allied casualties on D-Day. It could have been far worse, as the Germans squandered opportunities across Normandy to push the first waves back into the sea. An entire army still loitered in Calais, awaiting a Patton-led assault that would never come, and panzer reserves that could have been decisive in the opening hours also sat idle, as no one in the German chain of command wished to wake a slumbering Hitler and ask for their release.

Just as Rommel had foreseen, tens of thousands of Allied troops would land in Normandy in the days to come. Though the Germans had substantial reserves throughout France, they struggled to reach the coastal provinces, thwarted by inoperable railways, roads, and bridges marred by months of Allied bombings. French Resistance fighters were also instrumental, sabotaging rail and communications networks and ambushing German forces on the move.

The operation was an early success, with the Allies firmly ashore and gaining strength each day, but there was much fighting to come. With a substantial German army still entrenched in Normandy, defending ground favorable to the ever-cagey Rommel, the liberation of France had only just begun.

THE BREAKOUT

Three weeks into the invasion, the Allies remained in a precarious position, bottled up around their beachheads and unable to push past the German forces arrayed against them.

To the east, British and Canadian forces expecting to take Caen on D-Day had been frustrated by an unyielding German defense, led by Rommel's few panzer reserves. It would take more than a month for Montgomery to dislodge them. The Americans had also made little progress, bogged down in a patchwork of small farm fields and orchards that stretched across much of western Normandy. Known as the bocage, it was filled with seemingly endless hedgerows—windbreaks planted centuries earlier to protect vulnerable crops. Each had an earthen base, typically a few feet wide and a few feet tall, topped with dense, deeply rooted tangles of shrubbery and low trees, several feet thick and up to twenty feet high. The imposing hedgerows lined every field, and behind each one, the Germans were able to conceal snipers, machine-gun nests, and antitank weapons that turned the American advance into a bloody, grinding struggle. The two sides battled for yards at a time, as casualties on both sides climbed into the thousands. Hitler's generals pleaded for a strategic retreat, but the führer refused, unwilling to cede any ground to the Allies.

The slugfest in the hedgerows dragged on for weeks, until late July, when the town of Saint-Lô, a German strongpoint with a critical road juncture, finally fell to the Americans. That opened the door for Operation Cobra, the long-planned breakout from Normandy, beginning with a massive carpet-bombing operation that demolished the German armor and infantry blocking the Americans. With a path cleared for Allied forces to finally push forward, Patton's fresh Third Army — his real command — rolled into action, and the German defensive lines began to crumble.

Hitler still refused permission for an orderly withdrawal, ordering ill-fated counterattacks instead that allowed the Americans and British to easily outflank and encircle what was left of the German Seventh Army. By mid-August, an estimated 100,000 Germans were penned in and fighting for their lives near the town of Falaise. Hitler finally approved a general retreat, but it was too late. Half of his remaining men were killed or captured as they attempted to escape, and though tens of thousands of others made it out of the Falaise Pocket, their tanks, vehicles, and heavy weapons were all left behind. It was the final collapse of German resistance in northern France.

A second front opened that same month. Led by the American Seventh Army, more than 94,000 Allied troops came ashore in southern France, capturing key ports at Marseille and Toulon. As they drove northward, Patton and others continued to push east from Normandy, battling to the outskirts of Paris by late August. Hitler ordered the city destroyed by artillery, but General Dietrich von Choltitz, commanding the Wehrmacht garrison, refused, and on August 25, Paris was liberated by Allied troops.

Though von Choltitz's defiance was a rarity in the German command structure, Hitler had long been the target of assassination plots. Success came close during the battle for

France, when Colonel Claus von Stauffenberg, a disabled German war hero, attempted to end the Nazi madness. On July 20, he smuggled a powerful briefcase bomb into the "Wolf's Lair"—a heavily guarded headquarters compound in East Prussia—where Hitler had convened a staff conference in a fortified bunker. After Hitler miraculously escaped the blast with only minor wounds, von Stauffenberg and other conspirators in German political and military circles were quickly rounded up and either imprisoned or executed. The attempt had failed, but it had a profound impact on Hitler, both physically and psychologically, deepening his long-festering paranoia.

Aftermath

By early September, the Allies had chased the Germans almost entirely from France, at considerable cost to both sides. In the early weeks, Rommel and others had managed to slow the onslaught of invasion armies with limited resources, but Allied reinforcements and air power, coupled with Hitler's stubborn refusals to cede ground, made it a hopeless endeavor. An estimated 400,000 Germans were killed, wounded, or captured in Normandy alone, more than doubling Allied casualties in the province.

The loss of France was a devastating blow to Hitler. Through four years of occupation, the country had provided substantial food, labor, and raw materials to the Reich—resources that were essential to the German war machine. It also left powerful Allied armies on Germany's doorstep. With the onset of autumn, and those forces poised to make their first advance onto German soil, boastful predictions began circulating that the war would be over by Christmas. A looming supply crisis among the Allies took center stage, though, halting operations near the German border as the fighting shifted to Holland, where the Allies readied another high-stakes gamble that promised to turn wishful claims of impending final victory into reality.

* * * * *

ⓘ At the height of the fighting in Normandy, a pair of British *Spitfires* strafed the staff car of Field Marshal Rommel, leaving the revered leader with serious head wounds. His subsequent evacuation left the Germans without their most proven tactical commander in France, adding to their defensive woes and further diminishing morale.

The V-1 and V-2 Programs

Even as his forces were in wide retreat across both the Western and Eastern Fronts, Hitler remained defiant, convinced that new, groundbreaking weapons under secret development could shift the war in his favor once again. That included powerful rockets and missiles designed to reduce London and other Allied cities to rubble.

One of those weapons was the Luftwaffe's V-1 program — the world's first guided cruise missiles. Known as buzz bombs for the noise they made in flight, the V-1s were unmanned, winged aircraft catapulted from launch pads in occupied Europe and propelled by jet engines. The missiles could fly up to 400 miles per hour, and each carried a one-ton explosive. The first V-1 struck London on June 13, 1944, just one week after D-Day, and more than 10,000 others would follow. In the last months of the war, British air defenses brought down some 4,000 of the missiles, but too many others found their marks, killing at least 5,000 civilians and injuring 16,000 more.

The Germans also produced the revolutionary V-2 rocket, the first short-range ballistic missile. Capable of delivering a one-ton warhead from a range of 200 miles and reaching unprecedented speeds up to 3,600 miles per hour, they were immune from any defensive measures. More than 3,000 V-2s were launched against Britain, France, and Belgium, and though they had great destructive force, they proved inaccurate and unreliable.

Both programs were housed in secret underground production facilities hidden deep within the Harz Mountains in Germany. Thousands of Jews and other slave laborers assembled the weapons, and few survived the oppressive working conditions and meager food rations. In the end, the V-1 and V-2 weapons elicited the intended terror among civilian populations, but their impact was too little and too late, and did nothing to slow Allied armies on the march across Western Europe.

George S. Patton Jr.

George S. Patton, Jr. (1885—1945) was one of the most successful and controversial field commanders of the war. He graduated from West Point in 1909, and three years later, competed for the United States in the modern pentathlon at the 1912 Olympics in Stockholm, Sweden. During the First World War, he commanded a tank brigade in the fledgling US Army Tank Corps and became an enthusiastic advocate of mechanized forces. A quarter-century later, he was a lieutenant general, commanding multiple armored divisions in North Africa.

Fluent in French, Patton romanticized war and found lessons in battles from ancient times. He was an egoist and a strict disciplinarian, but also a colorful, flamboyant character, wearing ivory-handled pistols on his hips and designing flashy uniforms. On the battlefield, Patton was an aggressive, fearless combat leader, supremely confident in his own abilities and those of his men. He drove his forces relentlessly and was uncompromising, willing to relieve any subordinate who could not meet the pace he demanded. He bested the Germans in North Africa, Sicily, and France, and his zeal and persistent beseeching of

Eisenhower for fuel and supplies so he could push into Germany was rooted in an earnest conviction he could single-handedly end the war. Eisenhower heard much the same from British Field Marshal Bernard Montgomery, and the rivalry between the two leaders endured through the final months of war, the pair competing for resources, notoriety, and history.

The controversy Patton generated away from the battlefield never eclipsed his extraordinary triumphs on it, but he still emerged as a polarizing wartime figure. The slapping of enlisted soldiers in Sicily ignited an uproar among critics, and the provocative, politically charged claims he made in public threatened to fracture the Allied coalition. It all became an ongoing aggravation for Eisenhower, regardless of the decades-long friendship between the pair.

As promised, Patton led his Third Army into Germany. When the war ended, he was appointed military governor of Bavaria, but his outspoken support of former Nazis serving in the occupation government became a final straw for his superiors, resulting in his dismissal. Patton's service in Europe ended in December 1945, when a tragic automobile accident in Manheim, Germany left him with a fractured neck. He died less than two weeks later, just sixty years old.

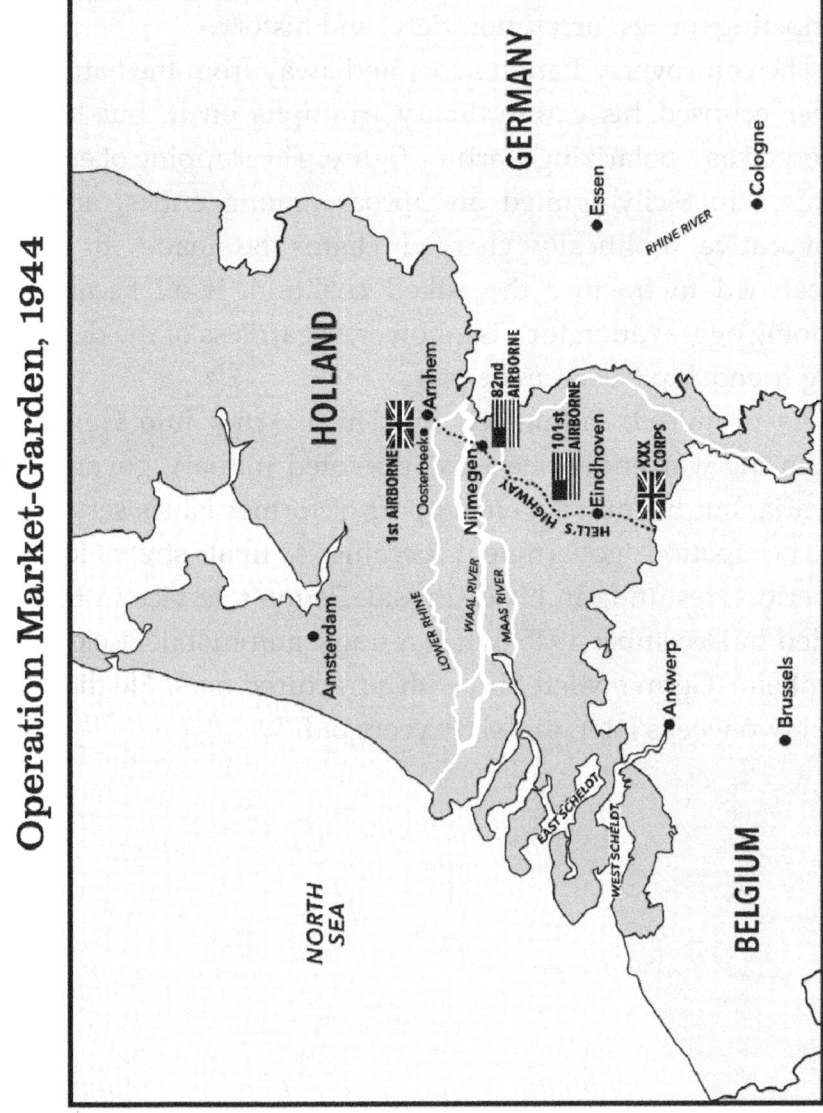

12
THE MARCH TOWARD GERMANY
SEPTEMBER 1944–NOVEMBER 1944

"VAST ALLIED AIRBORNE ARMY LANDS IN HOLLAND AS BRITISH STRIKE IN MOVE TO TURN WESTWALL."
–New York Times, 18 September 1944

"Out of ammo. God save the King."
–Final radio message from British paratroopers at Arnhem

By September 1944, the German Army was backpedaling across Western Europe and struggling to contain what must have seemed like an unstoppable juggernaut. After breaking out of Normandy, Allied forces swept across France at breakneck speed, ending the four-year occupation and liberating tens of millions of people. The British crossed into Belgium and pushed toward Holland, while farther south, American armies edged closer to the French-German border.

Amid the chaotic German retreat, Field Marshal Gerd von Rundstedt was called upon again to take charge. A legendary figure in the Wehrmacht, von Rundstedt was at the center of blitzkrieg triumphs early in the war. When Overlord began, he commanded all German forces in the West, including those of Rommel, but was sacked by Hitler after failing to halt the Allied advance. Two months later, with the German front in disarray, von Rundstedt was reappointed to his former command. He swiftly restored order and discipline to the ranks, stabilizing the

German lines, but it was only a temporary fix, as his men were exhausted, reinforcements were sparse, and morale had plummeted.

His counterpart, Eisenhower, faced challenges as well. The Allies had sizable tactical advantages, but British and American armies had become increasingly starved of fuel and ammunition as they marched farther from their Atlantic ports. Supply convoys crisscrossed France around the clock, but without rail transport—the French system was in shambles after months of Allied bombings—provisions trickled to the front lines. Eisenhower hoped to press the Germans from across a broad front, stretching out von Rundstedt's remaining forces, but with the scarcity of supplies limiting the Allies to a single major thrust, Eisenhower would have to choose among his field commanders to lead it. Patton and Montgomery, of course, clamored the loudest.

As always, Patton argued for blunt force. After dashing across much of France, his Third Army was closing in on Germany's frontier defenses. Known as the Westwall, it was a miles-deep network of bunkers, minefields, tank obstacles, and other fortifications extending across the length of Germany's border with France. Much bloodshed was expected there, giving Montgomery an opening. He offered Eisenhower an appealing alternative, proposing to skirt the Westwall entirely and strike in the north where the German lines were weak. By opening a more circuitous route into Germany. Montgomery's forces could bring the conflict, entering its sixth year, to a rapid conclusion. Eisenhower approved, setting in motion one of the most fateful operations of the war.

• • • • •

There was little evidence of Montgomery's trademark caution in the plan he conceived. It was loaded with gambles and dependencies and required his forces to move with far more alacrity than they were accustomed to. The man who had always insisted on ample time — weeks, or even months — to prepare for major clashes, now allotted mere days.

The plan, codenamed Market-Garden, was twofold. "Market" was the airborne operation, and with 35,000 men involved, it was the largest ever attempted. Three divisions of paratroopers would be airlifted into Holland, well behind enemy lines. Their objective was to quickly capture and hold the bridges spanning several waterways, including the imposing Meuse (Maas, in Dutch), Waal, and Rhine Rivers. British planners, confident the Dutch interior was only lightly defended, expected the paratroopers to capture the bridges with ease, well before the Germans could mobilize reinforcements.

"Garden" referred to the parallel ground operation. The British XXX Corps, a powerful force of armor and infantry, would smash through the German front lines near the Belgian-Dutch border. Racing north along a 60-mile corridor, the armored column would link up with the paratroopers at each successive bridge until reaching the city of Arnhem and crossing a final bridge over the Lower Rhine. That would place Allied forces within miles of the unfortified Dutch-German border, where a gateway could be opened into northern Germany and the prized Ruhr Valley. The Allies could then roll into Germany, choke off industrial production, and leave Hitler's war machine to wither.

Shortly before the operation began, intelligence reports revealed the recent movement of German armored forces into occupied Holland. It was an alarming development, as paratroopers, armed with just rifles and other lightweight weapons, would be no match for German panzers. The discovery, however, was dismissed — and quietly buried — by British officials, dubious the German armor was in fighting condition after thrashings across France.

The British assessment was partly accurate. Led by General Wilhelm Bittrich, an experienced and skilled tactical leader, the veteran II Waffen SS Panzer Corps had indeed been severely diminished by recent fighting in France. Though his corps needed substantial refitting, and had few serviceable tanks, Bittrich's two divisions were no pushovers, filled with thousands of veteran soldiers and enough armored vehicles to pose a significant threat to the Allied paratroopers. The SS forces had been moved to what was considered a quiet sector, away from the front lines, to rest and await replenishment. They arrived, coincidently, some miles outside Arnhem, just days before the Allied operation was to begin. Their presence was detected by British aerial reconnaissance, but it made little difference to those in command. The proximity of what were considered severely depleted German units to the British landing zones was still regarded as insignificant.

THE OPERATION BEGINS

On September 17, 20,000 British and American paratroopers and glider-borne infantry touched down in the Dutch countryside without incident. Near Eindhoven, the American 101st Airborne Division moved quickly to secure nearby canal crossings, while farther north, the 82nd Airborne Division began its march toward bridges over the Maas and Waal Rivers.

The British 1st Airborne Division also arrived safely, but in a landing zone far from ideal. With planners unwilling to risk losing valuable transport aircraft to nearby German anti-aircraft batteries, the division was dropped outside the village of Oosterbeek, eight miles from the Arnhem bridge. It was the most critical objective of the entire operation and quite a distance to cover for paratroopers on foot. Shortages of transport planes and gliders added to their challenge, allowing only part of the division to be delivered on the first day. The remainder of the 1st

Airborne was expected to follow on the second day, and a brigade of Polish paratroopers on the third.

As the 1st Airborne men began digging into perimeter defenses — the landing zone was needed for later drops — a single brigade set out for Arnhem. It was a four-hour march for the three battalions, but a squadron of armored jeeps would precede them, brought in by gliders to speed the first troops into town.

By that time, all surprise had been lost. German forces moved into blocking positions, pinning down the jeep squadron and two of the battalions before they could reach Arnhem. A third, led by Lieutenant Colonel John Frost, avoided the Germans and slipped into the still-undefended city. The paratroopers occupied the north end of the bridge and attempted to cross, but Germans holding the southern end easily repelled the assault, forcing Frost's men to settle into defensive positions to await XXX Corps. The Germans sensed an advantage against the paratroopers, and the next day, sent armored cars and personnel carriers filled with SS troops across the bridge. Frost and his men held, driving back the Germans with their light weapons, but the fight for Arnhem was just beginning.

Meanwhile, XXX Corps had begun its advance toward the main German defensive line in the south. Volleys of artillery, mortar, and machine-gun fire slammed into the lead tanks, but British fighter-bombers came to their aid, blazing a path through the German defenses. Thousands of vehicles journeyed north, forming a slow-moving column that stretched for miles along a single paved road. German ambushes were so frequent, the road became known as "Hell's Highway," and progress slowed considerably as they drove toward the Wilhelmina Canal. Ahead of them, elements of the 101st Airborne had found the crossing there destroyed by German demolitions, but British engineers achieved a remarkable feat, spanning the narrow waterway in a single night with a portable bridge capable of supporting tanks. After crossing the Wilhelmina, XXX Corps charged toward the next set of bridges, including the half-mile, steel-arch Goliath over the Waal River that would become a nightmare for American paratroopers.

The bridge was in the city of Nijmegen, and the 82nd Airborne likely could have commandeered it early on, but the paratroopers had been ordered to first clear a large patch of high ground outside the city. The Germans took advantage of the delay, fortifying the south end of the bridge and forcing the Americans to attempt a flanking maneuver. They sent an assault force across the Waal, with paratroopers and combat engineers crammed into twenty-six small boats made from canvas and wood. With just a thin smokescreen to mask their movement, the men rowed across the river in daylight, a distance of more than three football fields. As they paddled frantically, even rowing with their rifle butts, the Germans showered the small flotilla with artillery and mortar fire. The deadly shrapnel tore through the boats, as did machine-gun and small-arms fire from the far bank. Those who survived the firestorm hurried ashore, racing toward the road and railroad bridges, while the remaining engineers ran the deadly gauntlet again, rowing their boats back across the Waal to return with the next wave of paratroopers.

Pressed from both sides of the river, the German defenses fell apart. The road bridge had been wired with demolitions, but for reasons unknown, they failed to detonate, allowing the lead British tanks to cross safely. To the dismay of the paratroopers, the tanks then paused to await their infantry, still clearing out the Germans in Nijmegen, and replenish their ammunition.

Just eleven miles away, time was running out for the British paratroopers in Arnhem. It was the fourth day of the operation, and German reinforcements had pushed Frost's outgunned battalion off the bridge and into the streets. The paratroopers battled back, but panzers roamed the city at will, blasting houses and buildings apart and slowly squeezing the remaining resistance. With only a fraction of his men still in fighting condition, aid stations overflowing with wounded, and ammunition exhausted, Frost had no choice but to surrender.

Near Oosterbeek, the rest of the 1st Airborne fared little better. Backed up against the Lower Rhine by German armor and artillery, the division was fast running out of ammunition, food, and medical supplies. Inoperable radios prevented any contact outside the Arnhem area, and expected reinforcements were long overdue, with dense fog in England grounding transport aircraft assigned to the Polish brigade.

As the 1st Airborne neared its breaking point, XXX Corps fought to within artillery range of the surrounding Germans but could not close the distance. On the ninth day of an operation expected to last only three, the Allies finally called it off. Under cover of darkness, the remaining 1st Airborne men withdrew, leaving most of their wounded behind and the bridge at Arnhem firmly in German hands.

Market-Garden had been a bold, imaginative gambit, and Allied forces had pushed deep into occupied territory, but the operation fell short of Montgomery's promise to open a bridgehead into Germany. American paratroopers and XXX Corps endured their share of losses, but it was the British airborne forces that suffered the most. Doomed by poor planning, overly optimistic assumptions, and multiple strokes of misfortune, just one out of every five British paratroopers who landed in Holland made it out alive. The rest—some 8,000 men—were killed or captured.

A BLOODY AUTUMN

Both before and after Market-Garden concluded, logistical challenges continued to foil Allied progress. The early September capture of Antwerp, a deep-water Belgian port, was expected to ease the chronic supply shortages, but it was sixty miles inland, and the approaches along the Scheldt River remained under German control. Montgomery, preoccupied for weeks with Market-Garden, waited until October before finally ordering those approaches cleared so Allied shipping could reach the port. He assigned the task to the Canadian First Army, and after weeks of hard fighting and steep casualties among the Canadians, the docks and quays finally began operating in late November.

Slowed by shortages of fuel and ammunition throughout those autumn months, American forces pushing east made limited gains, most notably in Lorraine, the region of northeast France bordering Germany, Luxembourg, and Belgium. After brawling with the Germans along the Moselle River, Patton's Third Army converged on the stronghold of Metz, a medieval fortress city protected by a ring of forts, but a stingy German defense and the onset of heavy rains hindered the Americans for weeks before the city was finally taken.

To the north, the American First Army also drove toward the border, reaching the German city of Aachen in early October. Berlin ordered the garrison to hold at all costs, even after the city was leveled with heavy artillery, and when the Germans still refused to yield, the two sides battled in the city streets. Aachen fell—the first German city to do so—but not before the First Army suffered 10,000 casualties. More misery awaited the Americans in the nearby Huertgen Forest. In wretched weather, thousands of Germans, far more familiar with the forbidding terrain and fighting ferociously to protect their homeland, brought several US divisions to a standstill. Over 31,000 Americans were killed or wounded in the dense woods amid some of the most savage fighting in the European Theater.

Aftermath

The bitter clashes along the German border from north to south in late 1944 left both armies bloodied and exhausted. As early December arrived and the incessant rains gave way to wintry temperatures, weary American divisions in action since June were desperate for relief. They mostly stood down, with Allied leaders expecting a quiet respite for their armies as they awaited favorable weather. Once Allied air power returned to the skies, the likes of Patton and Montgomery were expected to sweep across the Rhine and into the heart of Germany, finally bringing the war to a close.

Hitler had other plans.

• • • • •

Penicillin

For generations, soldiers sidelined with battlefield wounds or stricken with disease had been dangerously susceptible to infections—a leading cause of death in the prior world war.

By the 1940s, with both Axis and Allied forces battling across multiple continents and oceans, straining manpower and resources, it became increasingly necessary to backfill armies with men recuperated from prior wounds and illness. Healing had become not only a humanitarian imperative, but a military one as well.

In 1943, the first doses of a groundbreaking antibiotic began arriving in combat theaters. Its origins traced to 1928, when a London bacteriologist, Alexander Fleming, discovered a substance from a mold that could destroy harmful microbes. He lacked the expertise to purify it, but years later, a team at Oxford University, led by Australian pathologist Howard Florey and a German-born biochemist, Ernst Chain, was able to take Fleming's discovery one step further. They purified the mold's active ingredient that was so effective against bacteria, and after successfully experimenting on mice and humans, they were ready to scale up production for what became known as penicillin.

By that time, Britain was at war again with Germany, and with its chemical and pharmaceutical industries already fully committed to the war effort, the Oxford team sailed across the Atlantic to enlist American drug companies in the manufacturing challenge. Several agreed to take part in what became a collaborative enterprise of government agencies, pharmaceutical manufacturers, and leading chemists. After the

Japanese attack on Pearl Harbor thrust the United States into the global conflict, production of penicillin became one of the War Department's highest priorities.

Forward medical units in combat theaters began receiving their first doses, reserving the limited supplies at first for life-threatening infections, but with twenty-one companies manufacturing the drug, the shortages soon vanished. Inventories grew, and by June 1944, over 2.3 million doses had been stocked for the invasion of Normandy. Dubbed the "miracle drug" of the war, penicillin became yet another Allied advantage, saving countless lives and restoring the health of so many who returned to the front lines.

For their extraordinary contributions to the discovery and development of penicillin, Fleming, Florey, and Chain shared the Nobel Prize for Medicine in 1945.

Arie Bestebreurtje

Arie Bestebreurtje, a native of Rotterdam, was just twenty-three years old when the war began. He was a competitive athlete as a teenager, qualifying as an alternate on the 1936 Olympic speed skating team, but by the time the Germans invaded Holland in 1940, Bestebreurtje was in Switzerland earning a law degree. He fled the continent a year later, eventually arriving in Britain.

Bestebreurtje became a British Army officer and later joined the Office of Strategic Services, a fledgling American spy agency. He was chosen to be part of the "Jedburghs" — small teams of men, including those who spoke native languages, which parachuted into enemy-held territory to carry out reconnaissance, sabotage, and other intelligence activities. Shortly before Operation Market-Garden began, Bestebreurtje was assigned to the American 82nd Airborne Division, filling a need for a Dutch-speaking intelligence officer familiar with the region. Bestebreurtje was a perfect fit, having spent many childhood summers hiking in the Nijmegen area.

When the 82nd Airborne made its jump into Holland, Bestebreurtje — known to many as "Captain Harry" because of their difficulty pronouncing his name—was paired with Major General James Gavin, the division's 37-year-old commanding officer. Shortly after the paratroopers landed, Bestebreurtje and Gavin came under fire from a German machine-gun nest. Bestebreurtje, a crack shot, quickly spotted the enemy crew and killed the gunner with his carbine, shooting from the hip.

During the fighting around Nijmegen, Bestebreurtje was everywhere, elated to be back in Holland and contributing to the fight for his homeland. After shrewdly using the local telephone system to call into the city and inquire about German strength there, he went into Nijmegen to make his own assessment, where he was lightly wounded in a firefight with the Germans. When a number of Dutch underground members volunteered to support the 82nd, Bestebreurtje coordinated their efforts to prevent the Germans from destroying the bridge. It remains a mystery why the German demolitions failed, but many have speculated that it may have been the work of Dutch Resistance fighters.

Bestebreurtje survived the war. He was later awarded the Military Order of Williams, Holland's highest military decoration, and the Legion of Merit, one of the United States' most prestigious honors. In peacetime, he became a successful attorney but was later drawn to theology, eventually becoming a Presbyterian minister. He immigrated to the United States and led parishes in Kentucky and Virginia before passing away in 1983.

The Western Front, December 1944

13
BATTLE OF THE BULGE
DECEMBER 1944—JANUARY 1945

"Soldiers of the West Front! Your great hour has arrived...We gamble everything."
–Field Marshal Gerd von Rundstedt

"The present situation is to be regarded as one of opportunity for us and not disaster."
–General Dwight D. Eisenhower

The trouncing of a single division of British paratroopers in Holland could not mask the fading might of the Third Reich in the last months of 1944. In the East, once-powerful army groups that had reached the fringes of Moscow three years earlier had been fully expelled from Soviet lands, pushed back across the Baltics and Central Europe by an unrelenting Red Army swelling in size and strength. In the West, Allied forces were badly bloodied, but Patton and others continued to press closer to German borders. On both fronts, Germany fought largely alone, abandoned by former cohorts Italy, Romania, Bulgaria, and Finland.

Though he had lost four million soldiers and the better part of his Fortress Europe, an increasingly erratic and delusional Hitler refused to concede his "master race" had been defeated. He was particularly derisive of American soldiers, disparaging their fighting abilities and attributing their battlefield success to a glut of industrial power. Convinced a well-planned strike would easily crush the American forces dug in across his lines, Hitler devised an elaborate winter counteroffensive—one he claimed would crush morale across the Anglo-American alliance, prolong the war, and force Western leaders to the negotiating table.

Many in the German High Command were dubious but still followed the führer's orders, discreetly assembling tanks, planes, fuel, and ammunition for the secret operation. To compensate for troop shortages, age requirements for conscripts and volunteers were loosened and new divisions formed by melding waves of the new inductees, most of them teenagers or grandfathers, with veteran soldiers. Other divisions, some of the best remaining in the Wehrmacht and Waffen SS, were quietly withdrawn from the front and moved to staging areas in Germany, even as those still fending off the Soviets and Americans pleaded for reinforcements.

As the buildup continued, Hitler settled on the location of his attack. He chose the rustic Ardennes in southern Belgium, a majestic expanse blanketed with steep ridges, farm pastures, and large patches of thick forestry. It was widely thought to be unsuitable for mechanized armies, but the Germans had defied such assumptions twice before, sweeping through the area in 1914 and 1940 with stunning speed and surprise. In late 1944, Hitler pushed his few remaining poker chips to the center of the table, betting they could do so again.

· · · · ·

The plan concocted by Hitler was called Operation "Wacht am Rhein" (Watch on the Rhine) and was slated to begin in December, when protracted bad weather would nullify Eisenhower's greatest advantage – his air power. Three German army groups would strike along a 60-mile front in the Ardennes, bulldozing past sparse and scattered American defenses. Panzer spearheads would then race to the Meuse River, reaching it before the dazed Americans could respond in force or destroy key crossings, then press on to Antwerp. Recapturing the vital port and supply base would drive a wedge between the British and Canadians in the north and the Americans in the south, and with the Allied armies divided and deprived once again of needed stocks, Churchill and Roosevelt would be compelled to reach an accord with Germany and end hostilities in the West.

Or so Hitler believed. Many of his top field generals considered the plan reckless and mad. A concentrated attack could certainly breach the thinly held American lines in the Ardennes, but few believed the panzer armies had any chance of withstanding Allied counterattacks and reaching Antwerp before their fuel was exhausted and the skies cleared. They hoped to convince Hitler to pursue more modest objectives, but the führer refused to budge, and with the Gestapo still jailing and executing those suspected of complicity in the July assassination attempt, further opposition was muted.

The Germans would certainly have an army to fight with. Hitler had achieved a remarkable feat, furtively assembling some thirty new and veteran divisions, one-third of them armored. Their success would hinge entirely on speed and surprise. The early prizes for the panzers—road nets in the center of the attack and high ground in the north—were critical stepping-stones to reaching the Meuse, and each had to be taken before the Allies could marshal their reserves. Fuel was another priority. Losses in the East had cut the Germans off from foreign oil sources, and Allied bombings had laid waste to their own synthetic oil production. With the early advance expected to consume most of the available fuel for the German armor, capturing American fuel depots was a pillar of Hitler's strategy. Any significant delays in reaching the depots would likely doom the panzers.

Just four American infantry divisions were posted across the sprawl of the Ardennes, with a single armored division in reserve. Three of the divisions were newly arrived in Europe and had been assigned to what was considered a quiet sector to gain needed experience and training. The others were deeply fatigued and understrength after punishing autumn battles. Throughout the Ardennes, the American defenses were anemic, but there was little internal concern, as no one believed the Germans could muster the strength for a meaningful offensive.

THE BATTLE BEGINS

Just before dawn on December 16, 1944, American troops in the Ardennes, slumbering in foxholes, farmhouses, barns, and other makeshift quarters, were awakened by an earsplitting artillery barrage. It hammered the American front for ninety minutes, and when it ended, 200,000 German troops and hundreds of panzers flooded into southern Belgium, easily overpowering any shaken defenders who had not yet fled to the rear.

The Germans made impressive progress in those early hours. Shrouded in thick fog, the panzers brazenly advanced in the open, reveling in the absence of American fighter-bombers overhead amid poor weather conditions and overcast skies. Chaos spreading across the American front was matched by mass confusion in the rear, with the loss of communications — the bombardment had severed telephone lines — leaving command posts in the dark. A small number of English-speaking German commandos had also slipped behind the lines, masquerading as military policemen to stir further confusion and hysteria.

Though his headquarters remained uncertain about what was unfolding, Eisenhower made a pivotal early move, ordering two nearby armored divisions into the Ardennes. Two other reserve units, the veteran 82nd and 101st Airborne Divisions, were also mobilized, and though it would take time for their arrival in Belgium, each would play an outsized role in the fighting to come.

By the end of the first day, the penetration by Hitler's lead divisions had created a massive bulge in the front line, one that ultimately extended forty miles wide and sixty miles deep. The mood among German generals, however, was far from celebratory, as the Americans had not completely collapsed as expected, and a patchwork of secondary defensive lines had already begun slowing much of the advance. Most disconcerting was the delay in the north, where the Sixth SS Panzer Army, Hitler's most powerful force, was leading the main thrust to Antwerp. The panzers met surprising resistance along the northern shoulder of the bulge, where they were blocked by elements of the 99th Infantry Division positioned on the Elsenborn Ridge. The heights controlled key routes leading to the Meuse, and the untested American infantrymen—later nicknamed the "Battle Babies"—were thought to be little match for the German armor. The men of the 99th proved otherwise, mounting a far stiffer defense than expected.

Elsewhere, other panzer forces gained considerable ground, slicing through two US infantry divisions and capturing two entire regiments of the 106th Infantry Division, nearly 8,000 men. Troubles arose, however, outside the town of St. Vith, site of a key road junction, where American infantry and armor, hastily cobbled together, impeded a German thrust. It would take days for the panzers to muscle past.

To the south, another spearhead, the Fifth Panzer Army, closed in on a second crucial gateway to the Meuse—the town of Bastogne. It was a strategic prize, sitting astride a tangle of hardtop roads ideal for moving tanks and other armor westward. As multiple German divisions converged on the town, newly arrived American forces awaited on the perimeter, ordered to hold the crossroads at all costs. It became the most epic stand in the history of the United States Army.

BASTOGNE

Even as Allied headquarters was still sorting out German objectives in the early hours of the offensive, the value of Bastogne was no mystery. Officials scrambled to barricade the town with any available troops, and a brigade-size force of the 10th Armored Division was the first to arrive. It rolled into Bastogne on the evening of December 18, sending teams of tanks and infantry to surrounding villages to block roads and slow the German armor until the nearest reserves could be mustered.

The 101st Airborne Division, bivouacked in France, received the emergency call. Assembled in the dead of night, the division was abruptly loaded onto a fleet of trucks and rushed north with only the food and ammunition it could carry. The paratroopers were lightly armed and a poor match against German tanks, but most were battle-hardened veterans of Normandy and Market-Garden. Arriving on the evening of the 19th, they were deployed in an arc around Bastogne. Lacking winter clothing and overcoats, the paratroopers shivered in the below-freezing temperatures as they dug in across the rolling hillsides and wooded groves ringing the town. Having stalled the German advance, the 10th Armored teams pulled back into Bastogne, joining the improvised defenses as the Germans began their push to take the town.

With overcast skies still grounding any air support, the Americans withstood repeated assaults and a dizzying array of artillery and mortar barrages, day and night. They slept on frozen ground under thin blankets, awakened in the early morning hours by shells that crashed into the trees above and showered them with deadly splinters and broken tree limbs. The Germans eventually encircled the paratroopers and tankers, and on December 22, a note was delivered across the lines demanding surrender. The acting commander of the 101st, Brigadier General Anthony McAuliffe, scribbled a one-word response—"Nuts!"—that baffled his German counterparts. News of the defiant missive rippled across the American positions, lifting the spirits of the exhausted, half-frozen men, as did clearing skies that finally allowed parcels of food, medicine, ammunition, and other supplies to be parachuted in. The ragged garrison fought on, refusing to bend.

German struggles also continued in the north. The vanguard of the Sixth SS Panzer Army—a first-rate battle group from the 1st SS Panzer Division led by Lieutenant Colonel Joachim Peiper—had fought past the frontline American defenses, knifing toward the Meuse. They would not make it, unable to punch through the assorted armored, infantry, and airborne forces thrown in their path. Drained of fuel and far out front of the main force, Peiper and his men had no choice but to abandon their tanks and armored vehicles and escape on foot.

With the center the only remaining option for reaching the Meuse, the Germans made one last desperate attempt to take Bastogne. The beleaguered paratroopers and tankers absorbed terrible punishment but refused to buckle, and a glimmer of hope soon emerged. Days earlier, Eisenhower had ordered Patton to break off his attacks in France and rush part of his Third Army north to Belgium. Patton, in turn, executed one of the great logistical feats of the war, reorienting several divisions, packing the troops onto tanks and trucks, and herding them over 100 miles to the Ardennes—all in mere days. The day after Christmas, lead tanks of his 4th Armored Division blasted through the German perimeter surrounding Bastogne, linking up with the outer ring of paratroopers. More of Patton's forces followed, and the siege was soon broken.

By early January, the Americans had poured hundreds of thousands of additional troops into the Ardennes. The threat of a German breakthrough had ended, but the two sides continued to brawl in the heavy snow, with steep losses among both. Many of the Germans had experienced extreme elements in Russia, but the Americans were new to winter warfare, and frostbite and trench foot became as crippling as German bullets and shrapnel. Still, the attrition was far more taxing on the Germans, who had no men or materiel to spare. Lacking fuel and reinforcements, and unable to hold the ground captured in December, what remained of Hitler's invasion force gradually withdrew to where it started from. By late January, the Battle of the Bulge was over.

Aftermath

The Ardennes offensive was a crushing defeat for Hitler. The loss of 100,000 men and innumerable tanks and other armored vehicles slashed his remaining forces in the West and consumed many of Germany's last strategic reserves. American losses were also alarmingly high—some 80,000 men had been killed, wounded, or captured—but unlike Hitler, Eisenhower still had resources to draw on, and his air forces continued to dominate the skies.

The failed operation also left massive Allied armies poised along the German border. Across the Westwall, the badly whipped Germans awaited the sea of Americans and British with dread, aware a concerted push into the German heartland was coming. In the East, a winter offensive by the Red Army had also notched significant gains, pushing German armies out of Poland and closer to their own borders. With both the Soviets and Americans readying their forces for one final push, the race to Berlin was on.

⋯ ⋯ ⋯ ⋯ ⋯

ⓘ On December 17, 1944, a Waffen-SS unit, acting under the orders of Lieutenant Colonel Joachim Peiper, massacred more than eighty American prisoners outside the town of Malmédy. Peiper's men carried out additional atrocities against American soldiers and Belgian civilians during their drive to the Meuse, and news of their butchery spread quickly across the American front, infuriating and galvanizing those facing the SS panzer forces. Peiper survived the war, and though he was later convicted by a war crimes tribunal, he claimed to be an ardent anti-communist—and thus a post-war ally of the West—and served just ten years in prison.

Lyle J. Bouck Jr.

Lieutenant Lyle J. Bouck Jr. of the 99th Infantry Division was one day short of his twenty-first birthday when the Ardennes offensive began. Commanding a reconnaissance platoon of just eighteen men, Bouck was ordered to hold valuable high ground along the Lanzerath Ridge. In the early hours of the German operation, Bouck's position was cut off from the rest of the division and charged by hundreds of German paratroopers attempting to clear a path for the lead panzer divisions in the north. Bouck's platoon held them off for most of that first day, but with their ammunition exhausted, Bouck and his surviving men were finally captured, and spent the rest of the war in German POW camps. So many Bronze Stars, Silver Stars, and Distinguished Service Crosses were awarded for their gallantry on the Lanzerath Ridge, the platoon became one of the most decorated units of the war.

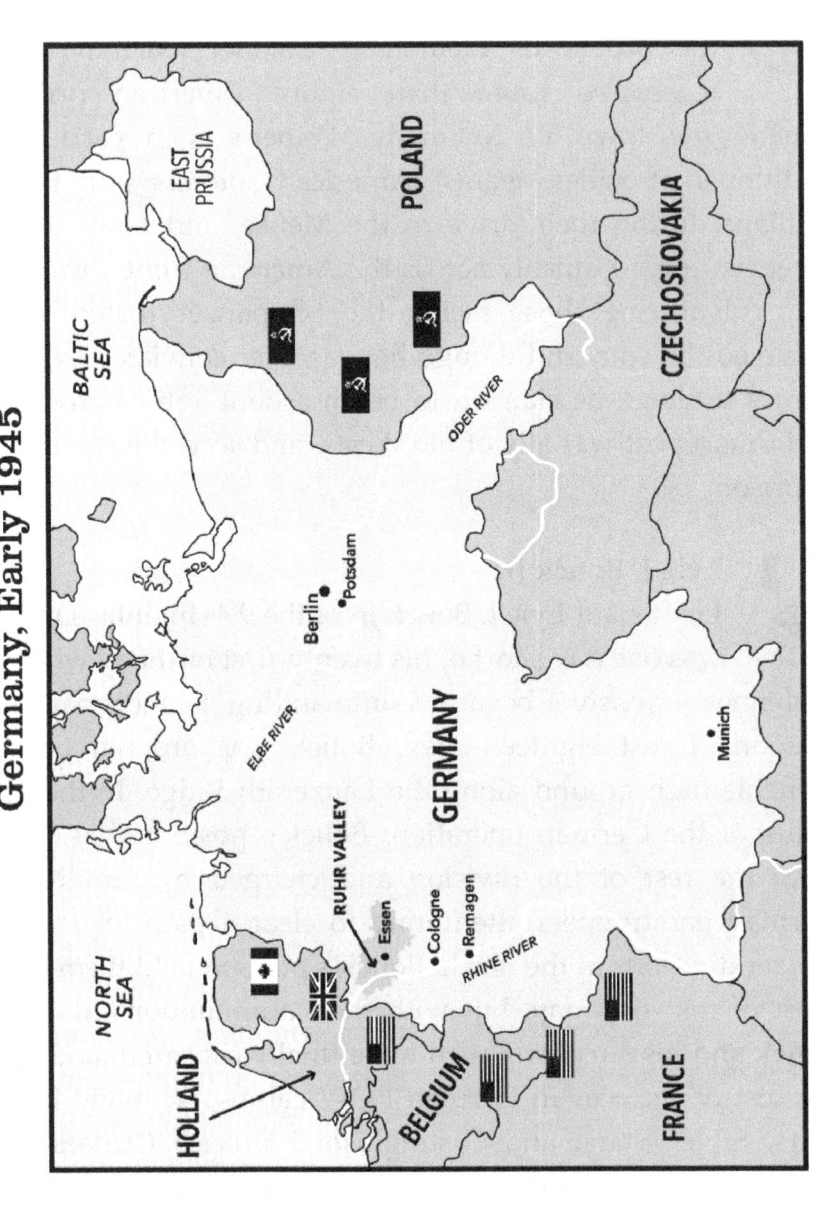

14
THE END OF THE THIRD REICH
FEBRUARY 1945–MAY 1945

"I expect every able-bodied German to fight with complete disregard for his personal safety; I expect the sick and the weak to work with their last strength; I expect all women and girls to continue supporting this struggle with utmost fanaticism."
–Adolf Hitler

"People of the strength and warlike tendencies of the Germans do not give in; they must be beaten to the ground."
–General Dwight D. Eisenhower

More than a year after their initial gathering in Tehran, the Big Three convened again, this time in Yalta, on the Crimean Peninsula. It was February 1945, and the Allied leaders were meeting to deliberate military strategies for the last phase of the war, as well as plans for occupying a vanquished Germany.

The stakes were high, as were tensions among the three men. The trust shared by Churchill and Roosevelt was lacking with their Soviet counterpart, the relations increasingly strained by mutual suspicion and competing visions for post-war Europe. Churchill was leery of Stalin and his maneuvering to absorb much of war-scarred Eastern and Central Europe into the Soviet sphere, while a more conciliatory Roosevelt hoped to persuade the Soviet premier to break his longstanding neutrality toward Japan and join America in ending the war in the Pacific.

The trio made some headway at Yalta, reaching tacit agreement to partition and share in the occupation of a defeated Germany, and to establish a post-war United Nations, with veto authority for the leading powers. The Soviets and Americans also reached a separate accord, with Stalin promising to move against the Japanese in exchange for territorial concessions in the Far East. More contentious matters, such as the future fate of Poland, were left unresolved, though Stalin assured the others the Poles would have self-determination.

As the leaders departed the Crimea, seemingly united, their armies prepared for the final marches into Germany. Awaiting them were the shattered vestiges of Hitler's forces, bracing for a torrent of foreign invaders and expecting retribution. For years, the Nazis had ruthlessly conducted a systematic campaign of mass murder and persecution among those they conquered, fueled by Hitler's fervent pursuit of racial supremacy and a thousand-year Reich. The blood of millions of innocents was on German hands, and a final reckoning was coming due.

• • • • •

On the heels of Hitler's failed Ardennes operation and the continued withdrawal of German forces from Western Europe, a multitude of American, British, and Canadian armies fought their way into the Rhineland, battling past the German border defenses. Poised for a broader push into the heart of Germany, a daunting obstacle loomed in their path—the mighty Rhine.

The meandering river flowed from the Swiss Alps to the North Sea, slicing neatly across western Germany, and its current, depth, and width—it averaged a quarter mile across—made it a formidable barrier. German engineers had destroyed key crossings, stalling the Allied advance, but in early March, lead elements of the US 9th Armored Division approaching the riverside town of Remagen discovered a railway bridge still intact. As the Americans dashed ahead to capture it, German demolitions exploded but failed to bring down the great structure. After easily overwhelming the few defenders, the 9th Armored men secured a foothold on the far bank, opening the first Allied bridgehead across the Rhine. Nearby divisions were hastily summoned, and thousands of soldiers and supporting vehicles began crossing in force.

Hitler was incensed. He ordered every officer responsible for the failure at Remagen to be executed and demanded the bridge be destroyed by all possible means. Artillery barrages, Luftwaffe bombs, and V-2 rockets all rained down on the structure, but to little avail. For ten days, American troops and tanks streamed across, until the bridge unexpectedly collapsed, killing more than two dozen soldiers. Five full divisions had reached the eastern bank, though, and would soon be joined by the balance of Eisenhower's forces after combat engineers managed to span other segments of the river.

By late March, the Allies were pressing into northwest Germany and the heavily industrialized Ruhr Valley, a hub of German coal mining and steel production. Months of bombing raids had flattened cities such as Cologne and Essen, but prized factories, mines, and steelworks throughout the region were still delivering armaments to German forces otherwise nearing defeat. Leading the defense of the Ruhr was one of Hitler's most capable subordinates, Field Marshal Walter Model, but his army could not match the mobility of the Americans and was swiftly encircled, trapping nineteen of Model's divisions in a large pocket. The besieged men were battered with daily artillery and aerial bombardments, leading to the surrender of more than 317,000 Germans by mid-April, including two dozen generals. It was the US Army's single greatest triumph of the war.

As the Ruhr pocket was crumbling, other Allied armies steamrolled east. They liberated POW and concentration camps hastily abandoned by guards and freed many of the eight million foreign workers laboring against their will in Reich factories and mines. To the surprise of his subordinates, though, Eisenhower halted the drive at the Elbe River, only a short distance from Berlin. Despite the swift progress, Eisenhower was wary of charging into the heavily defended city and risking so many lives in the waning days of the war. Nor was he willing to sacrifice his men for territory that would ultimately fall under Soviet control. Instead, he left the German capital to Stalin and his field marshals, who were already preparing their own invasion from the east, eager to repay the Germans for the untold atrocities and destruction wrought on Soviet soil.

THE BATTLE OF BERLIN
In 1941, Hitler's invasion force of some three million men drove deep into Soviet territory, marching toward Moscow, Leningrad, and Kiev with an aura of invincibility. But defeats from Stalingrad to Kursk had staggered once-swaggering Wehrmacht and SS armies, and for two years, the Germans had fallen back across the East, chased by a vengeful Red Army. As the Soviets ousted the Germans from long-occupied territories, they discovered evidence of the horrifying breadth of Nazi evils, including countless mass graves, charred ruins of homes and entire villages, and vast networks of concentration camps and killing centers.

By early 1945, the Soviets had swept across most of Poland, reaching the Oder River, less than fifty miles from Berlin, where they paused to gather strength for the final advance. The German defenders awaiting them — even those uninvolved with the atrocious crimes and cruelties in the East — were fatalistic about the looming battle, fully aware the Red Army had scores to settle. As for the civilian population, the German people had already endured much suffering, their cities and industrial centers bombed day and night, leaving hundreds of thousands already dead. But for those in the path of the Red Army, the worst was still to come.

In mid-April, some 2.5 million Soviets, backed by thousands of tanks, barreled into Germany. They were spurred on by Stalin, who happily took advantage of Eisenhower's pause. Stalin was both surprised and impressed by the speed of the Anglo-American advance since crossing the Rhine a month earlier, but unable to stomach the possibility of his allies raising their flags first over the German capital. The Americans and British had certainly borne their share of casualties, but the war had taken millions of Soviet lives. Berlin was his prize.

The eastern approaches were well-defended, and though the Germans fought with desperation, slowing the invasion army, they could not stop the Soviet onslaught. As mobs of Red Army soldiers spilled into local communities, millions of Germans panicked, conditioned by years of Nazi propaganda painting the Soviets as bloodthirsty barbarians. They fled west, clogging roads in hopes of reaching the protection of the Americans and British. Those unable to escape the Soviet rampage were swept up in a campaign of unmitigated terror, as marauding soldiers pillaged and looted towns, villages, homes, and farms. Tens of thousands of civilians were murdered, and many more brutalized in a frenzy of physical and sexual violence that left women and girls of all ages assaulted and raped, often repeatedly. No one was spared.

As Stalin's armies battled to the outskirts of Berlin, every German, young and old, was exhorted to give his or her life for the defense of the Reich. SS squads roamed the city and surrounding countryside, enforcing the decrees and executing deserters, while Hitler remained in the city, barricaded in a subterranean air raid shelter and bunker complex near the Reich Chancellery. Heavily medicated since the July bombing attempt on his life, delusion and paranoia consumed Hitler as he raged about the failures of his generals, the Luftwaffe, and even the

German people. Claiming Berlin would be saved by new "miracle weapons" and phantom armies rushing to the rescue, those who thought otherwise and counseled strategic withdrawals or negotiated settlements were berated and dismissed for defeatism, reducing Hitler's inner circle to his most devoted worshippers.

When the Soviets entered Berlin, a Volkssturm (citizen army) of old men and young boys, most without uniforms or training, met them in the streets, alongside a mix of fanatical SS men, regular Wehrmacht troops, and thousands of teenaged Hitler Youth. It was not enough, and by April 30, the defenders had exhausted the last of their ammunition. The Soviets charged into the city center, seizing control of the famous Reichstag building as Hitler, a short distance away in his bunker, put a handgun to his head and ended his life with a single gunshot. To prevent his corpse from falling into Soviet hands, it was taken outside to a courtyard, doused with gasoline, and set afire. Sporadic fighting in the city continued as German officials attempted to negotiate terms, but the Soviets refused any concessions. On May 2, all resistance ended.

An estimated 120,000 German soldiers and civilians were killed in the fight for Berlin. The Soviets lost three times that number. In the days to come, German armies, across what was left of the Third Reich, laid down their arms, and on May 8, one day after German leaders surrendered unconditionally, the last battlefields fell silent. Nearly six years after it began, the war in Europe was finally over.

Aftermath

Following the German surrender, Allied leaders assembled in Potsdam, a suburb of Berlin, to finalize plans for defeating the Japanese and revisit earlier discussions in Yalta concerning postwar Europe. New principals were in attendance, including President Harry S. Truman, having succeeded the deceased Roosevelt three months earlier, and Clement Attlee, the new

British prime minister. Winston Churchill was at Potsdam when deliberations began but gave way to Attlee days later after his political party fell out of power in London. Stalin remained the lone constant.

Japan was the first order of business. Despite the severity of losses across the Pacific and Far East, the country refused to acquiesce, prompting an emphatic demand from the Allies for Tokyo's unconditional surrender. Though Stalin would later honor his past pledge to join the Americans, British, and Chinese in that theater, he continued fencing with his Western counterparts over matters relating to Europe. The parties found some common ground — reaffirming their intent to prosecute war criminals and agreeing to demilitarize Germany and Japan and shut down their military industries — but broke sharply over matters of governance and elections. Poland remained at the center of their division. Britain had declared war six years earlier to defend Polish freedom, but Stalin objected to the notion of independence, citing a legacy of Russian suffering at the hands of Western armies tramping through Polish lands. Abandoning his prior assurances of free elections, Stalin plotted instead for Poland to anchor a bulwark of Soviet satellites and buffer states.

There was little the United States and Britain could do to prevent it. Soviet armies still stretched across Eastern and Central Europe, and their presence lent considerable weight to communist factions muscling their way into power in Poland, Czechoslovakia, Hungary, Romania, Bulgaria, and Albania. Facing an expected reduction of US forces in Europe — they were needed for an invasion of Japan — and little enthusiasm at home for risking renewed conflict in Europe, the Americans and British contented themselves instead with staking their territorial claims in Germany and pledging to contain Soviet influence. Berlin was partitioned, with the Soviets, Americans, British, and French each assigned occupation zones, and the country itself broken into what would eventually become West and East Germany. The contours of a new "Cold War" between the Soviets and their Western rivals gradually came into focus.

Long before the wartime alliance unraveled, there was still unfinished business half a world away. Japan had endured a series of stinging defeats in 1944 and 1945 and bombing raids had ravaged cities and infrastructure across the home islands, but hard-liners in Tokyo refused to concede. War-weary American forces began training for a long-anticipated invasion of Japan, where millions of soldiers and civilians remained devoted to their emperor and vowed a fight to the death. What was shaping into the grandest and most perilous operation in American military history would have been inconceivable just a few short years earlier, when Allied forces had been routed in a string of early clashes across the Pacific, beginning with a jarring and devastating strike on American soil.

· · · · ·

Absent from the führerbunker in Hitler's final days were his two most ardent and longest-serving accomplices. With the Third Reich on the cusp of defeat, Heinrich Himmler, the diabolical SS chief, had taken command of a field army outside Berlin, where he sought to broker a secret peace agreement with the Allies. The move enraged Hitler, who ordered Himmler taken into custody, but the SS man managed to elude his hunters in the final days of the war. Hermann Göring, head of the Luftwaffe and Hitler's onetime designated successor, also fell into disfavor when he attempted to take charge of the Nazi state from southern Germany. A seething Hitler viewed the act as a betrayal and ordered Göring apprehended as well. Though Göring and Himmler survived the war, each was later arrested by Allied authorities and shared a similar fate, taking their own lives before they could be brought before executioners.

Espionage

During the Potsdam Conference, President Truman quietly informed Stalin that the United States had successfully tested a powerful new weapon that could end the war. It was no surprise to Stalin, who was already aware of American-Anglo breakthroughs with atomic energy, as top scientists at the highest security laboratory in America had divulged some of the most closely guarded secrets of the war to Soviet spies. The betrayals came primarily from two men: British physicist Klaus Fuchs, who before the war had fled Nazi Germany for England, and Theodore Hall, an American physicist recruited to the atomic energy enterprise after graduating from Harvard at age eighteen. Both men were communist sympathizers, intent on aiding the Soviets to prevent the United States from gaining a monopoly on the fledgling technology. They succeeded, as the acquired secrets greatly accelerated the Soviet nuclear weapons program, with lasting implications for an escalating nuclear arms race that threatened to annihilate much of the globe.

THE WAR AT HOME

INTRODUCTION
ECONOMIC RESURGENCE AND THE
STRUGGLE FOR EQUALITY

For much of its early existence, the United States was mostly dismissed by the Old World as an unsophisticated newcomer, still testing the resiliency of high-minded democratic ideals against the fragility of a fledgling republic. By the end of the nineteenth century, America had weathered civil war, bridged a continental divide, and expanded its global commerce and trade. It was a nation that was no longer to be taken lightly, eager to assert itself on the world stage. It finally did so in 1898, waging war against Spain to end European imperialism in the Western Hemisphere. A decisive outcome gave America new territorial possessions from Puerto Rico to the Philippines, stretching its reach well beyond its own shores and birthing its own form of imperialism.

The rise continued in the early twentieth century, fueled by a rapidly evolving economy. Decades of immigration—the foreign-born population more than doubled from 1880 to 1930—created an abundance of low-wage labor at the same time American industry was developing new methods of accelerating production. The wealth of natural resources within America's borders was reflected in the growth of the steel industry, where the mining of vast iron ore deposits in the Midwest boosted annual steel production from just over one million tons in 1880 to sixty-three million tons a half century later. With enterprising industrialists and financiers pouring in investment dollars, the profuse mix of labor, innovation, raw materials, and financial resources transformed the country into a manufacturing powerhouse.

Much of the world first glimpsed this industrial heft in 1907, when President Theodore Roosevelt ordered a "Great White Fleet" of sixteen steam-powered battleships, their steel hulls painted white, to circumnavigate the globe. Six years later, the Ford Motor Company unveiled the first assembly line, producing Model T automobiles in less than ninety minutes. On the heels of this new age of mass production came the First World War, and though it began with the United States on the sidelines, the British and French became dependent early on American-made munitions shipped overseas to their armies.

America's unbridled economic growth continued after the war and into the 1920s. With the nation's wealth soaring and wages and consumer spending reaching historic levels, stock values skyrocketed, leading speculators to borrow heavily and gamble on high-yield investments. It was a high-wire act, dangerously susceptible to the unpredictable whims and volatility of a free market system, and in October 1929, it all came crashing down. A slide in stock prices led to panic on Wall Street, where jittery investors sold off sixteen million shares. The chaotic "Black Tuesday" sell-off triggered a sharp downward spiral, as investment and consumer spending plunged, commerce slowed to a trickle, and trade markets evaporated. As the banking system collapsed and factories and businesses folded everywhere, the worst economic crisis in American history took hold. It became known as the Great Depression.

Conditions worsened with time. Three years after the stock market crash, the economy was still in a dismal state, with one-quarter of all working adults jobless. Those employed earned barely half of what they made prior to the crash. Social safety net programs, such as welfare and food stamps, did not yet exist, nor was there any hint of rescue from a federal government ill-equipped to ease the suffering. President Herbert Hoover was mostly a bystander, and the corrective measures he pursued fell well short of aiding those in need. With millions out of work, thousands of banks failing, and savings fast vanishing, public faith in the Hoover Administration disintegrated.

In the fall of 1932, the American people voted for change, sweeping into office 51-year-old Franklin Delano Roosevelt. The cheerful, optimistic governor of New York coasted to victory after prevailing in forty-two of the forty-eight states. He inherited a severely ailing and despairing country, with nearly thirteen million Americans out of work and the economy still locked in a tailspin. Homes, businesses, and farms had been lost by the hundreds of thousands, and soup kitchens and bread lines remained fixtures across the country. Those joining the queues were desperate for work, scraps of food, and perhaps most of all, hope.

After campaigning on the promise of a more forceful government response to pull the country out of its economic malaise, Roosevelt began his presidency with a burst of policymaking energy. He put forward a collection of bold, sweeping initiatives to speed up a national recovery, delivering on his election year promise of a "New Deal" for the American people to help weather the economic hardship.

Over the next few years, a slew of new federal public works programs began putting the nation back to work while investing in growth and modernization. Millions of jobs were created, and ground was broken on new schools, roadways, airports, bridges, hospitals, and state parks. The Tennessee Valley Authority built dams and hydroelectric power plants from Virginia to Mississippi, increasing employment in deeply impoverished areas while delivering the first electricity to much of rural America. The Agricultural Adjustment Administration and Farm Credit Administration revitalized rural communities by stabilizing farm prices and offering subsidies to struggling farmers. Additional programs to aid underserved populations came later, including the landmark Social Security Act, which provided pensions to the elderly and help to dependent children and people with disabilities.

By 1937, the number of jobless Americans had fallen to under eight million, and foreclosures on homes and farms had steadily waned. A reduction in federal spending and a recession late that year led to some backsliding and more job losses, but many of Roosevelt's initiatives were successful in stanching the worst bleeding.

Throughout the 1930s, as the nation struggled to overcome its fiscal crisis, an increasingly pluralistic American society remained divided by social inequities. A country that trumpeted the nobility of freedom and liberty overseas continued to deny fundamental rights and privileges to nearly thirteen million African Americans – then one-tenth of the US population. Women, too, were treated as lesser citizens. Roosevelt's appointment of Frances Perkins as secretary of labor – the first female presidential cabinet official – was a milestone achievement, and other women filled high-level roles in several New Deal agencies and programs. Nationwide, however, employment opportunities and wages for women continued to lag far behind those of men.

With the United States awash in economic troubles and social division, conflicts began developing abroad among newly militarized belligerents. Most Americans were content watching from afar, their isolationist sentiments rooted in the experience of World War I, when political and ethnic disputes among smaller countries ensnared the world's great powers into four years of battlefield horrors. The result was millions of deaths, including 53,000 Americans.

Still in the throes of the Great Depression, the American public remained adamantly opposed to overseas intervention. Even after the Japanese brazenly bombed a US gunboat in China in 1937, killing two Americans and wounding four dozen others, the public favored a withdrawal from China rather than any sort of retaliation. Throughout those years, as Italian forces expanded their holdings in Africa, Japan invaded mainland China, and a pugnacious German leader began menacing his neighbors, the United States willingly added its voice to the diplomatic choir of critics but refused to involve itself any further. Britain's prime minister bemoaned the tepid response from Washington. "It is always best and safest to count on nothing from the Americans but words," he grumbled, shortly after the gunboat incident.

As a practical matter, there was little choice. A decade of austerity had taken a toll on the American military, and federal spending for Roosevelt's New Deal initiatives had forced drastic reductions in other programs deemed non-essential. With the country at peace and lacking serious threats to its shores, the defense budget was slashed, cutting down the size of the Army and Navy, and sharply reducing available funding for new equipment and weapons. As the 1930s came to a close, much of the world was at war, and the United States had fallen substantially behind potential adversaries.

Thus began a period of profound change. After a decade of decline, the sleeping giant of American industry stirred to life. A great reservoir of labor awaited, with idle workers jobless from the Depression keen to rejoin assembly lines, mills, and mines long out of action. Shuttered factories and shipyards reopened and expanded their operations. The unemployed returned to work, bolstered by millions of African Americans and women entering the industrial workforce for the very first time. By 1944, a jobless rate that stood at fourteen percent four years earlier had fallen to barely one percent, lowering the curtain on the Great Depression. Racial and social inequality would persist for years to come, but the contributions and sacrifices made by millions of Americans of all ethnic and socioeconomic classes on the home front produced extraordinary wartime results, carrying the United States and its allies to final victory.

· · · · ·

ⓘ With passage of the Selective Training and Service Act in 1940, all men between the ages of twenty-one (later lowered to eighteen) and thirty-five were required to register for the first peacetime draft in American history. Though more than forty-five million men registered during the war, just ten million were actually inducted, as many were excluded for underlying medical and health conditions, family hardships, or because they were in essential occupations, such as farming or manufacturing. Others declared themselves conscientious objectors, a status granted to those morally opposed to war, or followers of religious teachings that proscribed the taking of other lives. These individuals were permitted the choice of serving as noncombatants (medics, orderlies, etc.) or in alternative public service roles outside of the military.

Millions of other men and women volunteered for military service. When the war ended, most draftees and enlistees returned to civilian life, and the draft was suspended. It was reinstituted in 1948 amid rising Cold War tensions, then discontinued again in 1973 with the end of the conflict in Vietnam. The US military remains today an entirely all-volunteer force.

15
ARSENAL OF DEMOCRACY: AMERICA'S INDUSTRIAL MIGHT

"What is America but beauty queens, millionaires, stupid records, and Hollywood?"
–Adolf Hitler, 1941

"Give us the tools, and we will finish the job."
–Winston Churchill, 1941

The end of 1940 capped off one of the bleakest years in European history. From April to June, an unstoppable force of German panzer armies overpowered much of Western and Northern Europe, leaving Britain and its Commonwealth allies alone to face the full brunt of Hitler's military power. By autumn, the Luftwaffe was bombing London nightly and reducing parts of the great city to rubble, as the remnants of a sapped and demoralized British Army readied for an invasion.

On a late December evening that year, President Roosevelt leaned into a microphone at the White House to deliver another of his familiar fireside chats. In an era without television, the nationwide radio broadcasts were an effective means for Roosevelt to connect with American families and comfort them through troubles at home and abroad. His tone that evening, however, was more somber as he recounted Britain's predicament across the Atlantic, and the struggles of an imperiled China to withstand a Japanese onslaught. Roosevelt was no alarmist and had previously assured the country it would not become entangled in overseas conflicts, but he was also a realist and could plainly see diplomacy was failing to contain the maniacal aspirations of those in Berlin and Tokyo.

Roosevelt faced another reality; in 1940, the long-neglected US military was no match for the Axis powers. His December fireside chat thus became a clarion call, imploring Americans to prepare for a war that could very well reach their own shores. "[I]t is the purpose of the nation," Roosevelt told his radio listeners, "to build now with all possible speed every machine, every arsenal, every factory that we need to manufacture our defense material. We have the men, the skill, the wealth, and above all, the will...We must be the great arsenal of democracy."

So began the most ambitious domestic endeavor in American history. By tapping the country's industrial potential, Roosevelt intended to arm those battling forces of oppression, remake America's own aged and withered military, and usher in an era of sweeping domestic change. It would reshape and rescale American industry and labor for years to come.

From corporate board rooms to factory floors, the industrial base shifted into high gear. Production of consumer goods trickled to a halt as blueprints, resources, and tools for building instruments of war poured into factories and plants across the country. Steelworkers, coal miners, industrial and electrical engineers, welders, chemists, textile workers, and those in countless other trades and occupations became every bit as essential as the men in uniform.

Even before Roosevelt challenged the nation, the production of war goods had been quietly on the rise. New vessels for the Navy were on order, as were the new aircraft Roosevelt appealed for earlier in the year. Many had scoffed when Roosevelt first floated the idea of 50,000 new bombers and fighter planes, as the Army Air Corps (soon to be renamed the

Army Air Forces) had barely 1,200 planes in its entire existing inventory.

The uptick in production demands was compounded by passage of the Lend-Lease Act in early 1941, opening the floodgates of military aid for Britain and others, and the War Department's own needs. With 2.2 million American men expected to be in uniform by the end of 1941 — up from 458,000 in 1940 — rifles and machine guns, uniforms, bayonets, combat boots, and steel helmets were all needed. As were munitions, heavy and light artillery pieces, communications gear, medical supplies, and so many other weapons and goods.

By early 1942, with the United States fully at war, virtually every American felt the impact of the nation mobilizing. Limits were imposed on consumer purchases of commodities needed for the war effort, including gasoline, rubber, and metals. Food products, such as meat and coffee, were also rationed, as was sugar, a key ingredient not only in candy and chewing gum issued to soldiers, but gun powder and dynamite as well. Families planted "Victory Gardens" in backyards and public parks to supplement the ration coupons they were issued; neighborhoods organized scrap metal drives for recycling; and millions of Americans joined an expanding labor force assembling everything from battleships to cartridge belts.

The Factories

With mills, mines, and refineries beginning to deliver record volumes of raw materials, the country was ready to build. Detroit, Michigan — home of the automobile sector — became the epicenter, its world-class assembly plants best suited to produce the heavy weapons and machinery War Department officials were clamoring for.

The automakers mostly converted existing operations, but the Ford Motor Company took an additional step, opening a mammoth new production facility known as Willow Run. The plant specialized in four-engine bombers for the Army, and with a mile-long assembly line, employed some 42,000 workers at its peak, one-third of them women. By the beginning of 1944, a workforce that had never assembled an airplane was finishing over 500 B-24 *Liberators* every month, rolling out a new bomber every sixty-three minutes.

Ford's River Rouge facility was another assembly wonder, delivering more than 277,000 Jeeps and tens of thousands of trucks, armored vehicles, and airplane engines. Dodge added 23,000 ambulances and 403,000 trucks, and General Motors plants, formerly turning out Cadillacs, Buicks, Chevrolets, and Oldsmobiles, restructured their assembly lines to build tanks, armor plating, munitions, and heavy weapons instead. By mid-war, growing Allied advantages in air power, transport, and mobility were largely attributable to the Motor City titans.

They were hardly alone. Nationwide, hundreds of manufacturers of all sizes reinvented their operations to fabricate everything from amphibious landing craft to artillery shells and canteens. Workers at the Underwood Typewriter Company in New York City became expert assemblers of M-1 carbines. A Frigidaire refrigerator plant converted its production to .50-caliber machine guns, while Kellogg's contributed tens of millions of "K-rations" — individual boxes of non-perishable combat rations. The Lionel toy company even suspended model train production to make military compasses for the Army and Navy.

Most impressive, though, was the volume of new planes and tanks. In late 1941, the number of operational B-17 *Flying Fortresses*, one of the country's most advanced warplanes, numbered in the dozens. By 1945, Boeing plants had turned out 13,000 of them. A country that began the war with a paltry sum of warplanes managed to build more than 325,000 of them by the end. As for tanks, the Army's entire, antiquated inventory numbered less than 500 in 1940. Five years later, more than

50,000 M4 Shermans, one of the premier tanks of the war, had been delivered to Allied armies.

With domestic production in overdrive, even the most optimistic goals were met, delivering firepower to America's fighting forces and turning the tide wherever Allied and Axis forces clashed, from jungle-strewn islands to the skies over Berlin. At the same time, a parallel and equally inspiring manufacturing push was also underway, this one along America's shores.

The Shipbuilders

Well before the United States entered the war, doubts swirled through the Navy Department as to how the existing undersized and understrength fleet would fare in showdowns against a Japanese naval service considered among the world's best, and German U-boats terrorizing Allied shipping in the North Atlantic. The age of the American fleet was equally concerning; most vessels in service traced their lineage to the post-World War I years.

As war tensions continued to escalate, a shipbuilding industry that barely scraped by during the Great Depression began experiencing a rebirth. In mid-1940, Congress passed two bills—the Naval Expansion Act and the Two-Ocean Navy Act—that were like jolts of electricity to American shipyards, authorizing twenty-one new aircraft carriers and more than 200 battleships, cruisers, and destroyers. Such construction would take time, though, and few of the ships were expected to be completed before 1943. A new merchant fleet was another priority, as the British were pleading for new freighters to replace those lost to German submarines. Passage of the new Lend-Lease Act also brought a sharp increase in exported goods, all requiring transport.

In response, new shipyards began springing up along America's coastlines and waterways. Prior to passage of the naval expansion bills, just a handful were in operation, but less than a year later, there were sixty-eight. By the end of the war, eighty-four shipbuilding facilities dotted the East, West, and Gulf Coasts.

Aircraft carriers were the most immediate need. With naval air power relatively new and untested in the 1930s, the US was limited to a handful of aircraft carriers when the war began. Half of those were lost in the first ten months, and by late 1942, only the *Enterprise* and *Saratoga* remained in the Pacific. That changed with the arrival of new *Essex*-class carriers in mid-1943. Built with thicker armor and ringed with anti-aircraft guns, the speedy new "fleet" carriers were far superior to their Japanese counterparts. Fourteen of them sailed in the war, carrying newer *Hellcat* fighters, SB2C *Helldiver* bombers, and TBF *Avenger* torpedo-bombers, all substantial upgrades from previous models. The lone drawback of the *Essex*-class carriers was a significant one—there were simply too few of them to support operations in the Pacific and protect merchant convoys in the Atlantic. The shortfall led to one of the most innovative manufacturing gems of the war—the "escort" aircraft carriers.

Often referred to as "baby flattops" or "jeep carriers," escort carriers were a smaller and slower version of the fleet carriers, carrying little armored protection, few anti-aircraft guns, and just a third of the aircraft of their larger siblings. What the escort carriers lacked in size and strength, they made up for in quantity. Owing to a production process that lasted just months, 115 of these ships were produced during the war, including forty-nine by a single shipyard in Vancouver, Washington. They were indispensable in both the Atlantic and Pacific, escorting troop and supply convoys, providing air support to invasion forces, and ferrying Army and Marine Corps aircraft to forward bases.

Aside from the aircraft carriers and other new warships, another shipbuilding marvel came in response to the high demand for cargo ships. With American forces operating in multiple combat theaters, a great many freighters were needed to transport not only millions of soldiers and Marines across vast oceans, but tanks, trucks, jeeps, munitions, food, artillery, medical supplies, spare parts, and other goods and equipment. To expedite production, naval architects designed a large-capacity ship with prefabricated components that could be mass-assembled at shipyards. These "Liberty ships"—joined later by "Victory ships" of similar design but with greater speed—were each large enough to hold the equivalent of 440 tanks or 230 million rounds of rifle ammunition. By the end of the war, more than 3,200 Liberty and Victory ships were shuttling men, equipment, and supplies across the two oceans, literally carrying the fight to the enemy.

The proliferation of shipyards, evolution of mass assembly methods, and addition of millions of new workers revolutionized the domestic shipbuilding industry. Construction phases that once stretched into years were reduced to months or even weeks. The Portsmouth Naval Shipyard in Maine built seventy-nine submarines for the war, shrinking completion time from sixteen months to six. The Bath Iron Works along the Kennebec River in Maine launched sixty-seven destroyers in a three-year period, averaging a new ship every seventeen days. The Kaiser Shipyards in the Pacific Northwest completed Liberty ships in as little as six weeks, producing three finished ships every day.

It was a pace the Axis powers could not come close to matching. By 1943, Japanese shipyards were languishing from severe shortages of raw materials and cutting back new production; in the Atlantic, the Germans sharply curtailed U-boat operations after losses of submarines far exceeded the ability to replace them. The US Navy had become the dominate force in both oceans.

ECONOMIC AND SOCIAL IMPACT

In 1940, the United States was still struggling to reverse a decade-long economic decline, its unemployment rate drifting toward fifteen percent. The impending infusion of billions of dollars into wartime manufacturing would have a seismic effect, resuscitating the industrial base and sparking explosive employment growth. American manufacturing roared back to life, and the jobless rate tumbled as most factories and plants began operating around the clock, adding second and third shifts of workers.

Two years into the war, less than two percent of Americans remained unemployed, and with those new jobs came demands for new skills. Millions signed up to work in industrial plants, with the Fore River Shipyard in Quincy, Massachusetts a microcosm, its workforce of 800 laborers in 1931 ballooning to more than 17,000 a decade later. From coast to coast, job sites filled with new workers, many of whom had been farmers, housewives, clerical workers, salesmen, or working in other occupations. These workers often lacked a single day of industrial experience, but eagerly learned new trades, from riveting aluminum airframes to wiring electronic circuits.

Equally impressive as the stunning breadth and volume of what America produced was who produced it. With such steep demand for labor, and so many existing workers absorbed into the military, application offices flooded with those who had long been excluded from such workplaces. Among them, women and

African Americans were largely greeted with hostility from supervisors and co-workers who had little faith in their abilities and took exception to their presence. They were given lesser wages and rarely promoted into management roles, no matter how deserved. Wartime labor shortages compelled greater diversity in the workforce, and much of the wartime manufacturing boom is attributable to the contributions of women and African Americans, but the ongoing animus and inequities reflected the country's continued lack of social progress well into the twentieth century.

A Record-Setting Legacy

Though it would take more than a year for the home front to become fully industrialized, the results exceeded all expectations. US shipyards created the most powerful naval force ever put to sea, launching more than 1,100 aircraft carriers, battleships, cruisers, destroyers, and submarines. American factories and arsenals produced 6.5 million rifles, 2.6 million machine guns, and 257,000 pieces of field artillery — all just the tip of the manufacturing iceberg.

Americans not only contributed their labor to the war effort; they also contributed their earnings. The government spent close to $300 billion in those years - more than $4 trillion in present-day dollars. Part of it was financed through the Victory Tax — a large progressive tax increase that included a tax rate of ninety-four percent on those with incomes above $200,000 — but additional funds were raised from the sale of war bonds. Eighty-five million Americans invested in these bonds, providing short-term capital to the government for a promised return of modest value in future years. Promoted by decorated war heroes and the country's most recognized film stars and sports icons, bond sales raised $185 billion.

It is yet another example of how so many Americans, beyond the sixteen million men in uniform, sacrificed for the war effort. From assembly line workers and neighborhood children collecting tin cans, to farmers and Victory Garden growers, the eventual triumph over the Axis powers did not simply belong to those who shouldered rifles or climbed into cockpits and tank turrets. It also belonged to those who wielded riveting guns and welding torches, filling the factories, shipyards, mills, and mines, day and night. Their collective wartime output was extraordinary, and elemental to the Allied triumph.

• • • • •

Proximity Fuses

One of the most pivotal innovations of the war was the proximity fuse. Artillery and anti-aircraft shells at the time exploded either on contact or with timed fuses, detonating when they reached a pre-programmed altitude. Such conventional shells required gun crews to land a direct hit on a fast-moving object, or to fill the skies with exploding shells, hoping that one matched the precise range, altitude, and speed of an approaching target.

Proximity fuses were first tested in combat in early 1943, and once mass production began, they revolutionized heavy gunnery. The fuse, front-loaded into each shell, included a tiny mechanism that transmitted radio signals. When the shell neared a target, the radio signal would bounce back to a miniature receiver inside the shell, triggering a detonation. The shells would thus explode only when they were in close enough proximity to damage or destroy a target. Not only did this vastly improve anti-aircraft fire against enemy planes, but it also made ground-based artillery far more deadly to enemy infantry in foxholes and trenches, who were exposed to air bursts and showers of shrapnel from shells exploding above.

The new munitions were used to defend London against V-1 rocket attacks, repel German assault troops in the late-war Battle of the Bulge, and, in perhaps their most essential role, down kamikazes (Japanese suicide pilots) in the Pacific before they could crash their bomb-laden planes into American ships. Attempts by the Axis powers to develop similar technology never gained traction; the Germans in particular invested considerable resources to upgrade their fuses and munitions, but never matched the Allied breakthroughs.

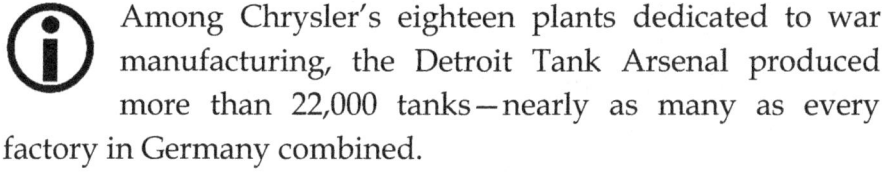 Among Chrysler's eighteen plants dedicated to war manufacturing, the Detroit Tank Arsenal produced more than 22,000 tanks—nearly as many as every factory in Germany combined.

16
WOMEN ON THE LINE

"Do the job HE left behind."
–World War II-era employment poster

"Women who stepped up were measured as citizens of the nation, not as women...this was a people's war, and everyone was in it."
–Colonel Oveta Culp Hobby
First commander of the Women's Army Auxiliary Corps

In extending voting rights to American women, the 1920 ratification of the Nineteenth Amendment to the United States Constitution marked a significant milestone in the historic struggle for political equality. Other barriers remained in place, particularly in employment, where sociocultural norms kept women in occupations deemed "appropriate" for their gender, such as nursing, teaching, and secretarial work. By 1940, some women had proven themselves against social prejudices and joined more prestigious fields, including medicine, the law, finance, and the sciences, but their numbers were few, and age-old paternalism persisted that women were better suited as homemakers and housewives.

At the dawn of World War II, much of the manufacturing base—the heart of industrial America—remained devoid of women, and other than nursing branches, the military services were similarly off-limits. The onset of war uprooted both practices. Though many clung to the view that assembly lines and army barracks were no places for women, the urgency to radically expand both the armed forces and domestic manufacturing left military and industrial leaders with little choice but to draw women more fully into each.

What followed was a fundamental transformation of America's social fabric, as women were absorbed into organizations and institutions that had long excluded them. They reversed perceptions about their abilities and potential, while blazing trails across manufacturing, aviation, and other previously forbidden trades. The progress was extraordinary, but short-lived, as the war economy eventually ramped down and former servicemen returned to the labor force, pushing out many of those who had backfilled their roles. It was a discouraging setback in the march toward equality, but it would not diminish all that had been achieved, or the remarkable legacy of wartime service and sacrifice by millions of women.

• • • • •

In Uniform

In the early 1900s, both the United States Army and Navy established small, all-women nursing auxiliaries to support their medical branches. By 1940, with Europe and the Far East already at war, the Army Nurse Corps began matching the sharp growth in the all-male Army, boosting its strength from 672 nurses in 1939 to more than 7,000 by December 1941. The Navy Nurse Corps remained more modest in size, numbering just 800 nurses when the war began, but grew exponentially along with the Navy beginning in early 1942. Thousands of new nurses enlisted, with some assigned to stateside facilities and others forward deployed to combat theaters, serving in field hospitals or on hospital ships. By mid-1944, the two organizations had been formally incorporated into their respective services and the women commissioned as officers. In total, over 70,000 nurses—all volunteers—served in World War II.

Women had also been providing clerical and other administrative support to the military for years, but as civilian contract workers, they were ineligible for military pay, government living quarters, and other benefits reserved for those in uniform. In 1940, Representative Edith Nourse Rogers of Massachusetts drafted legislation to remedy this by establishing a branch of the Army exclusively for women. Military leaders initially bristled at the idea, but over time agreed to collaborate with Rogers on compromise legislation, leading to the formation of the Women's Army Auxiliary Corps (WAAC) in 1942. Though the new WAAC was a civilian organization, it provided women with pay and benefits and a far greater variance of opportunities to aid in defeating the Axis powers. Some 25,000 volunteers eagerly signed up.

The WAAC proved a success, and as greater numbers of women stepped into key support roles across the Army's expanding footprint, Army leaders emerged as the organization's most vocal champions. Interest among women waned, however, due to noticeable gaps with the pay and benefits of male soldiers and the sudden availability of more lucrative employment in civilian factories and shipyards. To address these shortcomings, lawmakers and military leaders agreed to convert the WAAC into a regular service branch of the Army, similar to what existed for engineers and military police. In July 1943, the WAAC morphed into the new Women's Army Corps (WAC), drawing over 150,000 women into its ranks by the end of the war.

Companion legislation opened the Navy and Marine Corps to women as well. More than 90,000 were inducted into the Navy's version of the WAC, known as the Women Accepted for Volunteer Emergency Service (WAVES), supporting hundreds of shore-based installations and offices across the United States.

Another 10,000 volunteered for the first US Coast Guard Women's Reserve, known as Semper Paratus, Always Ready (SPAR), and 18,000 joined the newly formed US Marine Corps Women's Reserve. They were all part of the 350,000 American women who served in uniform during the war.

Expanding Roles

Opening each service branch to women was merely a first step; still to be determined were the capacities male leaders would permit them to serve in. Some in the Army and Navy hierarchy sought to mirror civilian practices and limit women to traditional positions such as typists, clerks, and switchboard operators. Many women served ably in such roles, but the military had far broader needs than administrative support; in particular, filling critical positions vacated by male soldiers and sailors reassigned to combat duty. Many required technical and other unique skills and were once considered unthinkable for women to occupy. No longer. The women who pursued and embraced such opportunities, no matter the challenge, proved every bit equal—if not superior—to their male predecessors.

Nowhere were their abilities more visible than in aviation. With defense plants producing new warplanes by the thousands, pilots were needed to ferry bombers and fighter planes rolling off assembly lines to training airbases across the country. As most male pilots were serving overseas, the responsibility was handed to a pair of small, fledgling civilian organizations—the Women's Auxiliary Ferrying Squadron and the Women's Flying Training Detachment—later consolidated into a single organization known as the Women Airforce Service Pilots (WASP). Among the 25,000 women who applied for the WASP program, barely 1,000 made it through a rigorous selection and training process. They became qualified to fly virtually every aircraft in the Army Air Forces' inventory, from single-engine fighter planes to four-engine heavy bombers.

Ferrying more than half of the combat aircraft produced during the war, WASP fliers proved so skillful, many were entrusted with more consequential duties, including the training of male cadets, testing new aircraft, and shuttling military personnel and cargo.

By mid-1944, support was building within the War Department for folding the WASP into the Army Air Forces, but legislation to do so failed in Congress, where opposition to female pilots in the military remained strong. Moreover, with German and Japanese air forces diminishing every day, demand for pilot training was tapering off, as was the need for civilian instructors. Many in Congress and the press began grumbling about the uncertain future of aviators returning from combat duty, and once Army leaders realized the continued use of female pilots would ground many of their male counterparts, support for the WASP program cratered. By the end of 1944, it had been quietly disbanded, with little debate or fanfare, let alone recognition of the thirty-eight women pilots who lost their lives in service to their country.

Women broke through other barriers beyond aviation during the war, most notably in military intelligence. A small number were recruited into espionage operations overseas, but it was signals intelligence where so many made their mark. Prior to the war, both the Army and Navy were engaged in rigorous efforts to break the military and diplomatic codes of Japan and Germany. Once the United States entered the war, cracking those codes became even more imperative, and thousands of women serving in the WAC and WAVES with an aptitude for mathematics and languages were drawn into cryptographic units in Washington, DC and Hawaii.

The instruction was intensive—many went through elementary and advanced cryptology and code compilation—and those trained as linguists became fluent in languages from Japanese and German to Portuguese. Code rooms began to fill with female cryptographic code clerks, cryptanalysts, translators, and high-speed radio operators, each with a role in picking apart the immense volume of intercepted communications. In time, the women became a central pillar of wartime signals intelligence operations.

It was not just American women stepping up to serve in the war. In Britain, half a million women supported the British armed forces, some as drivers and clerical workers, and others as radar operators, codebreakers, and anti-aircraft gunners. British intelligence also enlisted female operatives for clandestine work in occupied France, taking advantage of German presumptions about their abilities that allowed women to easily blend in and avoid suspicion. In France, Poland, and across Europe, women played a significant role in resistance operations, leading acts of sabotage, collecting intelligence, and smuggling downed Allied pilots back to friendly lines. The Soviet Union went the furthest. Desperate to fend off a German invasion early in the war, the Soviets sent more than 400,000 women directly into combat, where they operated artillery and anti-aircraft guns, served in tank crews or as sharpshooters, and even became some of the most feared bomber pilots on the Eastern Front.

The Manufacturing Sector

The drive to modernize the US Navy in 1940 and 1941, and to supply the British and other allies with wartime necessities, put tremendous pressure on a tenuous manufacturing workforce. With America's entry in the war, a labor pool already shrinking from the peacetime draft lost even more workers to the armed forces, at the same time production demands were on the rise. Women were a ready substitute, and industrial plants and facilities across the country, desperate to meet the government's production quotas, began inviting female applicants to work where few had ever set foot.

Less welcoming to the women were foremen and other male workers who deeply resented the change. Some were adamant that women lacked the requisite physical strength and ability to operate heavy machinery, while others complained about the women distracting male colleagues. Despite such overt hostility, legions of women signed up at factories, shipyards, steel mills, and coal mines, picking up welding torches and rivet hammers for the very first time. They were fast learners and overcame their inexperience, impressing male supervisors with their work ethic, diligence, and willingness to learn. Many women thrived in their new vocations, but few were recognized for promotion and advancement. Wages also remained uneven, with male counterparts, performing identical tasks, typically earning twice the wages that women were paid. Nonetheless, these women defied every expectation, becoming highly proficient welders, pipefitters, mechanics, riveters, crane operators, and more.

Women were also drawn to other occupations outside the defense industry, from truck drivers and lumberjacks to railroad workers and firefighters. They filled dozens of everyday roles, bolstering a civilian labor pool thinned by men marching off to war. As a whole, the number of working women sharply increased over the course of the war, climbing over forty percent. Most of it was in defense plants, where 80,000 women were hired within the first six months of war. Six months later, that number had swelled to three million and would eventually top five million before the end of the war. Considering the dearth of opportunities for women that existed just four years earlier, it was a stunning achievement.

RECORD OF ACCOMPLISHMENT
Historic progress had been made in the battle for social equality between men and women. The millions of women who joined the military services and industrial labor force during the war were pioneers, notching extraordinary feats that would have been nearly impossible to fathom in the 1930s. The value of their support to America's armed forces and wartime manufacturing was incalculable.

Inequities persisted, however, between male and female servicemembers and industrial workers, proving the journey was far from complete. When the war ended, millions of these women were sidelined again. Some by their own choosing, wishing to return to their homes and reunite with their families, but most others were involuntarily mustered out of the military or dismissed from the workforce. Men returning from overseas expected to reclaim their former jobs, and public opinion backed them. A Gallup survey in 1944 found fifty-nine percent of respondents in favor of women workers surrendering their jobs when the men came back from war.

It could not diminish the momentous contributions of women across American industry, or the heroics and sacrifices among those in uniform. Those contributions also extended to the highly secretive atomic energy project, where female engineers, technicians, analysts, and mathematicians proved women could succeed in any pursuit, including the science and technology fields that became foundational to America's security and prosperity in the post-war era. World War II provided a timely and unexpected opportunity for women to showcase their abilities and devotion to country. Millions delivered.

• • • • •

Virginia Hall

"Working in a region infested with enemy troops and continually at the risk of capture, torture, and death…Miss Hall displayed rare courage, perseverance, and ingenuity."
–Citation for the Distinguished Service Cross awarded to Virginia Hall

Virginia Hall was a native of Baltimore, Maryland. Born into affluence and privilege, she yearned for a life of travel and adventure. After attending several prestigious colleges in the United States, as well as in France and Austria, Hall decided she wanted to live abroad and work as an American diplomat. She started her career as a State Department clerk, but her career aspirations were thwarted when a shooting accident in Turkey required the amputation of her left leg below the knee. Under State Department policy at that time, the injury prevented a diplomatic career, and though Hall was disappointed, she was also determined and would look for other ways to serve.

In 1940, as German forces swept across the European continent, the 34-year-old volunteered to drive an ambulance in France. The speed of the German advance forced her to evacuate to Britain, where she came to the attention of the British Special Operations Executive (SOE). The SOE saw Hill's gender and disability as assets that would shield her from German suspicion and returned her to occupied France to spy in 1941. Working undercover as a journalist, Hall collected intelligence, supported British agents arriving in France, obtained money and supplies for the French Resistance, and aided agents and Allied soldiers in escaping safely to England. After being targeted by the Gestapo, Hall fled to neutral Spain by walking more than fifty miles in three days of heavy snow in the Pyrenees Mountains. At one point in her harrowing journey, Hall radioed London that Cuthbert—her nickname for her prosthetic limb—was giving her trouble. The London operator replied: "If Cuthbert is giving you trouble, have him eliminated."

Shortly after returning to England, Hall joined the Office of Strategic Services, the forerunner of the Central Intelligence Agency (CIA). The American organization was still in its infancy and in desperate need of tested agents to support the upcoming Allied invasion. After returning to France in 1944, Hall became a prolific operator, helping to organize, arm, and train Resistance forces. As their sabotage operations derailed freight trains, destroyed bridges, severed telephone lines, and captured prisoners, Hall's cadre of Resistance fighters grew to 1,500 men and women.

Hall survived the war and became the only civilian woman to be awarded the Distinguished Service Cross for service in

World War II. In the post-war years, she returned to work in US intelligence, joining the CIA in 1951. She died in 1982.

Mae Krier

Mae Krier was raised on a farm outside Dawson, North Dakota. When her brother and others from the Dawson area went off to fight in the war, the young women in the community sought to contribute as well. In 1943, the 17-year-old Mae, her sister, and a friend moved to Seattle, where they were hired to work in Boeing's aircraft factory.

After two weeks of training, Mae joined the assembly line for four-engine B-17 bombers, and later, the even larger B-29s. Her job was to crawl inside the wings of each airplane to rivet them together (a rivet is a thick, metal bolt or pin used to hold two components together). In May 1944, Krier was part of the team that built *5 Grand*, the 5,000th B-17 to take to the skies.

During the war, a Pittsburgh artist, J. Howard Miller, created an illustrated poster of a female factory worker in a denim shirt and red bandana with white polka dots, confidently flexing her biceps, with the exhortation of "We can do it!" The image was produced for a Pennsylvania manufacturer to motivate women in its production plant but received far greater attention after the war. The poster became forever associated with "Rosie the Riveter," an iconic symbol of the legions of women who built the ships, airplanes, and tanks that fueled the Allied victory.

Later in her life, Krier worked tirelessly to convince elected officials in Washington, DC to award Congressional Gold Medals—the nation's highest civilian honor—to the millions of wartime "Rosies." The legislation was signed into law in 2020. Today, visitors can learn more about these women at the Rosie the Riveter National Historic Park in Richmond, California.

ⓘ More than 500 nurses served in medical air evacuation transport squadrons during the war, most notably in the Pacific Theater where the air units shuttled wounded men great distances from forward combat zones to medical facilities hundreds of miles behind Allied lines. Of the 1.2 million patients evacuated by air during the war, just forty-six died during transport. Seventeen flight nurses also lost their lives, either from enemy air attacks or flight accidents.

17
SEGREGATION IN WARTIME AMERICA

You jim crowed me
Before hitler rose to power –
And you're STILL jim crowing me
Right now, this very hour.
–Langston Hughes, poet, *From Beaumont to Detroit* **(1943)**

In January 1941, President Roosevelt stood behind a lectern, forcefully delivering his annual State of the Union Address to the United States Congress. America was nearly a full year from entering the war, but Roosevelt intended to shake the country from its indifference toward the peril sweeping across Europe. Imploring Congress and the American people to support Britain in its hour of desperation against the Nazis, Roosevelt capped his remarks by citing America's moral obligation to stand for human freedoms that transcended geographic boundaries and cultural divides. Pulling on idealistic heartstrings, he voiced his hopes for a world that would one day universally embrace those essential freedoms, including the freedom of speech and expression; freedom to worship a God of one's own choosing; freedom from want – a reference to those lacking necessities – and freedom from fear of tyranny and oppression.

His "Four Freedoms" speech received a rousing ovation from those in attendance, but others were unmoved by Roosevelt's prose. For thirteen million African Americans, such lofty rhetoric contradicted the America they knew, a bigoted society where racial inequalities and injustices long-practiced by custom, and long-protected by law, made a mockery of their own supposed freedom.

As the country moved closer to war, African American leaders had little faith a government actively promulgating and enforcing racist policies would include their community in America's military mobilization and manufacturing surge. Pressure from civil rights organizations prodded the Roosevelt Administration into action, leading to the removal of barriers within the military and industrial sector, but the transition was hardly seamless, or without resistance. After two centuries of slavery and a generation of legalized discrimination, change would not come easily.

TWO AMERICAS

At the dawn of World War II, just seventy-four years had passed since the last slaves in America had been freed. Though slavery had been abolished, an 1896 Supreme Court ruling in *Plessy vs. Ferguson* upheld the constitutionality of laws that permitted segregated schools, buses, railway cars, lodging, theaters, and other public facilities and services, so long as all had equivalent access. This "separate but equal" framework, legalizing racial segregation, reigned until 1954, when the watershed Supreme Court decision in *Brown vs. Board of Education* landed a blow to *Plessy*, declaring segregated public schools unconstitutional and ushering in the modern civil rights era.

More than a decade before *Brown*, America remained deeply segregated. "Jim Crow" laws enacted by state and local governments to enforce segregation had effectively institutionalized inequality and further marginalized African Americans. Denied economic opportunities, and rarely allotted corresponding resources for segregated facilities and services, African Americans were relegated to a second-class citizenry, punctuated by rampant racial abuse and violence that extended well beyond the Deep South.

As for the military, few African Americans were serving in uniform when the war began. That changed in the weeks and months following the attack on Pearl Harbor, when African Americans enlisted by the thousands. Others answered the call for new workers from an industrial base under pressure to scale up in little time. It was a conundrum for African Americans, driven by a sense of obligation and duty to defend a country that so brazenly dehumanized them. A country that would not allow them to dine in restaurants alongside White patrons; where the Red Cross rejected their blood donations unless they could be stored in segregated blood banks; and where galling and humiliating forms of wartime discrimination emerged, such as the awarding of privileges to German soldiers held in POW camps on American soil—privileges denied to the Black soldiers assigned to guard them.

To reconcile the paradox of serving a country blighted with so much injustice, many African American leaders, political activists, and journalists rallied behind a "Double V" campaign, with the letter "V" standing for victory. They agreed to join the fight abroad for Roosevelt's noble ideals of freedom and liberty, but also vowed to defeat bigotry and discrimination at home. Victory became far more than simply squelching the evils sprouting from Germany and Japan; it also meant championing equality in their own communities and ending the pervasive social and economic disparities among races in America.

THE MILITARY DIVIDE

Prior to the war, African Americans were unwelcome in most occupations and work environments, and the military was no exception. The small number on active duty—less than 4,000—were confined to support billets with no opportunity for advancement. That changed in 1940, when a new law establishing the first peacetime draft in American history explicitly prohibited discrimination against any person on account of race or color. More than 2.5 million African Americans subsequently registered for military service, though far fewer were actually inducted. Draft boards composed entirely of White officers winnowed the numbers of those accepted, as did the limited space at the few segregated training facilities available for Black soldiers and sailors.

Every branch of service spurned those accepted, each steeped in its own history of racial exclusion. There were just a limited number of enlisted Black sailors in the pre-draft Navy, all serving as cooks or mess stewards, while the Army Air Corps had long refused to admit Black trainees, claiming the men lacked the requisite mental aptitude for piloting aircraft. The Marine Corps made no pretense of its racial bias; there had not been a single Black Marine since the Corps was re-established in 1798. "If it were a question of having a Marine Corps of 5,000 Whites or 250,000 Negroes," remarked Major General Thomas Holcomb, the seventeenth commandant of the Marine Corps, in early 1941, "I would rather have the Whites."

Despite staunch opposition from Army and Navy leaders, the necessities of war—and, in some cases, direct orders from above—began opening more doors. The armed forces gradually accepted large numbers of African Americans into their ranks, albeit into segregated units led by White officers, many of them natives of the South. The results were decidedly uneven.

Of the more than 900,000 African Americans who served in the Army during the war, just a fraction saw frontline duty. Among them were members of the Army's 92nd Infantry Division, known as the Buffalo Division after the famed Black frontier fighters from the late nineteenth century. The first predominantly Black ground force to be deployed in combat, the 92nd Division arrived in Italy in the fall of 1944. The division achieved some success, seizing more than 3,000 square miles of enemy-held territory through the end of the war and capturing 20,000 German prisoners. It also struggled at times, plagued by episodes of entire units and pockets of men refusing to fight or fleeing from the battlefield. The spotty performance was little surprise given how poorly trained and led the division was compared to its all-White counterparts. It was also hindered by a disproportionate share of recruits who were illiterate and had difficulty learning. The Army establishment was apathetic about the division underperforming, making little effort to correct its deficiencies.

Other African American units fared better, and some chalked up sterling combat records. One of the more fearsome outfits in the European Theater was the 761st Tank Battalion, known as the Black Panthers. Arriving in France in late 1944 with thirty Black officers, six White officers, and 676 enlisted Black men, the 761st skillfully fought its way across France, Belgium, Holland, Austria, and Germany, even liberating a Nazi concentration camp. The Black Panthers finished the war with a casualty rate of nearly fifty percent, while earning a lengthy list of commendations and individual medals for gallantry, including a Presidential Unit Citation for "extraordinary heroism."

More success could be found in the skies above. After finally bowing to pressure to allow Black pilots into its ranks, the Army Air Forces (formerly the Army Air Corps) established a separate training facility for its first African American air group in Tuskegee, Alabama. The base produced 1,000 pilots, navigators, and bombardiers during the war, and though all graduated with exceptional skills, some in the Army hierarchy remained convinced Black pilots would falter under enemy fire. Such doubts, coupled with antagonism and obstruction from White commanding officers, doomed one unit, the 477th Bombardment Group. With its progress repeatedly undermined, the 477th was unable to complete its training and never flew a single combat mission.

The 99th Pursuit Squadron had a far different experience. The first African American unit to fly in combat, it deployed to North Africa in 1943 and later to Italy, where it joined three other all-Black squadrons in forming the 332nd Fighter Group. Saddled with dated aircraft, the 332nd was initially limited to harbor and coastal patrols and lower-risk ground attacks, but after finally transitioning to modern P-47 *Thunderbolts* and P-51 *Mustangs* — marked with distinctive red tails — more hazardous missions awaited. The men of the 332nd proved their mettle, gaining their legendary acclaim flying protective escort missions for long-range bombers raiding industrial Germany. Notching more than 15,000 combat missions during the war, the pilots became so proficient at fending off German fighter planes that all-White bombing units began requesting the "Red Tails" as their escorts. The Tuskegee Airmen earned fourteen Bronze Stars for heroic and meritorious service during the war, as well as three Distinguished Unit Citations and ninety-six Distinguished Flying Crosses.

Though such achievements debunked claims that African Americans would not perform well in combat, the men assigned to frontline fighting units as infantrymen, tankers, and pilots were the exception. The majority were relegated to serving in support branches, but they, too, made invaluable contributions, none more so than the fabled "Red Ball Express."

Weeks after the invasion of Normandy in mid-1944, American and British forces finally broke out from their beachheads and began charging across the French countryside. As the forward surge stretched out already-thin supply lines, ammunition and gasoline stocks dwindled, threatening to halt the army and allow the Germans to regroup and fortify their lines. In response, a fleet of 6,000 trucks was organized to shuttle supplies overland from the Normandy beaches to forward areas. Most of the drivers on the Red Ball Express — named for the red dots used on rail maps to mark priority trains — were African

Americans, and few had any experience handling the large, cumbersome trucks. The two-man teams were in motion twenty-four hours a day, from August to November, their treacherous, fifty-four-hour journey frequently disrupted by enemy air and artillery strikes, as well as roadside accidents. It all took a toll on the drivers, but they successfully delivered thousands of tons of daily supplies to American ground forces, fueling the decisive advance toward Germany.

There were fewer success stories in the Navy. It was not until April 1942 that Secretary of the Navy Frank Knox finally succumbed to outside pressure and ordered the Navy and Marine Corps to accept African Americans into general service. The Navy initially inducted some 27,000 Black sailors, but continued to assign the majority as stewards, cooks, or manual laborers. Thousands of others served in segregated Naval Construction Battalions (nicknamed "Seabees"), building airstrips and fortifications on island bases across the Pacific. By January 1944, African American enlistment in the Navy had climbed to 100,000, yet there was not a single Black officer among them. The Navy relented, agreeing in March of that year to commission a small group of thirteen officers, limited to commanding work details of Black sailors. Another milestone came that month with the launching of the USS *Mason*; the destroyer escort was the first US Naval warship to sail with a crew of majority Black sailors.

In the Marine Corps, the first African American enlistees to join were trained separately from White recruits. Many were eventually organized into segregated defense battalions and assigned to coastal and air defenses in the Pacific Theater, while others provided logistics support during amphibious operations. Though such assignments were designed to release White Marines for combat duty, manpower shortages often brought Black Marines into the fighting on hotly contested islands, where they joined in repelling Japanese assaults and evacuating wounded men. "The Negro Marines are no longer on trial," declared Lieutenant General Alexander A. Vandegrift, the eighteenth commandant of the Marine Corps, in January 1944. "They are Marines, period." More than 19,000 African Americans served with the Marines, but the Corps was even stingier than the Navy when it came to promotion. Not a single Black Marine was elevated to the officer ranks during the war.

Wartime volunteerism extended beyond African American men. The first officer candidate class for the WAAC (later, the WAC) began training in July 1941 in Fort Des Moines, Iowa. Of the 440 women in the first class, ten percent were African American. By 1945, 6,500 African American women had joined, but their proportional representation had fallen, comprising just four percent of the 162,500 women serving. The Navy was as indisposed to inducting African American women as it was to men, refusing to accept the first into the WAVES until October 1944, more than two years after the organization was initially established. Of the 90,000 women who served in the WAVES during the war, just seventy were African American. Worse yet, the Marine Corps refused to induct a single African American woman. That wall did not come down until 1949.

FROM FARM FIELDS TO FACTORY FLOORS
In 1940, with the industrial base ramping up war production, the Roosevelt Administration faced growing political pressure to include African Americans in the expanding economy. The aircraft industry was a prime example of the under-representation, with just 250 African Americans among its workforce of more than 100,000. Nationwide, Black unemployment was double that of White unemployment.

With their political influence on the rise, African Americans intensified their appeals to the White House. Black voters had tilted Republican since the post-Civil War era, reliably favoring the party of Abraham Lincoln, but that support began to shift to

Democrats in the 1930s as those in the working- and middle-classes were increasingly drawn to Roosevelt's more progressive social and economic policies. When A. Philip Randolph, a prominent Black labor leader, demanded an end to racial discrimination in hiring and threatened to march on the Nation's capital with 100,000 supporters, the White House took notice. In mid-1941, Roosevelt issued Executive Order 8802, explicitly prohibiting federal defense contractors from discriminatory hiring based on race, creed, color, or national origin. That decree, coupled with the hiring frenzy among factory and shipyard operators to meet surging demand, led to masses of African American men and women joining the manufacturing sector. Black employment in the defense industry more than doubled during the war years, from three to eight percent.

Scores of Black workers migrated from the rural South to industrial plants and shipyards in the North and the West, but their eagerness to learn new trades collided with a caustic social climate that was little better than the one they left behind. Stark wage inequities were also commonplace, and though some plants and factories permitted White and Black laborers to work side by side, others remained segregated, with cordoned-off workspaces, cafeterias, and restrooms.

Labor unions resisted the hiring of Black workers, fearing a threat to White employment, and as resentment among White laborers became increasingly palpable, violence was not far behind. Plans to promote Black workers sparked riots at facilities in Alabama and Texas, but the unrest was not confined to the South. In June 1943, 25,000 workers at a Packard Motors plant in Detroit walked off the job, irate over plans to elevate African Americans to more skilled positions. Weeks later, on a blistering-hot day, long-simmering racial tensions over jobs and sparse housing in Detroit erupted into a violent race riot that spilled into the streets. The melee left thirty-four dead—twenty-five of the victims Black—and injured hundreds more, many of them by police who turned on the African American community with batons. Order was not restored until the next day, when Roosevelt ordered 6,000 soldiers into the city to quell the violence.

After the War

More than one million African American men and women served in the Army, Navy, and Marine Corps during World War II, and thousands more with the Coast Guard and Merchant Marine. Contributing to the final triumphs in both the Pacific and European Theaters, African Americans had undoubtably achieved the first "V" in their Double V campaign, but the fight to prevail against discrimination and racism at home continued well into the next generation and beyond.

African American war veterans, who mustered out of the military and hoped to find an appreciative and more accepting society at home, instead found pre-war inequalities and attitudes unchanged. Many had acquired specialized skills during their war service, from electronics to mechanics, but workplace obstacles and hostilities persisted. Congress had passed the GI Bill to assist returning veterans with job, education, and loan benefits, regardless of race, but Black veterans still found themselves unjustly denied mortgages and other needed services. Worst of all were the appalling assaults, lynchings, and murders of Black servicemen and veterans, often when wearing their uniforms.

On July 26, 1948, President Harry S. Truman signed Executive Order 9981 directing "equality of treatment and opportunity for all persons in the armed services without regard to race, color, religion, or national origin." His order set the stage for desegregating the military, six years before the Supreme Court struck down wider segregation across the country. Racism within venerable military institutions would not vanish overnight, but the eventual integration of the armed forces became a lasting tribute to the trailblazing efforts of the scores of African American men and women who so ably and courageously served their country during the Second World War.

* * * * *

In 1944, Jackie Robinson, a former collegiate sports star, was a second lieutenant in the 761st Tank Battalion as it neared the completion of its training. Prior to the unit shipping out overseas, the 25-year-old Robinson was court-martialed after refusing to move to the back of a segregated bus at Fort Hood, Texas. He was acquitted, but unable to join his former unit in combat and was instead honorably discharged from the Army. He later broke one of the country's most visible color barriers in 1947, becoming the first African American to play in Major League Baseball.

Waverly B. Woodson Jr.

Trained as a medic, Corporal Waverly B. Woodson Jr. was attached to the only all-Black unit to land in Normandy on D-Day in 1944. His landing craft hit a mine as it approached Omaha Beach, wounding the 21-year-old, but he still managed to wade ashore and give aid to other injured men as the Germans peppered the landing beaches with machine-gun fire. Woodson labored for thirty consecutive hours, removing bullets, administering plasma, and even performing an emergency amputation. He saved numerous lives before finally collapsing from his own wounds. Woodson survived the war and was awarded a Bronze Star and Purple Heart for his actions that day, and while his heroics at Normandy likely merited the Medal of Honor, not a single African American serviceman was awarded the Nation's highest military honor during the war years. Such recognition would come for some, but not until decades later.

Rothacker Smith

Rothacker Smith was a native of New York City who moved to Detroit in his early years. A devoutly spiritual young man, Smith was attending Emmanuel Missionary College in Berrien Springs, Michigan when the war began. By early 1943, with his tuition no longer affordable and the 19-year-old out of school, Smith was drafted into the US Army.

Smith had limited exposure to racism in the northern cities where he was raised and was jolted by his early experience in the segregated Army. It began as Smith was traveling by rail to Camp Stewart, Georgia, where he was to report for basic training. When the train stopped in Cincinnati, just across the border from Kentucky, Smith and other African Americans aboard were ordered to transfer from their coach car to one far less comfortable. It would get worse. From his training in Georgia to his first overseas deployment in North Africa, Smith was an eyewitness to the overt racism pervading the Army, including harassment of African American soldiers by the military police and grossly unfair treatment by White officers. Such practices routinely ended with punishments and demotions.

Smith was eventually assigned to an all-Black infantry regiment. Because of his religious convictions, he declared himself a conscientious objector, a status that allowed those with moral or religious concerns to serve in non-combat roles. He became a medic and saw his first combat action in Italy in December 1944. After his unit's forward position was shelled by the Germans, gravely wounding Smith, he was taken prisoner and barely survived an excruciating, 35-mile journey on foot to a POW camp in Italy. He was later moved to another POW camp in Germany, where he remained until liberated in April 1945.

Like many servicemen returning from combat, Smith had difficulty adjusting to civilian life again. He slept on the floor for months because the bed was so much softer than what he became accustomed to as a soldier and prisoner, and his near-death trauma strained his everyday conversations with others, leaving him unable and unwilling to share his war experiences with anyone, including his father. Smith persevered and used the GI Bill to finish college and complete a lengthy career in teaching while earning five academic degrees. A devoted husband, father, and grandfather, Smith died in 2021 at the age of ninety-seven.

18
WARTIME INJUSTICE: THE FATE OF JAPANESE AMERICANS

"When the gates were shut, we knew that we had lost something that was very precious; that we were no longer free."
–Mary Tsukamoto, recalling her 1942 arrival at a relocation camp in Arkansas

"A Jap's a Jap. It makes no difference whether the Jap is a citizen or not."
–General John L DeWitt, US Army Western Defense Command, 1942

For generations after America's founding, waves of immigrants from foreign lands fueled the young nation's soaring population growth. By the time the United States entered the Second World War, millions of Americans shared a common ancestry with their German and Italian adversaries. These Americans were either immigrants themselves or had parents or grandparents who had once journeyed across the Atlantic, pursuing fortune, equality, and liberty.

Far fewer could trace their roots to Japan. In 1940, just 127,000 persons of Japanese ancestry lived in the continental United States—most of them in California—and only one-third were Japanese-born. The majority, known as Nisei, were born in the United States, the children and grandchildren of Japanese immigrants. Along with those immigrants (Issei) who had met citizenship requirements, most were United States citizens.

In the wake of the attack on Pearl Harbor, with the nation gripped by heated emotions, the birthplace and citizenship of Japanese Americans became immaterial. Anyone who shared bloodlines and physical traits with America's hated foe was berated, scorned, and branded a national security risk, their ethnicity proof enough of potential disloyalty and enemy collaboration. It was an early step toward the unthinkable—the opening of internment camps, likened by many to concentration camps, on American soil.

It would not be the first time Constitutional boundaries had been stretched under the guise of safeguarding the country. Previous government overreaches included the Alien and Sedition Acts of 1798 and President Lincoln's suspension of writ of habeas corpus in 1861. Added to that ignominious list was an order from President Roosevelt leading to the incarceration of some 120,000 Japanese Americans without trial for the duration of the war. It stands as one of the most shameful episodes of World War II and one of the worst injustices in American history.

"Exclusion"

A swirl of emotions consumed America following the shocking attack on Pearl Harbor, including rage. The public fumed over Japanese duplicity in attacking the United States prior to a formal declaration of war—a breach of time-honored norms— and those of Japanese ancestry were assumed to be prone to similar treachery. Fears of a possible Japanese invasion spread quickly, as did speculation that collaborators on the mainland were conspiring to aid such an operation. This toxic mix of fear and fury led to the shunning of Japanese Americans in communities where they had long lived and worked. With little evidence of any wrongdoing, the Federal Bureau of

Investigation opened a flurry of espionage cases across Hawaii and the West Coast, leading to arrests, the ransacking of homes and businesses, and the confiscation of guns, radios, and cameras.

It was just the beginning. Urged on by the public and his military advisors, President Roosevelt issued Executive Order 9066 in February 1942, authorizing the War Department to establish restricted military areas and "exclude" designated persons from those areas for any reason. The War Department subsequently identified California, Washington, Oregon, and parts of Arizona as military zones, and excluded Japanese Americans from living, working, or traveling in those areas. The decree was applied to not only Issei, but American-born Nisei as well.

The government next divided the West Coast into 108 exclusion zones, with roughly 1,000 Japanese Americans living inside each. All were ordered to report to neighborhood gathering places, then transported to makeshift assembly centers located on vacant racetracks and county fairgrounds. The government limited evacuees to the clothes and possessions they could carry, forcing them to abandon family pets, heirlooms, and other valuables. Few were able to make arrangements for homes and businesses in such a brief time, and much of their property became lost forever. They arrived at the assembly centers, where poor sanitation, meager food service, and temporary living quarters—often in vile-smelling horse stalls—awaited. The detainees endured such miserable conditions for months as construction of longer-term facilities was completed.

THE PRISON CAMPS

As the blazing summer heat finally began to ebb in 1942, the new War Relocation Authority (WRA) began transferring tens of thousands of detainees from the assembly centers into more permanent camps, known by their euphemism of "relocation centers." The War Department had considered allowing Japanese American evacuees to resettle in other states and live freely there with new employment, but governors from those states vehemently objected. Opponents included Nels H. Smith, who warned the War Department that "The people of Wyoming have a dislike for any Orientals and simply will not stand for being California's dumping ground. If you bring Japanese into my state, I promise you they will be hanging from every tree." Bert Miller, the attorney general of Idaho, echoed such sentiments, declaring that "All Japanese must be in concentration camps for the remainder of the war…We want to keep this a White man's country."

Ten camps were built in California, Arizona, Utah, Wyoming, Idaho, Colorado, and Arkansas, all in remote locales and surrounded by mountain ranges, swamps, and barren deserts. They were primitive, with crude, military-style barracks constructed of wood planks and tar paper that did little to provide warmth or relief from the outdoor elements. In the desert camps, the mercury reached as high as 110 degrees in summer and dipped to well below freezing in the colder months. Many facilities were shrouded in perpetual dust, kicked up by whipping winds sweeping across dry, desolate landscapes. The dust became a fixture, settling inside housing structures, coating faces and clothing, and invariably mixing into food and drinking water.

Living barracks were divided into rooms twenty feet wide and sixteen to twenty-five feet long, with each room housing at least one family, no matter the family size. They used Army blankets for partitions and straw-filled sacks for mattresses. Showers, toilets, and dining facilities were all communal, and privacy, even within shared bathrooms, was non-existent. The largest such facility was the Manzanar Relocation Center in Owens Valley, California, roughly 200 miles northeast of Los

Angeles, where more than 10,000 people were crammed into barracks, each without indoor plumbing, kitchens, or adequate heat.

Security was tight, and the camps were ringed with barbed wire fencing, watchtowers, and armed sentries. The detainees nonetheless did their best to make camp life tolerable. They opened schools, held religious services and musical performances, and organized internal governance councils. They started camp newspapers, youth sports leagues, and scouting troops, and eventually established post offices and fire stations. Many of the detainees worked in the camps as teachers, mess hall staff, doctors, nurses, and police officers, while others planted gardens or received permission to work on nearby farms to improve the supply and quality of their food.

Despite the public hysteria and racial invective, and the abominable living conditions within the prison camps, the Japanese American community endured. Many of the younger men even took the extraordinary step of volunteering for military service. Driven by allegiance and a desire to contribute, they set aside their bitterness and resentment toward the government that had wronged them, eagerly stepping forward to defend their birth country.

JOINING THE FIGHT

Considered enemy aliens after the Pearl Harbor attack, Japanese Americans had been ineligible for the military draft since the beginning of the war. That changed in early 1943, when the US Army, desperate for additional manpower, sent Army recruiters to the camps in search of volunteers. More than 800 detainees immediately enlisted, but they would not be the first Japanese Americans to fight in the war.

In 1941, there were approximately 158,000 Japanese Americans living in Hawaii, then a US territory. Oddly, the islanders fared far better after the Pearl Harbor attack than those living on the mainland. With Japanese Americans representing one-third of the population in Hawaii, the islands were more ethnically diverse and culturally tolerant than the West Coast, and authorities there only took a small number of Japanese Americans into custody during the war. The rest, Issei and Nisei alike, remained free to live and work in their home communities—far different conditions than what those on the mainland experienced.

When the Army first agreed to form all-Japanese American units, hundreds of Hawaiian Nisei enthusiastically volunteered. Many were already National Guardsmen or former Reserve Officer Training Corps cadets at the University of Hawaii and formed the core of what became the 100th Infantry Battalion. With the Army hierarchy dubious of their willingness to fight the Japanese, the battalion was sent to the European Theater, arriving in August 1943, shortly before the Allied invasion of Italy. They became the first Japanese Americans to serve in combat, and in early fighting across the Italian Peninsula, the 1,400 men performed exceptionally well, impressing War Department officials but sustaining heavy casualties along the way. Earning more than 900 medals for combat wounds, the 100th was forever branded the "Purple Heart Battalion."

Back in the United States, a mix of new volunteers from Hawaii and the mainland detention camps had completed their own training. Like the 100th Infantry Battalion, the commanding officer and senior subordinates of the 442nd Regimental Combat Team (RCT) were White, but the remaining officers and all enlisted men were Japanese American. Arriving in the Mediterranean in June 1944, the 442nd RCT absorbed the 100th Infantry Battalion into its ranks as it battled the Germans in central Italy. It later participated in the invasion of southern France before returning to Italy and fighting alongside the all-Black 92nd Infantry Division.

Throughout the final, decisive months of the war, the 442nd RCT distinguished itself as much as any single unit of comparable size during the war. The men were awarded some 18,000 individual decorations, including 21 Medals of Honor and more than 350 Silver Stars, 800 Bronze Stars, and 3,600 Purple Hearts. The regiment itself received seven Presidential Unit Citations, the highest military award for a unit.

The service of Japanese Americans in the war was not limited to the infantry. The intelligence services, desperate for native or fluent Japanese speakers to serve as translators and interpreters, recruited more than 6,000 Japanese Americans, many straight from the detention camps. In island campaigns across the Pacific, they interrogated prisoners, translated enemy communications and captured documents, and persuaded enemy soldiers and civilians to leave their bunkers and caves, saving many from certain death. Like so many others who served in intelligence, the vital contributions of these linguists preserved scores of lives, though their role remained unheralded until decades later.

THE END OF THE INCARCERATION

Throughout their domestic imprisonment, not a single Japanese American was ever formally accused of espionage or sabotage. Some sought to use the courts to secure their release, including Fred Korematsu, a second-generation US citizen living in San Francisco when the war began. Fearing a vindictive public following the strike on Pearl Harbor, Korematsu changed his name and had his physical appearance surgically altered, leading to his subsequent arrest for attempting to conceal his Japanese ethnicity. After challenging his detention in lower courts and losing, Korematsu appealed his case to the US Supreme Court. In *Korematsu vs. United States* (1944), the Court upheld the government's action in a six-to-three ruling, finding the claim reasonable that Korematsu and other Japanese

Americans posed a national security threat. The Court therefore deemed his forced evacuation from the Pacific Coast lawful.

However, in a simultaneous ruling in *Endo vs. United States*, the Supreme Court also found that in the absence of any evidence of disloyalty, the government could not detain US citizens without cause or simply because of their ethnicity. The ruling freed detainee Mitsuye Endo from a camp in Topaz, Utah and ended the government's legal authority for incarcerating other US citizens on merely ethnic or racial grounds.

As these court challenges were adjudicated, Roosevelt's own attorney general and secretary of the interior voiced their support for closing the camps and ending the detention. Roosevelt relented in December 1944, the day before the Supreme Court handed down their rulings in *Korematsu* and *Endo*, having likely received advance notice of the Court's findings. With the government declaring there was no longer a military necessity for evacuation—a somewhat hollow claim considering there had been no real threat of a Japanese attack on the West Coast for over two years—those behind the barbed wire fences were finally released. The exodus was slower than what might have been expected, as many older Issei, fearful of the hostility that might await them in their home communities, were reluctant to leave the relative safety of the camps and had to be convinced otherwise. Most detainees were stranded hundreds of miles from their former homes. Provided just a train ticket and little cash, some returned to the Pacific Coast, while others found new homes elsewhere in the country.

In 1948, Congress took the first step in recognizing the extraordinary wartime injustices, allowing the filing of compensation claims for lost property. Though more than 26,000 claims were filed for losses totaling $148 million, the final disbursement approved by the government was just $38 million. Forty years later, legislation was finally enacted providing $20,000 to every survivor, along with a long overdue public admission of wrongdoing and an apology on behalf of the government.

* * * * *

Daniel Inouye

During late-war fighting in Italy, Hawaiian-born Daniel Inouye was serving as a junior officer with the US Army's 442nd Regimental Combat Team. Just two weeks before the war ended in Europe, the 22-year-old Inouye was leading his platoon up a German-held ridge when it came under heavy fire from a trio of machine-gun nests. Wounded in the torso, Inouye crawled forward, taking out two of the machine-guns with hand grenades and his submachine gun. As he was hurling a grenade at the third enemy position, an exploding rifle grenade shattered his arm. Inouye continued to advance until another bullet in the leg finally stopped him. He miraculously survived the battle, but a grueling recovery followed, including the amputation of his arm. Initially awarded the Distinguished Service Cross for his valor, the decoration was later upgraded to the Medal of Honor. In 1959, Hawaiians elected Inouye to the House of Representatives, and later to the United States Senate. The war hero served on Capitol Hill for fifty-three years before his death in 2012.

19
THE MANHATTAN PROJECT

"We had the full backing of our government, combined with the nearly infinite potential of American science, engineering and industry, and an almost unlimited supply of people endowed with ingenuity and determination."
–General Leslie R. Groves

"We felt as if the fate of the world was in our hands."
–Peter Lax, 19-year-old mathematician

In August 1939, just weeks before the first German tanks began rolling across Poland, correspondence arrived at the White House from Albert Einstein, the German-born, Nobel Prize-winning physicist residing then in Long Island. The letter was signed by Einstein but mostly authored by another physicist, Leo Szilard, a Hungarian refugee who also fled Europe as the Nazis swept into power.

The men were reaching out to President Roosevelt to share new discoveries in the emerging field of atomic energy. The letter detailed developments in fission, a process of splitting microscopic atoms to release energy and split additional atoms, sparking a chain reaction. Such nuclear chain reactions, the scientists noted, could generate tremendous amounts of energy, capable of unimaginable destructive force. After urging Roosevelt to fund continuing research, Einstein and Szilard warned of German efforts to stockpile uranium—the same fissionable element that teams in the United States were experimenting with.

Roosevelt responded with caution at first, appointing a presidential advisory committee of civilian scientists and military officials to assess the feasibility of atomic weapons, and recommend an appropriate role for the government in the development process. By late 1941, with the Nazis occupying much of Europe and Hitler's forces pressing deep into the Soviet Union, Roosevelt quietly ordered a more vigorous pursuit, eager to understand the potential of atomic energy and harness it before the Germans. The US Army took charge, and with resources from Washington pouring in, progress in the scientific and academic communities began to accelerate.

• • • • •

Shortly after Roosevelt issued his directive, the United States was at war with the Axis powers. Consecutive defeats from Pearl Harbor to the Philippines staggered the country, but the news was more encouraging from university laboratories, where scientific teams made remarkable inroads. They were eager to test their theories about nuclear chain reactions, but experimentation required significant volumes of fissionable material.

The most suitable fuel sources were uranium, which could be mined from the earth, and plutonium, a synthetic element derived from uranium ore. Generating sufficient quantities for fission required an enrichment process within specialized production facilities that did not yet exist. Building those facilities was delegated to the Army Corps of Engineers, an organization with plenty of experience tackling large-scale government construction needs. The Army was also entrusted with an additional mandate — shielding America's atomic energy secrets from German and Japanese spies.

In August 1942, an umbrella office was established in New York City to manage the secretive energy program. It was given the intentionally cryptic name of the Manhattan Engineer District, and the man chosen to lead it, Colonel Leslie R. Groves, was a highly regarded Army engineer who had managed construction of the new War Department headquarters, commonly referred to as the Pentagon. Promoted to brigadier general, the hard-charging Groves wasted little time making his mark, gaining approval to assign the highest emergency prioritization to any materials his program required. He also selected building sites for new production and research facilities and enlisted key personnel to manage what would become a vast enterprise spanning the North American continent and multiple scientific disciplines. Among those he recruited was 38-year-old J. Robert Oppenheimer, a respected theoretical physicist from the University of California, who would direct Project Y — the design and assembly of the first atomic bomb.

Experimentation with fission continued. In December 1942, researchers at the University of Chicago, led by Enrico Fermi, another European refugee, achieved a historic breakthrough inside a small reactor they had fashioned under the grandstands of the school football stadium. Though their uranium-based experiment produced little energy — Fermi quickly shut down the reactor as a precaution — it generated the very first self-sustaining nuclear chain reaction. It was an extraordinary achievement, and just weeks later, with the promise of atomic energy no longer merely theoretical, Roosevelt gave formal approval to build needed facilities for producing enriched uranium and plutonium. The scope of the Manhattan Project, as it was now known, was about to expand significantly.

Tennessee and Washington

Enriching uranium was a complicated and painstaking process. It required a multitude of new industrial plants and reactors, each sprawling in size and operated by an army of technicians, engineers, and other skilled workers. After reviewing proposed sites for building these new facilities, Groves made his first selection—a sparsely populated patch of land in eastern Tennessee. The planned facility, sixteen miles long and seven miles wide, was originally referred to as the Clinton Engineer Works, but the site name was later changed to Oak Ridge, sharing its name with the town hastily constructed to accommodate the expected 30,000 workers and their families. The four main production complexes at Oak Ridge—one would stretch for a mile—were sited in separate valleys to limit the impact of accidental explosions. Hydroelectric plants of the Tennessee Valley Authority would supply the requisite electrical power, and laborers would be drawn from the city of Knoxville, less than twenty miles away. By the time the facility reached peak production, the wartime population of Oak Ridge had swelled to 75,000 people, making it the fifth largest city in Tennessee.

A second, even more remote site in Hanford, Washington was chosen for producing plutonium. Proximity to the Columbia River would provide sufficient hydroelectric power and coolant for the nuclear reactors, but the location also ensured the facility would be safely distant from major population centers, minimizing potential radiation exposure in the event of an accident.

From the time the facilities in Oak Ridge and Hanford first opened, their workforces operated in complete secrecy, leaving the public with no inkling of what the plants were actually producing. The government informed the workers of little beyond their individual responsibilities, and only a select few were aware of what the enriched material was intended for. That aura of secrecy was also prevalent at a third site selected by Groves, nestled atop one of the many picturesque plateaus of the American Southwest, where the most sensitive phase of the entire Manhattan Project would be carried out.

New Mexico

As Oak Ridge and Hanford began developing potential fuel sources, project leaders turned to their greatest puzzle—designing and building the weapon itself. Among the many challenges was uncertainty about how to trigger a chain reaction in a device dropped from high altitude, with an optimal detonation in mid-air.

Groves and Oppenheimer agreed that centralizing all research and testing within a single laboratory would ease the sharing of information and ideas, speeding progress. They ruled out existing facilities in Chicago and New York, as the work had to be concealed from prying eyes and those involved sequestered from the public. The pair ultimately settled on a large, secluded plot of land adjoining the Jemez Mountains of northern New Mexico, sixteen miles from the nearest town. Much of the land was a national forest under federal control, easing the path to approval. It was also home to the Los Alamos Ranch School for young boys, leading to the hasty relocation of staff and students, told only that the land and buildings were needed for military purposes.

Los Alamos, as it was simply known, opened in April 1943, with Oppenheimer as its civilian director and scientific chief. He was joined by hundreds of physicists, chemists, engineers, machinists, and explosive experts recruited from across government, industry, and academia. By early 1945, nearly 6,000 of these workers and their family members were living inside the facility—the most unique government installation in American history. Both a scientific research center and a military post, Army officials managed it accordingly. Military policemen guarded every entry point, and anyone arriving or departing the camp was required to pass through checkpoints where identities and badges were carefully inspected. Armed patrols roamed outside the barbed wire fences, and inside the camp, the civilians adhered to rigorous and burdensome security protocols. All contact with the outside world was cut off, mail was censored, and no one was permitted private telephones or mailing addresses.

With most workers and their families confined to the camp for long stretches of time, amenities were provided, including a school, hospital, and even a ski hill. Social functions were common, and the civilians bonded with one another, organizing backyard barbeques, baseball and softball leagues, dances, and horseback rides. Inside the labs, the work continued at a brisk pace. By February 1945, Los Alamos had received its first plutonium from Hanford, as assembly of the world's first atomic device neared completion.

AMERICA IN THE LEAD
Despite early premonitions, the building of a bomb evolved into more of a race against time than a race against rival developmental efforts. The Axis powers had made little headway during the war beyond early research and experimentation. Limited resources and the lack of uranium ore hindered Japan from the outset, and any hopes of advancement ended after American heavy bombers destroyed its most prominent research facilities. Germany faltered as well, unable to progress beyond its breakthrough achievement in 1938 when it became the first country to split a uranium atom. Poor coordination among Reich leaders and scientists stalled momentum, as did demands on the German industrial base to prioritize the production of more tanks, planes, and munitions for Hitler's armies. America's boundless means and industrial prowess proved a decisive advantage once again.

Among allies, Britain simply no longer had the financial means to capitalize on its own groundbreaking studies, but its expertise would not be wasted. The British became essential contributors to the Manhattan Project, lending a considerable number of skilled scientists and engineers to North American laboratories and production facilities. As for the Soviet Union, a concerted, late-war effort was made to develop its own weapons, but the country lagged far behind the United States, and eventually turned to espionage against its wartime ally to close the distance.

A little more than two years after the facility opened, Los Alamos was ready to test its first atomic device. On July 16, 1945, a plutonium-fueled bomb named Trinity was lifted atop a 110-foot steel tower in the New Mexico desert. It detonated with blinding light, the explosive force of 19,000 tons of TNT vaporizing the steel tower and obliterating virtually everything for miles around. Oppenheimer witnessed the earthshaking blast and mushroom-shaped cloud from a concrete bunker six miles away. Awed by its destructive power and perhaps a bit apprehensive about its potential, he famously uttered a line from an ancient Hindu scripture—"Now I am become Death, the destroyer of worlds."

Aftermath

In just three years, the Manhattan Project evolved into the largest program of research, testing, and development the world had ever known. More than thirty project sites and 130,000 civilian workers and military personnel were involved, costing some $2.2 billion—more than $32 billion in present-day dollars. In the end, the enterprise produced one of the greatest scientific and technological achievements in history.

The success of Trinity came at an opportune time. The Nazis had fully surrendered two months earlier, but Japanese forces—mostly penned up in their home islands and on the Asian mainland after three years of defeats across the Pacific—refused to concede. Preparations continued for a long-expected invasion of Japan itself, but recent experiences with other island campaigns made clear there would be fanatical resistance from

Japanese soldiers and civilians alike. Combined casualties on both sides were expected to reach into the hundreds of thousands, if not higher.

Just three months after he was sworn in to succeed the fallen Roosevelt, it was up to President Harry S. Truman as to whether and how an atomic weapon would be used against Japan. It was one of the weightiest questions ever put before an American president, with moral implications that were sure to be scrutinized and debated for generations to come. For Truman, the scale of expected bloodshed resulting from an invasion was inconceivable, but the fate of immense numbers of non-combatants, including children and the elderly, was also in his hands.

Nine days after the Trinity test, Truman reached his final verdict.

• • • • •

Theodore Hall

With a brilliant mind and keen aptitude for the sciences, Theodore Hall graduated from Harvard University just after reaching adulthood, and in January 1944, the 19-year-old became the youngest physicist recruited into the Manhattan Project.

As with other new hires, Hall did not learn the purpose of the atomic weapons program until his secretive work began—a potential use that deeply troubled the young man. The Great Depression had hit his family hard, drawing Hall to Marxist ideals that promoted greater economic and social equality between the classes. In his new position, Hall saw an opportunity to safeguard humanity from the scourge of atomic weapons and prevent the United States from gaining an unfair advantage over the Soviet Union, a country tethered to what

Hall considered more equitable and just political and social ideologies.

In late 1944, Hall began his espionage, sharing extremely sensitive technical information from the Los Alamos laboratory with Soviet contacts. The disclosures advanced the development of Moscow's atomic weapons program by several years, and when the Soviets tested their first atomic device in 1949, it was a near-replica of the plutonium-fueled bomb the United States dropped on Japan in 1945.

Hall was just one of several Americans and British inside the Manhattan Project who shared atomic energy secrets with the Soviets. The espionage network was unraveled after the war, leading to the arrests of spies at Los Alamos and the execution of others found to be their handlers, but Hall was never caught or prosecuted. He maintained his innocence until 1995, half a century after his espionage ended, when decrypted, decades-old Soviet cables clearly implicated him as a spy. Prosecutors declined to act, as Hall was suffering from Parkinson's disease and kidney cancer, and others who could have testified against him were no longer alive. It mattered little; Hall succumbed to his illnesses in 1999.

THE PACIFIC THEATER

INTRODUCTION
A GATHERING STORM IN THE FAR EAST

Until the mid-nineteenth century, Westerners knew little of the Japanese, a devoutly spiritual people with a rich cultural heritage. Inhabiting a cluster of mountainous, volcanic islands in the Far East, they had remained secluded from the developing world for generations. Foreign trade was almost non-existent, and few Japanese traveled abroad. The people were ruled by a feudal regime comprised of small, medieval fiefs, each governed by a lord and his soldiers, known as samurai. By custom, a divine emperor presided over the country, but he reigned largely as a symbolic figure rather than an authoritative one. Civil and military powers were vested in an appointed shogun instead.

The isolation ended in 1853 when an American emissary, Commodore Matthew C. Perry of the United States Navy, sailed into what is known today as Tokyo Bay. Perry commanded a squadron of four warships, their decks lined with far more firepower than any vessel Japan had ever put to sea. With commercial trade budding between the United States and China, Perry's mission was to persuade the Japanese—by gunpoint, if necessary—to open their ports to American ships for fueling and provisioning and provide aid to shipwrecked sailors stranded on their shores. Perry delivered a personal letter to the emperor from President Millard Fillmore and offered gifts designed to impress the Japanese, such as a steam locomotive and a telegraph. He returned to Japan the following year and formalized an official treaty, one that led to closer relations between the two countries.

Having finally re-opened its doors to outsiders, a new Japan slowly emerged, enticed by the promise of modernization and global commerce. A longtime self-supporting, agrarian society evolved into a more industrial one, increasingly dependent on access to foreign raw materials and trade markets for its manufactured goods. The feudal system was dissolved, and a constitution adopted in 1889 revolutionized governance in Japan, vesting greater political and military authorities in the emperor.

In the decades following Perry's visit, a national army was formed, and a more militarized Japan began eying an Asian mainland teeming with natural resources the home islands lacked. Though China had long been the dominant regional power, many Japanese were eager to challenge the Qing Dynasty over control of Korea, a Chinese protectorate just across the sea from southern Japan. Hostilities broke out in 1894, and the First Sino-Japanese War ended in a surprise triumph for Japan the following year. Besides loosening China's grip on Korea, Japan also won possession of Formosa (present-day Taiwan), its first significant colony and later one of its most prized military bases. The balance of political and military power in the Far East fundamentally shifted, and Japan's longtime admiration of Chinese strength was replaced by contempt for a vanquished foe, seen now as a lesser race tainted by weakness and defeat.

A decade later, an emboldened Japan went to war again, this time with the Russian czar. Once more, Japan outfought a well-regarded adversary, picking up several war trophies from the Russian Empire, including a foothold in Manchuria, a province in northern China with abundant raw materials. In 1910, Japan annexed Korea, colonizing and robbing the country of its independence and economic resources. An oppressive, thirty-five-year occupation followed, marked by systemic abuse, confiscation of lands, and enslavement.

Having triumphed over both China and Russia, the Imperial Japanese Army began cultivating an aura of cultural superiority and infusing it across its officer corps. For these modern warriors, Japan was on the cusp of a historic ascendancy — one that promised military supremacy and territorial conquest across the Far East. Military leaders became zealously wedded to the dream of a greater destiny, and civilian authorities who protested or attempted to rein in such ambitions were often slain for their dissent.

Many in Tokyo still advocated a more restrained and peaceful imperialism, fearful of riling the West and jeopardizing future access to commercial markets for Japanese goods. The militants held far more clout, though, and were determined to blaze a different path. Buoyed by the drubbings delivered to China and Russia, they continued to trumpet Japanese preeminence while denouncing European colonization in the Far East and Western thievery of precious Asian resources. Some even sought their own brand of colonization, calling for parts of Japan's surging population to be resettled on the Asian mainland and elsewhere in the Pacific.

Japan's bid to broaden its reach and influence in the world was hardly without precedent. Others had long ruled over or carried out forcible displacements of indigenous populations after deeming them culturally inferior and unworthy of such land and treasure. That included the United States, a colonial power itself in the Pacific with territories in the Philippines and Hawaii. Indeed, Americans were well familiar with the idea of exceptionalism, as claims of Manifest Destiny had once fueled a westward expansion and expropriation of sacred lands inhabited by others. Western Europeans were equally complicit, with a history of exploiting colonies in the Caribbean, Africa, and Asia for their native riches.

By the 1930s, Japan's domestic struggles were matching those of other nations mired in the global economic depression. Joblessness and diminished food stores quickly spread among more than seventy million people packed onto islands collectively the size of California. Arable land for planting crops was limited, and natural resources for industrial production were few, leading to declining trade. With the country's survival and prestige in the balance, and a pernicious mix of nationalist sentiment and racial superiority rippling across the military, Japan's belligerence overseas became increasingly brazen. Powerful forces began maneuvering in Tokyo and beyond to capitalize on opportunities to expand the Japanese empire, boost its industrial output and military prowess, and fulfill its long-awaited destiny.

PRELUDE TO WAR: A TIMELINE OF EVENTS

1914-1918

In August 1914, Japan declares war on Germany, aligning itself with France, Britain, and Russia in the Great War. Though a minor participant in the fighting in Europe, Japanese forces take control of the German-held Marshall, Caroline, and Mariana Island chains in the Pacific. Apart from Guam, a US territory since the Spanish-American War, all are awarded to Japan in the 1919 Treaty of Versailles. The Japanese Empire later develops several Central Pacific islands into air and naval bases as it quietly expands its eastward reach.

1926

Hirohito, just twenty-five years old, becomes the 124th emperor of Japan. The early years of his reign coincide with the rise of ultranationalists in the Imperial Army and Navy, and a ballooning population with inadequate food production and other natural resources to support it.

1927

In China, a fragmented country ruled by regional warlords, Generalissimo Chiang Kai-Shek unifies much of the population under his Nationalist Party. He orders a violent purge of communists, seen as a threat to China's future, sparking a civil war that rages for more than two decades.

1931

SEPTEMBER: Local Japanese troops orchestrate an explosion along a Japanese-operated rail line in Manchuria, a province in northeast China with large coal and iron ore deposits, and immediately blame Chinese saboteurs. Without approval from civilian authorities in Tokyo, Japanese forces seize the nearby town of Mukden, and eventually all of Manchuria, establishing a puppet state under Imperial Army control. The move is seen by the United States as a threat to the longtime "Open Door" policy in China, where all nations had been provided equal trade and commerce opportunities, in return for respecting Chinese territorial sovereignty.

1932

JANUARY: In the first diplomatic move to blunt future Japanese aggression in the Pacific, US Secretary of State Henry Stimson declares the United States will not recognize territorial changes in China brought upon by force or coercion. That same month, protesters in China angered by the occupation of Manchuria stir up boycotts of Japanese products, sparking a wave of violence in the coastal city of Shanghai. Clashes between Chinese and Japanese troops continue until a ceasefire agreement is signed months later.

MAY: Zealous Imperial Navy cadets gun down Japanese Prime Minister Tsuyoshi Inukai, an outspoken opponent of his country's aggression in China and attempts by military figures to usurp the civilian government in Tokyo.

1933

FEBRUARY: With Japan the lone dissenting member, the League of Nations votes to adopt a report blaming the Japanese for the incident in Manchuria. Irked by the condemnation, Japan withdraws from the League.

MARCH: Franklin Delano Roosevelt is inaugurated as the thirty-second president of the United States. The country is ravaged by the Great Depression, and domestic affairs consume the early years of the Roosevelt presidency, as a public wallowing in joblessness and poverty shows little interest in conflicts brewing beyond America's shores.

1936

NOVEMBER: Germany and Japan sign the Anti-Comintern Pact, named for the Communist International, a Soviet organization that promotes worldwide communism. It is the first formal accord between Berlin and Tokyo.

1937

JULY: The Japanese government accuses Chinese soldiers of attacking Imperial Army troops near the city of Peking (present-day Beijing). Tensions escalate, leading to a wider Japanese invasion of China.

AUGUST: Fighting erupts in Shanghai between Japanese and Chinese armies. It is the first major battle of the war, and three months later, the city falls to the Japanese. The Imperial Army occupies cities and coastal areas across much of eastern China but struggles to deliver a decisive defeat to Chiang Kai-Shek's Nationalist army, requiring hundreds of thousands of Japanese troops to remain on the Asian mainland for years to come.

DECEMBER: On the Yangtze River, Japanese planes attack and sink the US Navy gunboat *Panay* as it evacuates American diplomatic personnel from the city of Nanking. Two US sailors are killed, and forty-eight other sailors and civilians are wounded in the bombing, which Japan apologizes for, and claims was a mistake. The next day, Imperial Army forces occupy Nanking, and for six weeks, terrorize the civilian population with a campaign of murder and sexual violence. An estimated 200,000 to 300,000 Chinese are massacred, and tens of thousands of women of all ages are assaulted and raped. The rampage becomes known as the Rape of Nanking and ranks among the worst atrocities of the twentieth century.

1938

JANUARY: The war between China and Japan becomes deadlocked, but the American public—unaware of the carnage in Nanking and unmoved by the attack on the *Panay*—remains wary of possible US entanglement. A Gallup poll finds seventy percent of the country favoring a complete withdraw of American military and civilian personnel from China.

1939

JULY: President Roosevelt views ongoing Japanese encroachment in the Far East and Western Pacific as a direct threat to US strategic interests, but public support for military intervention remains tepid. More than half of all voters favor more measured sanctions instead, such as halting the sale of war goods to Japan, heavily dependent on the United States for most of its oil and aviation fuel.

SEPTEMBER: Germany invades Poland, igniting the start of a larger war that draws in close US allies France and Britain, and gradually sweeps across the European continent.

1940

MAY: In hopes of deterring further Japanese aggression, the United States Fleet is temporarily relocated from the West Coast to a forward position at Pearl Harbor, a naval base in the Hawaiian Islands.

JULY: The US Congress authorizes production of nearly 200 new warships. Though such a boom will expand the Navy by seventy percent, none of the ships are expected to be completed before 1942. The United States also imposes additional economic sanctions on Japan, subjecting steel, scrap iron, aviation fuel, and other raw materials to export licenses, clamping down on sales to Japanese interests.

AUGUST: Leaders in Tokyo call for a Greater East Asia Co-Prosperity Sphere, a self-sustaining political and economic union among Asian countries. Though purportedly a move to counter Western colonialism, the proclamation is regarded by the United States and others as a ploy to legitimize Japan's military aspirations, which likely include the commandeering of resource-producing territories long-held by Western powers.

SEPTEMBER: To elevate its global standing and negotiating power with the United States, Japan joins with the fascist governments of Germany and Italy in signing the Tripartite Pact. With the signees pledging to provide mutual military assistance if any party is attacked by a power not yet at war, the agreement is widely interpreted as an attempt to discourage US intervention in Europe and Asia. That same month, Congress passes the Selective Training and Service Act, requiring all American males between the ages of twenty-one (later lowered to eighteen) and thirty-five to register for the military draft.

DECEMBER: With the British faltering against the Nazi war machine, Roosevelt challenges the country in a national radio address to draw upon its vast manufacturing capacity to create an "Arsenal of Democracy." A nationwide enterprise is soon underway to build record volumes of ships, planes, tanks, and other weapons of war for both the US and friendly nations.

1941

January: Roosevelt is inaugurated for an unprecedented third term in office.

February: The United States Fleet is reorganized, with the Atlantic Fleet permanently assigned to the East Coast, the Asiatic Fleet to the Philippines, and the Pacific Fleet to Pearl Harbor.

April: Officials from Tokyo and Moscow sign a nonaggression pact, assuring the Japanese they will face no opposition from the Soviet military while expanding their empire. The two countries maintain their neutrality until 1945.

June: To bolster the protection of North American shipping convoys from German submarines, the US Navy transfers an aircraft carrier and two dozen battleships, cruisers, and destroyers from the Pacific Fleet to the Atlantic Fleet, reducing its naval forces in the Pacific by over twenty percent.

July: After Japanese troops move into French Indochina (present-day Vietnam), within striking distance of nearby British and Dutch territories, the White House orders all Japanese assets in the United States frozen. American exports of oil and aviation fuel to Japan are also halted, and Japanese leaders conclude they must choose between abandoning their campaigns in China and Southeast Asia in hopes of relieving the sanctions or going to war with their Pacific rivals.

September: Diplomatic efforts fail to defuse tensions, and the two sides reach a stalemate. Washington refuses to accept any Japanese occupation of China, insisting military operations there must end, while Tokyo demands America cut off all aid to

Chiang Kai-Shek's forces and resume oil and fuel exports to Japan.

OCTOBER: Prince Fumimaro Konoe, the prime minister of Japan and an advocate for peaceful settlement with the United States, resigns from office. Konoe supported a withdrawal of Japanese troops from China, but his replacement, General Hideki Tojo, is a hawkish Imperial Army minister who adamantly opposes such concessions.

NOVEMBER 26: In Washington, Secretary of State Cordell Hull submits a set of conditions to the Japanese ambassador for lifting the US trade embargo, including the removal of Japanese forces from China and Indochina. Japan wrongly interprets this as an ultimatum—one that promises dire consequences if Japan fails to comply with American demands. Five days later, Emperor Hirohito endorses the decision to go to war.

NOVEMBER 27: Admiral Harold R. Stark, Chief of US Naval Operations, sends an urgent message to American bases in the Pacific: "This dispatch is to be considered a war warning. Negotiations with Japan…have ceased. An aggressive move by Japan is expected within the next few days."

• • • • •

Hirohito

Hirohito (1901–1989) was the longest serving Japanese emperor, with a reign that lasted from 1926 until his death sixty-three years later. Considered a living god, he enjoyed boundless reverence among his subjects, who worshipped their spiritual leader unconditionally, feeling bonded to him as they would a beloved parent.

A constitutional monarchy since the late nineteenth century, Japan operated under a parliamentary system of government, with elected representatives serving in a legislative body known as the Diet. The constitution also vested substantial executive powers with the emperor, who served as both head of government and commander-in-chief of the armed forces. Advised by a Cabinet and Privy Council, Hirohito delegated the daily machinations of governance to ministers and other surrogates.

Hirohito was no firebrand, but like those leading Japan into war, he was a nationalist. He sought to emulate the British model of constitutional monarchy, reigning without ruling, and allowed his government to sort out questions of policy and politics. Though he generally refrained from the micromanagement of military operations, he did weigh in on several momentous decisions, including the invasion of China and the attack on Pearl Harbor, approving plans for both and siding with the militants pushing the country into war.

Following the Japanese surrender in 1945, many demanded Hirohito be tried as a war criminal and accept full responsibility for Japanese atrocities against civilian populations and POWs. Allied authorities concluded Hirohito was likely aware of wrongdoing in China, the Philippines, and other conquered lands, but decided his public trial and potential removal from the throne might jeopardize post-war political stability Japan desperately needed. As an alternative, Hirohito agreed to renounce his divinity, an act that reduced the emperor to a powerless figurehead. In the years that followed, the country continued to distance itself from its imperial legacy and traditions, adopting a new constitution and sweeping political and social reforms. Japan eventually developed into a leading democratic and economic power.

Genevieve Grotjan

Genevieve Grotjan graduated from the University of Buffalo with a passion for mathematics. With the Great Depression ravaging the economy and few teaching opportunities available, she accepted a position as a statistician with a small federal agency. In 1939, Grotjan left that post to join the US Army Signal Intelligence Service, aiming to put her math skills to greater use. As Japan and the United States edged closer to war, Grotjan was trained as a cryptanalyst, and joined a secretive effort to decipher coded messages intercepted from the Japanese diplomatic corps. In late 1940, the 27-year-old achieved a breakthrough, discovering a key correlation that enabled the team to unlock the diplomatic codes and translate the intercepts.

For years, this codebreaking coup provided invaluable early warnings and pivotal insights about Tokyo's foreign policy objectives that often guided Japanese military strategies. Grotjan worked on other Japanese codes as well, then turned her attention to a trove of intercepted cables from the Soviet Union, a US ally. Here, too, Grotjan led the way in solving the puzzle, eventually unmasking a network of Soviet spies embedded across American government and industry. In 2010, four years after her death, Grotjan was inducted into the National Security Agency's Cryptologic Hall of Honor.

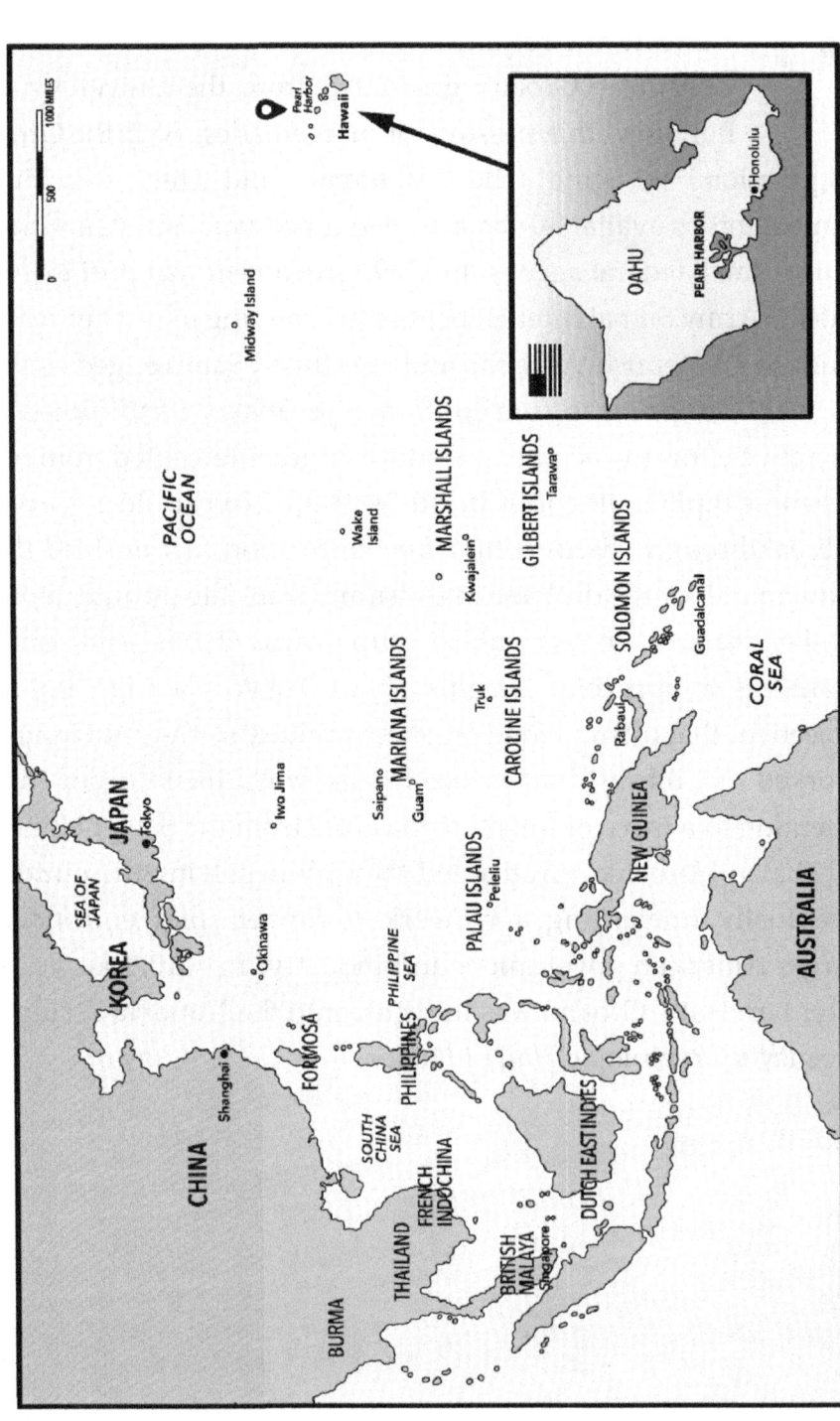

20
DAY OF INFAMY
DECEMBER 1941

"I have said this before, but I shall say it again and again and again: Your boys are not going to be sent into any foreign wars."
–**President Franklin D. Roosevelt, 1940**

"Nine minutes after 8 a.m., we blew up."
–**Louis Conter, 19-year-old sailor aboard the USS *Arizona***

In the early months of 1941, the Imperial Japanese Army was on the march, sweeping across stretches of China and Southeast Asia with relative ease. As it pushed closer to Western-held territories with abundant raw materials, the United States levied new economic sanctions against Tokyo, suspending exports of oil and military-related goods. The measures, intended to deter further aggression, only antagonized Japanese officials, who refused to be cowed by those they considered their lessors. Nor were they willing to slow their pursuit of a greater destiny.

As the two rivals continued to drift toward war, the Japanese held a clear advantage. Their military was already mobilized and seasoned by years of battling the Chinese, while America's armed forces remained woefully unprepared. Stocks of planes and tanks were few, weapons and machinery were dated, and recently approved naval modernization plans were still in their infancy. As autumn approached, diplomatic sparring intensified, and with little hope of bridging the divide, Japanese leaders quietly approved plans to end the standoff. They plotted to unleash their military might, beginning with a surprise, preemptive move against America's largest base of operations in the Pacific.

· · · · ·

With the Nazi onslaught consuming much of the European continent and preoccupying the most prominent colonial powers on the globe, the Japanese sensed opportunity. Across the Far East, lightly defended British and Dutch territories brimmed with prized resources that could transform Japan into a self-sustaining regional power and end its dependency on American and European imports.

Viewing war as their only viable path to survival, the Japanese hierarchy weighed where to strike first. Britain and Holland each maintained a military presence in the Far East, but their forces were modest and posed little threat to Japanese ambitions. It was the United States Navy that loomed instead as the most formidable obstacle in the Pacific. Admiral Isoroku Yamamoto, commander-in-chief of the Japanese Combined Fleet, thus devised a plan to raid Pearl Harbor, the large naval base on the Hawaiian island of Oahu. Crippling the American fleet anchored there would isolate bases and territories thousands of miles from the nearest aid, clearing a path for the Japanese.

The operation began in late November. A powerful armada commanded by Admiral Chūichi Nagumo steamed from the Japanese home islands, led by six of Japan's premier aircraft carriers, their flights decks and hangar bays filled with hundreds of torpedo-bombers, dive-bombers, and fighter planes. With war not yet declared, the operation depended on secrecy, and to their fortune, the ships steamed across the expanse of the Pacific undetected. As they reached the end of their journey, Nagumo received discouraging reconnaissance reports suggesting the three American aircraft carriers in the Pacific were missing from the Hawaiian base. It was true, as two of the carriers were ferrying aircraft to island outposts, while the third was operating off the West Coast.

There was better news about the American battleships. Widely considered the backbone of the Pacific Fleet—aircraft carriers had not yet been tested in war and were thus an unknown commodity in 1941—all were accounted for. Seven of the battleships were reportedly moored together alongside Ford Island, in the center of Pearl Harbor, forming what was commonly known as Battleship Row, as an eighth rested in a nearby dry dock, undergoing repairs. Also at anchor and sprinkled across the large harbor were two heavy cruisers, six light cruisers, twenty-nine destroyers, and dozens of auxiliary ships, submarines, and other smaller vessels. An extensive supporting infrastructure surrounded the fleet, including ship repair and maintenance facilities, the largest fuel repository in the Pacific, and a naval air station on Ford Island.

Other than offshore naval patrols, primary responsibility for defending the harbor from air attacks fell to US Army fighter squadrons operating from airfields dispersed across the island. With both Army and Navy elements based on Oahu, a shared command structure was in place. Admiral Husband E. Kimmel, commander-in-chief of the Pacific Fleet, managed all naval air and sea activities, while Lieutenant General Walter C. Short commanded the Army air forces, anti-aircraft batteries, and infantry troops responsible for safeguarding the anchored ships.

The pair would later be harshly reprimanded for lax preparations. A cable had arrived from Washington on November 27, explicitly warning of likely hostilities in the Pacific, yet Kimmel and Short implemented few changes in Hawaii. Both were convinced the Japanese would strike first far closer to their home islands, with American bases in the Philippines and British and Dutch colonies in Southeast Asia the most inviting targets. Their analysis correctly identified targets of interest to the Japanese, but wrongly assumed the Japanese were incapable of executing multiple operations at once and indisposed to venturing far from their own waters.

It was a significant miscalculation, but Kimmel and Short were hardly alone, as Western military commanders across the Pacific were equally complacent. Still, the lack of readiness at Pearl Harbor was egregious. Kimmel had taken comfort in the harbor's forty-foot waters, aware plane-launched torpedoes required a minimum depth of seventy-five feet to function properly. Short, his Army counterpart, mostly concerned himself with the native population, many of whom were of Japanese ancestry. To prevent sabotage, he ordered Army fighter planes clustered on open tarmacs, wingtip to wingtip, to allow easier nighttime guarding. Their removal from protective shelters would prove disastrous.

After days of navigating hazardous weather, the Japanese fleet reached its destination on December 7, some 230 miles north of Oahu. Nagumo issued the launch order, and in the pre-dawn twilight, the first wave of attack aircraft—183 total planes—lifted off from the wooden flight decks of the six carriers. As the large formation drew closer to its target, the ships and air defenses in Hawaii should have had some warning, but a series of miscommunications derailed any chance of alarms sounding prior to the attack.

The first opportunity came hours before the Japanese air groups took to the sky, when multiple messages from Tokyo to its embassy in Washington were intercepted and decrypted by US intelligence operators. With the intercepts signaling an attack was imminent somewhere in the Pacific, alerts were hastily wired to key military posts from the West Coast to the Philippines. The one exception was Hawaii, where atmospheric conditions blocked the transmission of military cables. A coded, commercial telegram was sent instead, arriving in downtown Honolulu at 7:33 a.m., with the incoming Japanese planes just thirty-five miles away. Unaware of its urgency, the telegram was carefully decoded and then passed to a messenger for delivery to Army headquarters miles away. It was eventually handed to General Short, hours after the attack ended.

Another opportunity came at 6:53 that morning when a message arrived at a Pearl Harbor command center from the USS *Ward*, patrolling the harbor approaches. The destroyer reported tracking and sinking a two-man "midget" Japanese submarine surreptitiously attempting to enter the main channel. Nearly twenty minutes passed before news of the incident reached Admiral Kimmel's staff, but even then, Kimmel opted against issuing an immediate alert to the base. Reluctant to sound a general alarm on an early Sunday morning, he waited instead for confirmation of the sinking.

The submarine was not the only early sighting. Minutes after the *Ward* made its report, an Army radar station operating from the island's northern coast spotted a large formation of planes approaching Oahu. It was brand-new technology at the time and manned by two trainees, who reported their findings to an information center. An equally inexperienced duty officer dismissed the report, mistaking the formation for a flight of American B-17 bombers expected to arrive that morning from California. The information went no further.

"Tora, Tora, Tora"

As the Japanese strike force closed to within visual range of Pearl Harbor, it was clear the Americans were not expecting an attack. The skies and waters were devoid of air or shipping traffic, and with Sundays generally a day off, most naval crewmen were still slumbering below decks or having breakfast with shipmates. Others, including many senior commanders, were ashore on liberty. Anti-aircraft guns were unmanned and unloaded, with most of the ammunition stowed away under lock and key.

Just before eight o'clock, the Japanese flight commander radioed the coded message "Tora, Tora, Tora" to Admiral Nagumo and others, signaling surprise had been achieved. The planes broke off to pre-assigned targets across Oahu, with torpedo-bombers and high-altitude bombers concentrating on the ships at anchor, and dive-bombers targeting the surrounding airfields. Fighter planes were to provide air cover and join in strafing the tarmacs.

The Japanese pilots descended on their targets and the Sunday morning serenity vanished in an instant. The harbor erupted, rocked with explosion after explosion as bombs and torpedoes slammed into battleships trapped helplessly at their moorings. Just minutes after the first bombs fell from the sky, all of Battleship Row was ablaze.

Sailors scurried to their battle stations and gun crews joined the action, but just minutes into the attack, an armor-piercing bomb struck the venerable USS *Arizona*. It penetrated a forward ammunition magazine stocked with gunpowder and shells, and the earsplitting blast ripped apart the front of the ship, producing a shock wave felt miles away. Enveloped by flames, the doomed ship quickly sank beneath the harbor surface, taking more than 1,100 sailors and Marines with it, including twenty-three sets of brothers. Losses on the *Arizona* accounted for nearly half of all American fatalities suffered that morning in Hawaii.

Unable to maneuver, the other battleships were also mauled. Several torpedoes penetrated the hull of the USS *Oklahoma*—the Japanese had modified the weapons to overcome the shallow water depths—causing the ship to capsize and trap hundreds of crewmen below flooded decks. Bombs and torpedoes also tore open holes on the USS *West Virginia* and USS *California*, filling their hulls with seawater and sending both ships to the harbor bottom.

The airfields fared little better. Bombing and strafing attacks destroyed entire squadrons parked in the open, leaving the airstrips strewn with burning wreckage. Several Army pilots gamely attempted to get their planes in the air, but few made it aloft.

An hour after the mayhem began, a second wave of 170 planes swooped in, pasting the harbor and airfields again. Battleship Row became an apocalyptic scene, the fiery ships surrounded by pools of burning oil, floating corpses, and injured seamen swimming for their lives. Amid the horrors came an inspiring sight, as junior officers aboard the USS *Nevada* managed to get the battleship underway, hoping to reach the open sea. As the wounded dreadnought limped down the channel past the other vessels engulfed in flames, Japanese bombers converged, walloping her repeatedly and slowing the great ship as it neared the channel entrance. In danger of sinking, the *Nevada* was intentionally beached to avoid blocking the narrow opening and trapping the fleet inside.

After two hours, the raid was over. Fires still raged across the harbor as Nagumo considered a third wave to destroy fuel stores and ship repair facilities. But with the American aircraft carriers still unaccounted for, and anti-aircraft fire over the island intensifying, Nagumo considered the risk to his fleet too great and ended the attack. He withdrew, leading his ships to safer waters.

Aftermath

With the heart of the Pacific Fleet out of commission, the attack on Pearl Harbor was widely perceived as a disaster for the United States. The Japanese were jubilant, steaming away after sinking four American battleships, damaging others, and decimating air defenses on Oahu. News of the air strike reached the US mainland, where Americans from coast to coast gathered around their radios and glumly tuned in to the shocking reports filling the airwaves. The casualty count—2,403 Americans killed and 1,178 wounded—stunned the nation.

Regardless of the one-sided outcome—the Japanese lost just twenty-nine planes—it was far less a victory than Yamamoto hoped. His forces had demonstrated the value of naval air power, yet the American aircraft carriers had escaped any damage and remained a threat to Japanese aspirations in the Pacific. Moreover, the failure to target the harbor's fuel storage tanks, shipyards, dry docks, and submarine pens—all undefended—proved a grievous error. Had Nagumo's planes destroyed the base infrastructure, including the only stockpile of fuel in the Pacific, the American fleet might have been compelled to retreat to the West Coast, drastically limiting its radius of future operations. Repair facilities were also still functional, allowing six of the eight battleships to eventually return to service. Only the *Arizona* and *Oklahoma* never saw action again.

Nonetheless, the raid had incapacitated the US Pacific Fleet in the near-term, and Imperial Army and Navy operations were soon underway across the breadth of the Far East and Pacific. In a matter of months, the Japanese Empire would expand to its farthest reaches.

The day after the attack, with fires still smoldering across Pearl Harbor, a somber President Roosevelt stood before Congress and requested a formal declaration of war. The senators and congressmen in attendance responded with rousing applause, their shared grief and wrath uniting partisans from across the political divide. Roosevelt's opening words resounded across the nation and world, signifying the Nation's resolve and a watershed moment in American history: "Yesterday, December 7, 1941—a date which will live in infamy—the United States of America was suddenly and deliberately attacked by naval and air forces of the Empire of Japan."

Within hours, Congress passed the declaration, and the president signed it into law. The United States was at war.

* * * * *

Isoroku Yamamoto
As a young naval officer, Isoroku Yamamoto (1884 – 1943) traveled extensively in America, first as a student at Harvard University and later while serving as a military attaché in Washington. He became an observer and admirer of the country's industrial capacity, quickly grasping the strategic advantages of such unrivaled production means. By the time Yamamoto advanced to command the Japanese Combined Fleet, his experiences in the United States had become profoundly influential to his decision making.

Yamamoto privately doubted Japan could prevail in prolonged conflict, having concluded America's resources and manufacturing power were simply too much to overcome. As the two countries crept closer to war, he crafted a strategy to overcome American strengths, beginning with a decisive strike against the Pacific Fleet that would gash the American Navy in the short-term and clear a path for territorial gains. Still, Yamamoto understood far better than others that the United States would not be subdued for long.

Through the highs and lows of the first year of war, Yamamoto remained the most iconic and consequential figure in the Japanese military. In April 1943, American codebreakers discovered details of his arranged visit to forward bases in the South Pacific. With approval from the highest levels, eighteen P-38 *Lightning* long-range fighter planes ambushed Yamamoto's transport plane and escorts, killing the revered admiral. The shootdown deprived the Imperial Navy of its most accomplished and irreplaceable leader and delivered a deflating blow to Japanese naval operations in the Pacific.

At the time of the Pearl Harbor attack, the USS *Arizona* was filled with hundreds of thousands of gallons of fuel oil. To this day, oil continues to leak from the sunken hulk at the bottom of the harbor.

Dorie Miller

Doris "Dorie" Miller, a 22-year-old grandson of slaves and native of Waco, Texas, was a crewman aboard the battleship *West Virginia*. With African American sailors only permitted to serve as mess stewards and barred from other billets and duties, Miller was assigned to the ship's galley. During the raid on Pearl Harbor, Miller carried the ship's mortally wounded captain to safety, then took position behind an unmanned .50-caliber machine gun he had never fired, shooting at the attacking planes until he expended his ammunition. After aiding other sailors, Miller was among the last to abandon ship. The first African American sailor to be awarded the Navy Cross for gallantry in combat, Miller was killed two years later when his ship was torpedoed by a Japanese submarine.

Naval Modernization

Once considered the most powerful element of the US Pacific Fleet, the aging, lumbering battleships were already surpassed in late 1941 by more contemporary Japanese battleships as well as newer American models in production. In time, the battleship losses at Pearl Harbor became mostly inconsequential as aircraft carriers and their air groups, unproven in combat before World War II, became the preeminent weapons in the Pacific Theater.

Donald Stratton

Donald Stratton was born in 1922 in rural Nebraska. His father was a sharecropper, farming land owned by others, and the family struggled to make ends meet during the Great Depression years. After graduating high school in 1940, the 18-year-old enlisted in the United States Navy, where he was billeted to the USS *Arizona*, one of the finest battleships in the Pacific Fleet.

On the morning of December 7, 1941, Stratton had just finished breakfast below decks and was delivering fresh fruit to a sick shipmate when the first bombs began to fall across Pearl Harbor. As the general alarm sounded, Stratton raced to his battle station and joined his gun crew in firing at the Japanese dive-bombers and torpedo planes aiming for the anchored ships. Unable to maneuver, the *Arizona* was struck by several torpedoes and armor-piercing bombs, including one that penetrated several decks and detonated in one of the ship's ammunition magazines. The *Arizona* exploded from within, tearing apart the ship with a massive blast. Protected from the thunderous explosion by a steel enclosure, Stratton found himself in an inferno with intense heat and flames enveloping the ship. With severe burns on much of his body and part of his ear missing, Stratton found a path of escape. A sailor on a vessel anchored nearby had secured a line of rope between the two ships, allowing Stratton and a handful of others to scamper over.

It took months for Stratton to recover from his injuries, including numerous surgeries and skin grafts. During his painful recovery, Stratton's weight dropped from 170 to 92 pounds, but he survived, and was medically discharged from the Navy in September 1942. He returned to Nebraska to continue recuperating, but ultimately rejoined the fight, re-enlisting in the Navy in early 1944. Assigned as a gunner aboard a destroyer, Stratton saw extensive action throughout the final months of the war in the Pacific. He died in 2020.

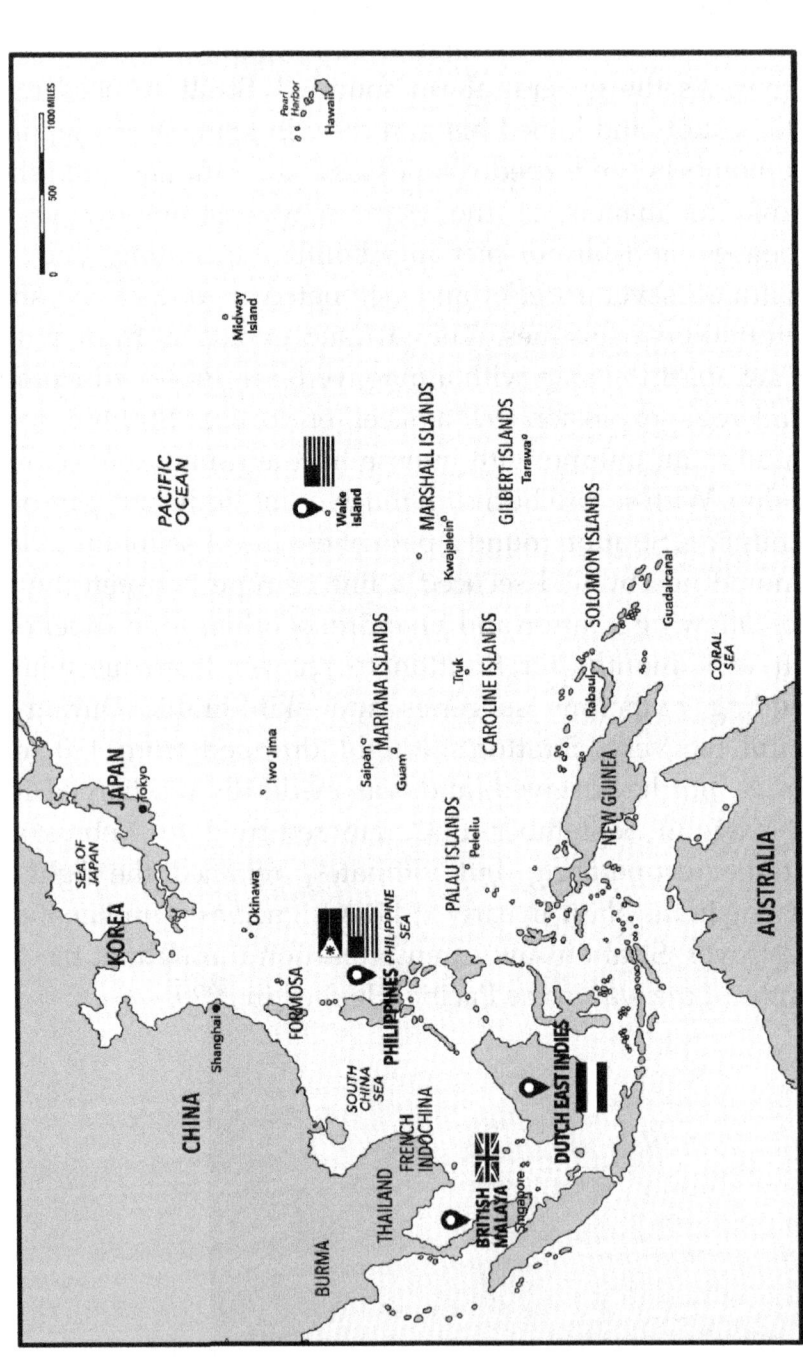

21
PACIFIC RETREAT
DECEMBER 1941–APRIL 1942

"If I am told to fight regardless of the consequences, I shall run wild considerably for the first six months or a year."
–Admiral Isoroku Yamamoto, October 1940

"We are shutting down. Goodbye 'till better times. Long live the Queen!"
–Final radio message from the Dutch East Indies, March 1942

With billowing smoke still darkening the skies over Pearl Harbor, the Japanese turned to the next phase of their strategy — the seizure of British, Dutch, and American territories across the Far East and Western Pacific. They bombed far-flung bases with deadly precision, followed by meticulously planned ground assaults against undermanned and isolated garrisons. The proficiency and experience of the Imperial Army was on full display, with the Japanese proving far more capable tacticians than anticipated, skillfully coordinating and executing multiple operations thousands of miles apart.

The Philippines posed the greatest challenge. The archipelago of more than 7,000 islands was home to the largest concentration of American air and sea power outside Hawaii, as well as America's most acclaimed military leader. Amid plummeting morale after a string of early defeats in the Pacific, US-led forces in the Philippines began a defiant, months-long stand, enduring unbearable conditions and hardships. Their resolve was welcome news at home, offering faint but desperately needed hope and inspiration to those monitoring the unexpected trouncing from afar.

• • • • •

WAKE ISLAND

A US territory since 1898, Wake Island was a desolate atoll. More than 2,000 miles from both Japan and Hawaii, its three islets barely covered three square miles, and the highest elevation topped off at twenty feet. It was of little value until 1935, when it became a refueling stop for the Pan American *Clipper*, a four-engine seaplane flying the airline's signature transpacific route.

In early 1941, more than 1,100 civilian engineers and construction workers arrived on Wake, commissioned to build new facilities for expanded air and submarine operations. A battalion of Marines soon followed, and defensive preparations continued into late autumn, when heavy artillery batteries were sited along the shoreline. The base lacked radar—still in early development and limited use—but a squadron of Marine Corps F4F *Wildcat* fighter planes was welcomed in early December, adding not only its firepower but aerial reconnaissance to the island defenses.

Days later, the small garrison had just learned of the Pearl Harbor attack when Japanese bombers struck without warning. Casualties were light, but the raid hit the air squadron hard, destroying more than half of the Marine fighter planes on the ground. The bombings continued until December 11, when Japanese troop transports churned toward the coastline, accompanied by three light cruisers and six destroyers. Attempting to land an invasion force, the Japanese ships were driven away by exemplary, long-range gunnery from the

Marines, who sank two of the destroyers with their coastal batteries.

As the Japanese resumed their bombing campaign, determined to chip away at the Marine air and ground defenses, a relief expedition sailed from Pearl Harbor. The task force, led by the aircraft carrier USS *Saratoga* and laden with additional Marines and fighter planes for Wake, was slowed by delays and refueling mishaps, allowing a second and much larger Japanese armada to arrive first. Backed by two aircraft carriers, they attempted another amphibious assault on December 23, this time successfully putting ashore 1,600 troops.

The Marines were outnumbered four-to-one, but as the two sides grappled in the early morning darkness, the *Saratoga* and her escorts were just 400 miles away, closing in on Wake. Officials at Pearl Harbor, wary of the Japanese naval forces offshore and unwilling to risk losing one of the Pacific Fleet's few aircraft carriers, ordered the ships to turn back. Those aboard were enraged, with Marine and Naval officers alike aghast at the idea of abandoning the Americans on Wake. Heated words were exchanged on the bridge of the *Saratoga*, bordering on mutiny, but the admiral in command ultimately complied with his orders. The Wake Island Marines were on their own.

To bolster the thin defenses, stranded civilian construction workers shouldered rifles and joined the Marines in the trenches, but the Japanese continued to surge forward, overrunning many of the outer defensive lines. Just before dawn, the island's command post wired a grim message to Pacific Fleet headquarters in Hawaii: "Enemy on island. Issue in doubt." With ammunition dwindling, internal communications severed, and the lives of so many civilians in jeopardy, the garrison surrendered. Forty-nine Marines, three sailors, and seventy civilians died in the fighting, with hundreds of Marines and other base personnel, along with more than 1,000 civilian contractors, taken prisoner. Japanese casualties were substantially higher—an estimated 800 to 1,000 of their marines and sailors were dead—but the United States had suffered its first significant defeat.

MALAYA AND SINGAPORE

Two hours before Admiral Nagumo's planes appeared above Pearl Harbor, the Imperial Navy began shelling British Malaya (present-day Malaysia). Brimming with raw materials essential to the production of war goods, the colony was also a stepping-stone from mainland Asia to the oil-rich Dutch East Indies. When the naval bombardment lifted, Imperial Army troops flooded across the border from adjoining Thailand, joined later by troops landing on the Malayan coast. They marched down the peninsula, steamrolling past the paltry Commonwealth forces in their path.

In response, the British Royal Navy dispatched the mightiest Allied warships in the region to attack the Japanese beachheads. Sailing without air cover, the battleship HMS *Prince of Wales* and battle cruiser HMS *Repulse* were soon swarmed by waves of Japanese land-based bombers. Struck by multiple bombs and torpedoes, each of the Goliaths sank in little time. The losses, a shocking and dispiriting blow to the Royal Navy, provided a vivid demonstration of the impact of air power at sea, with even the most powerful naval vessels no longer free to venture wherever they pleased.

By the end of January, the Japanese were in full control of the Malayan Peninsula. They turned their attention to Singapore, the British naval base and strategic jewel just off Malaya's southern tip. The stronghold controlled the sea lanes between the Pacific and Indian Oceans, and was defended by a robust garrison, including tens of thousands of British, Australian, Indian, and Malayan troops. In command was British Lieutenant General Arthur Percival, and though he outnumbered the invaders, most of his Commonwealth troops had little training and carried dated weapons. When the Japanese began their assault on the island-fortress, the garrison exhausted its ammunition and water supplies within days, forcing Percival to surrender after just a single week of resistance. The swift fall stunned Britain and much of the world, with Winston Churchill branding it the "worst disaster and largest capitulation in British military history."

In less than two months, the Japanese had achieved an extraordinary feat, capturing Malaya, its invaluable natural resources, and more than 130,000 Allied prisoners. It cost the Imperial Army fewer than 10,000 casualties.

Dutch East Indies

With Japan's early objectives hinging on the ability of its naval forces to traverse the sprawl of the Pacific, winning control of the East Indies (present-day Indonesia) was imperative. The Japanese had limited reserves of petroleum, and the archipelago, a centuries-old Dutch colony comprising thousands of islands, produced sixty million barrels of oil each year, as well as abundant other resources Japan coveted.

The campaign began in mid-December with assault troops landing on the islands of Celebes and Borneo, followed by an invasion of Sumatra in February. As the Imperial Army battled the Dutch-led defenders on land, the opposing naval fleets clashed in nearby waters, leading to the first large-scale, ship-to-ship battle in the Pacific. It happened in the Java Sea, where a mix of British, American, Australian, and Dutch cruisers and destroyers attempting to block an invasion armada were met by a comparable force of Japanese cruisers and destroyers. The Japanese dominated the action, drubbing the Allies and topping off the rout with the sinking of the USS *Houston*, a heavy cruiser. The loss of the flagship of the US Asiatic Fleet and largest American warship west of Hawaii, coupled with the earlier sinkings of the *Prince of Wales* and *Repulse*, shattered Allied sea power in the region and opened the door for Imperial Army forces to storm onto Java, the grandest prize in the East Indies chain. By early March, the entire territory and its oil reserves were in Japanese hands.

THE PHILIPPINES

The Philippines, acquired by the United States following the Spanish-American War in 1898, became a self-governing commonwealth in 1935. The American military continued to operate there, drawing the ire of officials in Tokyo, who viewed those forces as a threat to planned operations in China and Southeast Asia, as well as the sea lanes connecting Japan to its greater empire.

In truth, US-led forces on the Philippines were of mixed strength. A professional army of 19,000 American soldiers and 12,000 American-trained Filipino scouts was ably led by a US Army legend, General Douglas A. MacArthur, but several divisions of Philippine Army troops MacArthur relied on to augment his forces were mostly reservists with little training and poor weapons. There was a potent air element in the Philippines — thirty-five modern B-17 *Flying Fortress* bombers and more than 100 P-40 *Warhawk* fighter planes — but the US Asiatic Fleet at Cavite Naval Base, America's largest Pacific outpost outside Hawaii, was a collection of relics. The Fleet's single heavy cruiser, later sunk in the Java Sea, was supported by just two light cruisers and thirteen World War I-era destroyers. Other than submarines and auxiliary ships, that was the extent of naval power available in the Western Pacific to thwart the might of the Imperial Japanese Navy.

There was also poor communication and coordination among the American forces, rooted in longstanding interservice rivalries. Once Navy officials in the Philippines were notified by Pearl Harbor of the strike in Hawaii, they rushed to mobilize their fleet in case of a similar attack at Cavite. No one bothered to inform Army headquarters in Manila, the Philippine capital. MacArthur would not learn of the news from Pearl Harbor until one of his radio operators heard reports over the commercial airwaves while listening to a California radio station.

Army ground forces were immediately placed on alert, and General Lewis Brereton, commanding the air groups, sought out MacArthur for permission to raid a large Japanese airbase on nearby Formosa with his B-17s. MacArthur, however, was oddly in seclusion and uncommunicative, preventing Brereton from taking offensive action. Concerned Japanese bombers might raid the Philippine airfields, Brereton ordered his planes aloft to prevent their loss on the ground. After several hours, no raid had materialized, and most of the circling aircraft returned to refuel. As ground servicing of those planes was underway, radar detected a large formation of incoming aircraft. Like Pearl Harbor, communications faltered, failing to provide early warning, and the Japanese bombers and fighter planes pummeled the airfields. By the end of the very first day of the war, half of the aircraft in MacArthur's inventory had been destroyed on the ground, crippling his defenses.

In the days ahead, small detachments of Japanese began landing on the main island of Luzon, followed by a full invasion force of 43,000 men. As they pushed toward Manila, MacArthur ceded the capital and shifted his army into more defensible positions in the jungles of the Bataan, a peninsula some twenty-five miles wide. With few provisions, the plucky Americans and Filipinos, known as "the battling bastards of Bataan," held out for weeks, fending off relentless Japanese attacks while running short of food, ammunition, and medicine. Scores fell ill to tropical disease.

In early March, with the front lines beginning to buckle, President Roosevelt ordered MacArthur to personally evacuate the islands. The consequences of his potential death or capture—

both to enemy propaganda and morale on the home front—were unthinkable, and though MacArthur was resistant at first, he ultimately followed orders. After transferring command to his immediate subordinate, Major General Jonathan Wainwright, MacArthur departed on a Patrol, Torpedo (PT) boat, slipping past the Japanese and eventually reaching the island of Mindanao in the southern Philippines. From there, the general was flown to Australia in a B-17.

By early April, the remaining men on the Bataan Peninsula were starving and on the brink of collapse. Three out of every four were so weakened by malaria and dysentery they were deemed unfit for duty. Unable to further resist, some 76,000 debilitated Americans and Filipinos surrendered, hoping to receive desperately needed food and medical attention. Their ordeal was just beginning, though, as conditions proved even worse in Japanese captivity. In blazing heat, the survivors were marched at gunpoint to prison camps nearly sixty-five miles away, deprived of food, water, and care for the wounded and sickly. Those who passed out from exhaustion or illness, or attempted to aid others on the jungle trail, were bayoneted or savagely beaten, as others were randomly executed and beheaded. An estimated 10,000 prisoners died on what became known as the Bataan Death March, the vast majority Filipinos.

Despite the mass surrender—the largest in American history—smaller pockets of US-led forces still battled across the islands, including on the small, rocky island of Corregidor, just off the mouth of Manila Bay. Wainwright led some 11,000 malnourished men there, most wounded or wilted by disease, and ensconced in an intricate underground tunnel system. Japanese bombers and heavy artillery hammered the tunnels and defensive perimeter day and night, until early May, when the first assault troops and tanks rumbled ashore. The remaining able-bodied Americans and Filipinos attempted to hold them back, but they were far too few, and with no hope of reinforcement or evacuation, and thousands of sick and wounded men continuing to suffer, Wainwright surrendered Corregidor and the Philippines the next day.

Aftermath

Yamamoto's opening strategy delivered as promised, chalking up a number of early conquests. Among them was Guam, an island base in the Central Pacific, where a few hundred lightly armed US Marines succumbed to more than 6,000 Japanese just days after the Pearl Harbor attack. Two noteworthy British possessions also fell. The strategic port of Hong Kong, defended by a mix of Commonwealth and Chinese troops, was attacked shortly after Pearl Harbor and surrendered on Christmas Day. Coupled with the later seizure of Burma (present-day Myanmar), the Japanese effectively sealed off the last pipelines for shuttling supplies and ammunition to Chinese Nationalists still resisting the Imperial Army. Chiang Kai-Shek's forces continued to battle with limited means, but closure of the supply routes mostly cut off the Chinese from the outside world.

Throughout those early months, tens of thousands of Allied soldiers became prisoners of war. Much abuse and suffering followed, as the Japanese adhered to an ancient ethos that considered surrender a mark of dishonor and an affront to their sacred warrior code. It fueled contempt and rage toward those they defeated and led to the torturing and beating of prisoners. Those who survived the barbaric conditions languished in slave labor camps for the duration of the war.

In the United States, demoralizing news continued to trickle in from across the Pacific Theater, badly shaking the American people. Many became fixated on avenging Pearl Harbor and thirsted for any sort of victory, no matter how small or large. It was a sentiment shared by the White House, and an audacious scheme soon came together to bloody the Japanese on their own soil. It was such a closely guarded secret, only President

Roosevelt and a handful of military officials were privy to the plans.

It was time for the United States to strike back.

• • • • •

Douglas A. MacArthur

Douglas A. MacArthur (1880–1964) was one of the towering figures of the war, and one of the most familiar, often posing for photographs with his trademark sunglasses and corn-cob pipe. He had retired in 1937 after a lengthy career that included service in World War I, as superintendent of West Point, and as chief of staff of the US Army. With war tensions swirling in the Pacific, MacArthur was recalled to active duty in July 1941 and named commander of US Army Forces in the Far East. Headquartered in the Philippines, he developed a close attachment to the Filipino people, and when his subordinate surrendered the territory in early 1942 after his departure, it was a stinging blow. MacArthur's famous declaration after arriving in Australia—"I shall return"—would have great bearing on Allied strategy once the United States began turning the tide in the Pacific.

MacArthur was later appointed to lead the Southwest Pacific Area, commanding all Allied ground, naval, and air forces in Australia and New Guinea. His wartime record was a mix of success and failure, beginning with the paralysis in the Philippines that led to the early destruction of US air forces. MacArthur rebounded, though, and from his base in Australia, deftly assembled great masses of men and materiel for a counteroffensive in the Pacific. Within months, his armies were pushing the Japanese back in New Guinea and across other jungle islands, and by the middle of 1944, MacArthur was poised to reclaim the Philippines. To some critics, that subsequent invasion—a victory with much bloodshed among US forces and the Filipino population—may have been driven as much by MacArthur's sense of personal obligation as it was by larger US strategic objectives.

On September 2, 1945, MacArthur presided over the final Japanese surrender aboard the battleship USS *Missouri* and later commanded American occupation forces in Tokyo. He became a revered figure there, and after North Korea invaded South Korea in 1950, MacArthur was appointed head of all United Nations forces in the region. His record there, too, was mixed, and his repeated clashes with President Truman over strategy led to his controversial removal in 1951. Though he was often mentioned as a possible Republican presidential contender, he never embarked on a political career. MacArthur died in 1964 at the age of eighty-four.

Henry Elrod

Captain Henry Elrod was a 36-year-old Marine Corps aviator who embodied the resolve of the Wake Island Marines. An exceptional fighter pilot, Elrod tangled at one point with twenty-two Japanese planes by himself, downing two of them, and later single-handedly sank an enemy destroyer, an extraordinary feat for a fighter pilot. When he no longer had an operable plane to fly, Elrod joined the beach defenses as a rifleman. The day Wake fell to the Japanese, Elrod was killed while protecting fellow Marines carrying ammunition to a gun emplacement. He was later awarded the Medal of Honor, posthumously.

Fighter Planes

In 1941, the most advanced US fighter planes in the Pacific were the Navy's F4F *Wildcat* and the Army's P-40 *Warhawk*, each outclassed by the Japanese A6M *Zero*. The *Zero*, a speedy, highly maneuverable aircraft, remained Japan's stalwart fighter for the entire war, but it was surpassed in 1943 by a trio of newly arrived and advanced American fighters. In the final two years of war, the Navy F6F *Hellcat*, the Army P-38 *Lightning*, and the Navy/Marine Corps F4U *Corsair* came to dominate the Pacific skies, with the *Hellcats* alone downing more than 5,100 enemy planes. Nearly 35,000 of the new American fighters were manufactured during the war, compared to fewer than 11,000 *Zeros* produced by Japanese factories.

ⓘ Many Japanese weapons were superior to those of the United States early in the war, torpedoes foremost among them. The nearly thirty-foot-long, Type 93, "Long Lance" torpedoes launched from submarines and destroyers took a deadly toll on American ships throughout the opening months of the war, most notably in the Solomon Islands. American torpedoes, in contrast, were plagued with deficiencies. Far less speedy and dependable than Japanese variants, they routinely failed to explode upon contact, often breaking in two when slamming into the hull of a ship. Such defects were not remedied until the third year of the war.

Ann Bernatitus

Ann Bernatitus, a native of Exeter, Pennsylvania, was one of 11,000 women to serve as nurses with the US Navy during the war. In the early 1930s, with the country immersed in the Great Depression and her parents unable to afford college, Ann turned to medicine, eventually joining the Navy Nurse Corps. When the war began, the 29-year-old surgical nurse was stationed in the Philippines, and once General MacArthur moved his ground forces into the jungles of Bataan, Bernatitus joined dozens of other Army and Navy medical personnel in staffing makeshift field hospitals. As the two armies battled across Bataan, Bernatitus and the other nurses and doctors treated thousands of wounded and sickened soldiers, even as Japanese planes bombed their hospital compound. Those nurses who stayed with the wounded soldiers became known as the "Angels of Bataan."

In early April, Bernatitus was ordered to the island of Corregidor, where the remaining American-led forces would make their final stand. Thousands were stricken with disease, including Bernatitus, who suffered from severe dysentery, a debilitating intestinal infection. She was evacuated by submarine in early May with a small group of other nurses and civilians shortly before the final US surrender, but sixty-six Army and Navy nurses who remained behind were eventually taken prisoner. Joined later by eleven Navy nurses captured in Manila, the women were held by the Japanese until their liberation in 1945.

Six months after her evacuation, Bernatitus became the first US servicemember to be awarded the newly created Legion of Merit, one of the most prestigious American military decorations. She returned to the Pacific Theater later in the war, serving as the senior nurse aboard a hospital ship during the 1945 invasion of Okinawa, where she survived a battery of kamikaze attacks by suicidal Japanese pilots who ignored the large, red crosses marking the hospital ship from bow to stern.

After the war, Bernatitus continued to serve in the Navy, advancing to the senior rank of captain, a rarity for a woman in those years. She retired in 1959 and died in 2003.

22
THE DOOLITTLE RAID
APRIL 1942

"I was scared to death...Anyone who says they weren't is a goddamned liar."
–Richard Joyce, 22-year-old bomber pilot

In the weeks following the attack on Pearl Harbor, President Roosevelt continued to stew over the Navy's losses in Hawaii. Increasingly flustered by the spate of demoralizing setbacks across the Pacific, and aware of the dim public mood, he convened a White House meeting of his senior military advisors. Filled with resolve, he ordered a retaliatory strike against the Japanese home islands—one that would lift the morale of distraught Americans and signal to the enemy the United States was not without power and reach.

His generals and admirals were flummoxed at first, unable to conceive of such an attack. Not only were American forces in poor condition from years of neglect, both the Army and Navy were reeling across the Pacific. Guam was lost, the Marines on Wake Island were hanging by a thread, and soldiers in the Philippines equipped with World War I-era rifles and helmets were bracing for a full-scale invasion. With no practical means in sight for delivering any form of retribution, the meeting adjourned without a solution, as the Japanese continued their stampede across the Pacific.

· · · · ·

The new year arrived, and Roosevelt's top military minds were still wrestling with the challenge of delivering a meaningful blow to the Japanese. The once-powerful battleships of the Pacific Fleet were off the table, as all were either resting on the bottom of Pearl Harbor or undergoing extensive repairs. The handful of aircraft carriers in the Pacific were a more viable option, but carrier-based planes had limited fuel capacity, requiring a launch relatively close to Japan. That would leave the flattops, already outnumbered by a three-to-one ratio in the Pacific, easily detectable by enemy air and sea patrols — a gamble the Navy could ill-afford.

The Army Air Forces had more suitable aircraft, including longer-range bombers that could deliver substantial payloads, but with the Philippines under assault, the Army lacked an air base within reach of Japan. The Soviet Union, just across the Sea of Japan, was close enough, and an American ally in the war against Nazi Germany, but the Soviets had signed a neutrality pact with the Japanese in 1941. With a massive German army already penetrating deep into Soviet territory, the Kremlin had little interest in risking its accord with Japan by aiding the United States.

Three weeks after Roosevelt's White House meeting, an aide to Admiral Ernest J. King, the newly appointed commander-in-chief of the United States Fleet, pitched a novel idea. If long-range Army bombers could be launched from an aircraft carrier, the ships could remain safely distant from Japanese waters and undetected by offshore patrols. It had never been attempted, as heavier bombers typically required an airstrip of at least 1,200 feet to lift off, and a carrier deck allowed barely a third of that, but Admiral King thought the idea was worth exploring.

Though subsequent test flights proved such a launch was plausible, landing the bombers on a short deck in a pitching sea was a nonstarter. An alternative was proposed—one that depended on the bombers completing their mission with enough remaining fuel to reach mainland China rather than return to an aircraft carrier. They could land at makeshift airfields in the coastal provinces, but with Japanese occupation troops nearby, the bombers would have to be quickly refueled and flown farther inland to areas under Chinese control. It was an exceedingly risky proposition for the bomber pilots, and left little room for error or unforeseen variables, but with no other tenable options, the mission was swiftly approved.

The aircraft chosen for the operation was the sturdy, twin-engine B-25 *Mitchell* bomber. The B-25s were larger than naval carrier planes and could carry more ordnance and fuel, but to keep the planes light and maximize their flight range, each was limited to just four conventional or incendiary bombs. Stripped of other excess weight, the bombers were fitted with special internal tanks to carry every possible drop of additional fuel. They would strike their targets at night, limiting the exposure of the bombers to Japanese air defenses.

There were sixteen total planes—the most that could be squeezed onto the end of a flight deck—crewed by five men each. The eighty officers and enlisted men, all volunteers, were led by Lieutenant Colonel James Doolittle, an iconic figure in Army aviation who left college in the final year of World War I to become an Army fighter pilot. He quickly proved to be an exceptional, natural flier—so much so, he was held out of the last months of the war to train other young airmen.

In between the two wars, Doolittle separated from the Army but continued to hone his flying skills. After visiting Germany in 1939 and witnessing its rapid mobilization and embrace of air power, he urged the War Department to expand and modernize its modest inventory of warplanes. He rejoined the Army, and after the Pearl Harbor attack became a top aide to General Henry "Hap" Arnold, head of the Army Air Forces. When it came time to select an officer with the requisite skill and temperament to lead the bombing raid against Japan, Doolittle was the obvious choice.

For security purposes, he shared nothing with his bomber group about their destination and targets. The information remained secret and known just to a handful of those involved, with the pilots and crewmen informed only that the mission would be exceptionally hazardous. They trained for weeks in Florida, practicing short takeoffs, night flying, and low altitude bombing before ferrying their planes to the West Coast in March. The Army bombers were then loaded onto the USS *Hornet*, the Pacific Fleet's newest aircraft carrier, in San Francisco Bay, and lashed topside to one end of the flight deck. With no space to spare, the ship's own aircraft were consigned to the hangar bay below, the naval pilots relegated to bystanders for the mission.

The *Hornet* was joined at sea by its protective escorts, including another aircraft carrier, the USS *Enterprise*, and several cruisers, destroyers, and oil tankers. Leading the task force was Admiral William Halsey Jr. — gruff, tough-minded, and the most respected sea commander in the Navy. By April 17, his ships were less than 1,000 miles from Japan and still unspotted. The aircraft carriers and cruisers refueled one last time before leaving the destroyers and slow-moving oilers behind, knifing their way closer to Japan.

THE RAID

The next morning, Halsey and Doolittle faced an urgent dilemma. A small Japanese patrol craft had spied the task force and radioed a warning, and Japanese ships and planes were expected to soon converge on their position. The *Hornet* would have to launch the B-25s immediately for the task force to make a safe escape, but the ships were more than 200 miles away from the planned launch point, a distance that would jeopardize available fuel for the bombers' 1,000-mile leg to China. An immediate launch would also result in a daylight raid, leaving the bombers susceptible to enemy fighter planes and anti-aircraft batteries.

Halsey and Doolittle never wavered. In heaving seas, the sixteen B-25s rumbled down the flight deck of the *Hornet* one at a time, lifting off and assembling into formation as they raced toward the Japanese shore. Hours later, the squadron reached land, passing over the coastline at treetop level. Most of the planes continued toward Tokyo, with others breaking off for Yokohama, Nagoya, Kobe, and Osaka. Targets included industrial plants, airplane factories, oil refineries, dockyards, and other essential infrastructure. Residential areas were to be avoided, as were hospitals, schools, and the Imperial Palace, the sacred home of Emperor Hirohito.

As the B-25s approached their targets, they were surprised by the absence of any enemy fighter planes. Hours had passed since the American ships had been sighted, but Japanese air defenses were dormant, as home defense officials had wrongly presumed the aircraft carriers carried only short-range naval planes. Expecting the ships to steam far closer to Japan before launching their planes, an attack was not anticipated until the next morning.

Once the bombers appeared over Tokyo, air raid sirens finally sounded, bringing Japanese air defenses to life. Anti-aircraft guns blanketed the sky with heavy flak, but it was mostly inaccurate—none of the planes sustained serious damage—nor did enemy fighter planes have time to intercept the raiders. The B-25s reached their drop point unscathed, releasing their payloads over several industrial targets. With so few bombers, only a small number of structures were hit, and the handful of fires were soon brought under control. Damage was light, but the impact on the Japanese was precisely as intended. Conditioned to believe their homeland was impenetrable, millions watched in shock and horror as plumes of smoke drifted above their cities, the first inkling the Japanese had of their own vulnerabilities.

Escape and Retribution

With their bomb bays empty, the B-25s banked away from their targets and began the long trek toward China. One plane developed fuel problems and was forced to navigate to the Soviet Union, where it touched down safely at a Siberian airfield. The Soviets, predictably loath to provoke Japan, interred the five men and refused to allow them to continue their journey. They were held for thirteen months before their release in 1943 and eventual safe return home.

The other fifteen planes flew on, their fuel tanks beginning to empty, but a miraculous tailwind came to their aid, pushing the bombers closer to the Chinese coastline. Out of fuel, they were unable to reach the temporary airfields, forcing the crews to either crash-land their planes or bail out and parachute to the surface. Three raiders lost their lives while ditching, with the survivors left scattered across the Chinese coast. Local villagers and peasants reached the airmen in little time, smuggling them away from Japanese patrols and overland to safe harbor.

In the weeks following the raid, sixty-four of the Doolittle Raiders made it to friendly territory, but not all were so fortunate. Eight fliers were captured by the Japanese, who mercilessly tortured the men before executing three of them. The remaining airmen were imprisoned until the end of the war, with all but one surviving captivity.

Enraged by the role of the Chinese, the Japanese ordered reprisals across the occupied territories. Reminiscent of their atrocities five years earlier in Nanking, Imperial Army troops tramped through villages and towns, murdering, torturing, and raping civilians by the thousands, few of whom had any involvement with the American fliers. The Japanese even employed biological weapons, contaminating farm fields, food supplies, and water wells and reservoirs with typhoid and other deadly toxins. In the end, an estimated 250,000 Chinese were killed in retaliation for a raid that claimed just eighty-seven Japanese lives.

Aftermath

Compared to what the Japanese had wrought at Pearl Harbor, the Doolittle Raid caused little meaningful damage to military and industrial facilities in the home islands. Still, to American officials unaware of the Chinese suffering to come, the mission was a resounding success. It demonstrated the ability of the United States to carry the war to Japanese soil and lifted morale across the American military and home front, galvanizing servicemen and civilians alike after so many early defeats.

Beyond the powerful, psychological blow that shattered Japanese illusions of invincibility, there were practical repercussions as well. To defend the home islands, several fighter squadrons were ordered to return to Japan, pulling many of the Imperial Army's best pilots and planes away from combat theaters. For Admiral Yamamoto, the raid validated his long-held anxiety about the American aircraft carriers and the threat they posed to Japanese aspirations in the Pacific. Unnerved by the bombing attack, Yamamoto's superiors heartily approved his plan to lure the American carriers into a fight on the open sea, leading to the most consequential naval engagement of the entire war.

· · · · ·

 Not counting the 46-year-old Doolittle, the average age among the fifteen other B-25 pilots was twenty-six years.

Thomas White

First Lieutenant Thomas White, just five years out of Harvard Medical School, volunteered to serve as the flight surgeon for the Doolittle Raid. When his plane crash landed in water, White remained onboard the sinking aircraft until he could retrieve his medical kit and surgical instruments, barely escaping before the plane plunged beneath the surface. He was later awarded the Silver Star for his care of wounded fliers during their escape in China, including one pilot who suffered several gruesome and painful injuries in his crash-landing and had to have his leg amputated by White.

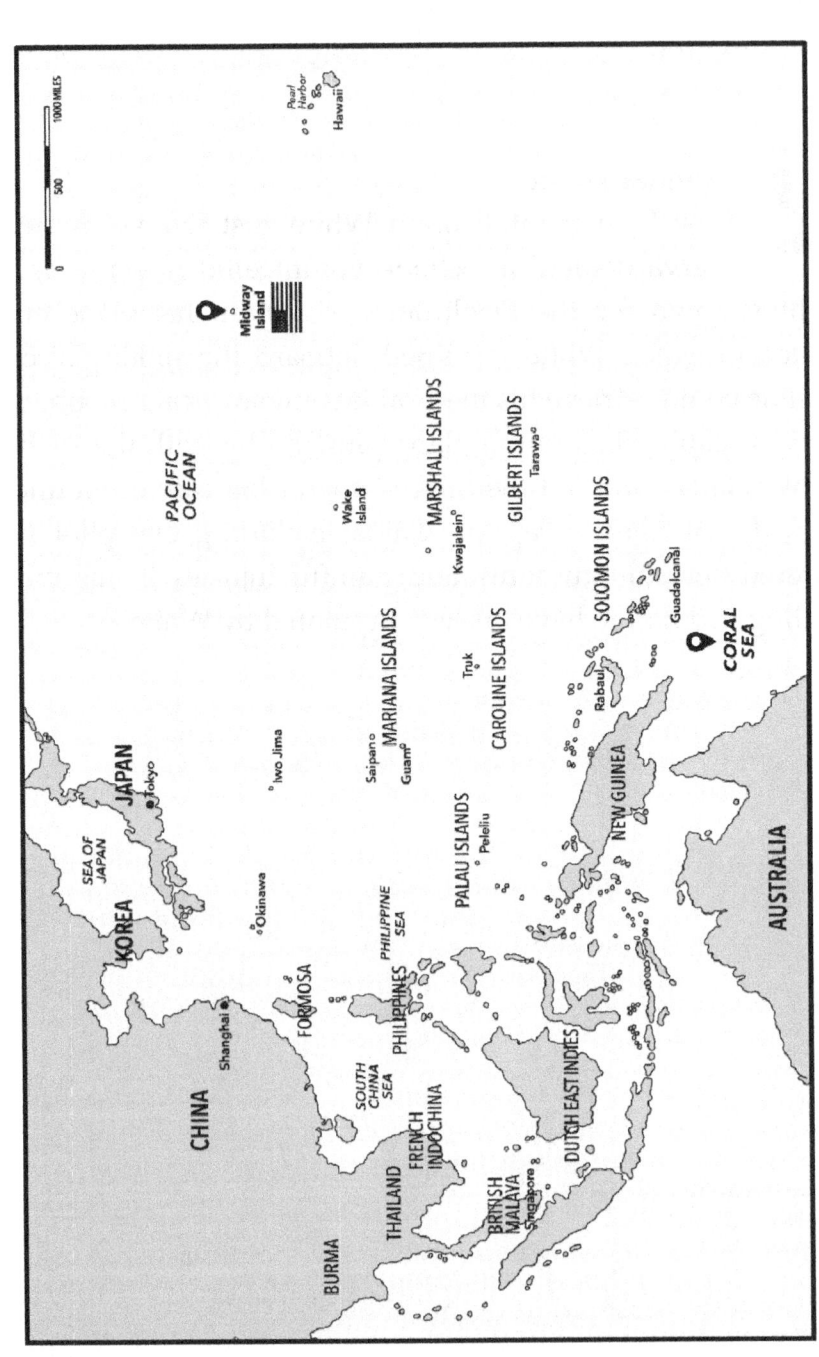

23
MIDWAY: THE TURNING POINT
JUNE 1942

"I used the red circle on the bow as my target."
–US Navy pilot Norman "Dusty" Kleiss, describing his dive-bombing attack on the *Kaga*

"We started this war and we are responsible for this disaster. We should all commit hara-kiri."
–Imperial Japanese Navy staff officer, using the term for ceremonial suicide, June 1942

News of the Doolittle Raid rippled across the United States, sparking waves of euphoria and exultant headlines entirely absent from the opening months of the war. Among military officials, the festive mood soon gave way to sobering reality, as the Japanese still held advantages in every corner of the Pacific.

Just two weeks after the bombs fell on Tokyo, a Japanese armada steamed toward Port Moresby, an Allied base on the large island of New Guinea. The outpost was vital to the defense of Australia, a country vulnerable to invasion and where the Americans planned to rebuild their forces for a counteroffensive. The approaching Japanese fleet was no surprise, as message traffic decrypted weeks earlier by US Naval intelligence signaled such an operation was brewing. In response, Admiral Chester W. Nimitz, commanding the US Pacific Fleet, ordered a pair of aircraft carriers into the Coral Sea to intercept the Japanese ships.

The ensuing battle marked a pivotal moment in naval history. Until that time, opposing fleets had fought their duels under the heavy guns of great warships, lobbing massive shells across open water. In the Coral Sea, attacks on ship formations were conducted exclusively by competing air groups, launched from ships never in sight of each other. It was a first, and a precursor of what was to come, with naval air power emerging as a core element of the war in the Pacific.

Nimitz's move successfully thwarted the planned Japanese invasion, but it came at great cost. The Pacific Fleet, already limited to just a few aircraft carriers, lost the USS *Lexington*, while another, the USS *Yorktown*, suffered a bomb hit that carved a massive hole in its flight deck. The Japanese fared slightly better, losing only a small aircraft carrier, but of greater consequence was the fate of two top-line aircraft carriers. With one sustaining substantial damage and the other losing much of its air group, neither would be available just a month later for what became Japan's most ambitious naval operation to date, a ploy by Yamamoto to bait the remaining US aircraft carriers into a lethal trap.

• • • • •

Midway was another small Pacific atoll, with each of its two islands barely two miles across. Just 1,100 miles from Pearl Harbor, Midway's greatest asset was its airstrip, from where a mix of Army, Navy, and Marine Corps planes guarded the northern approach to Hawaii.

Yamamoto's plan was elaborate. After a diversionary raid far to the north in the Aleutian Islands, his aircraft carriers would strike Midway with sudden surprise, just as they had Pearl Harbor six months earlier. The objective was to destroy Midway's air group, clearing the path for 5,000 assault troops to land on the atoll and overpower the Marine garrison.

Yamamoto, an avid poker player, was gambling such an aggressive move so close to Hawaii would draw the remaining US aircraft carriers from the safety of Pearl Harbor, allowing his own massive fleet to deliver a crushing and decisive blow to American naval power in the Pacific.

Unfortunately for Yamamoto, his grand operation was no secret. In May 1942, US Naval intelligence acquired several Japanese intercepts pointing to a future attack on a target codenamed "AF." With cross-references to other intercepts suggesting AF might be Midway, radio operators on the atoll were secretly instructed to send a cable over open channels reporting problems with their water distillation plant. Falling for the ruse, another Japanese message was subsequently intercepted suggesting fresh water may be in short supply at "AF." Midway had become the confirmed target, providing one of the great intelligence coups of World War II.

With details of Yamamoto's plan in hand, Nimitz saw an opportunity to turn the tables. He dispatched his only available aircraft carriers, the USS *Enterprise* and USS *Hornet*, to meet the Japanese forces head-on, long before Yamamoto expected them. Nimitz had one other card up his sleeve. The *Yorktown*, severely damaged in the Coral Sea, was expected to be sidelined for the coming battle, but after limping into Pearl Harbor, Nimitz had the ship boarded by a work party of 1,400 welders, carpenters, electricians, and other tradesmen. Laboring around the clock to repair the flight deck and make the ship seaworthy, the patched-up *Yorktown* was soon steaming toward Midway, only two days behind its sister ships.

Even with the *Yorktown*, the odds were squarely in Yamamoto's favor. He had a superior number of aircraft carriers and escort ships, and his air squadrons were piloted by veterans of the Pearl Harbor attack. Commanding his carrier group once again was Admiral Nagumo, while Admiral Halsey, the most skilled and experienced American fleet commander, was hospitalized, suffering from a severe skin condition. As the two forces converged on Midway from opposite directions, the Americans were not without their own advantages. Their airplanes were generally less maneuverable than those of the Japanese, but far more durable, and the *Enterprise*, *Hornet*, and *Yorktown* were all fitted with radar systems, capable of providing early warning of inbound Japanese attacks. Most of all, they had the element of surprise.

THE BATTLE

Just before daybreak on the morning of June 4, Nagumo launched his first wave of aircraft against Midway. Though the Japanese plan assumed the American carriers were still safely anchored at Pearl Harbor, Nagumo held back half of his planes as a precaution, armed with torpedoes and armor-piercing bombs should any threats unexpectedly appear. Lacking radar, he also ordered scout planes to fan out across the open sea and search for dangers lurking in the waters below.

Once Midway's radar station picked up the incoming Japanese strike force, every operable aircraft was sent aloft. Army B-17s and Navy and Marine dive-bombers flew off in search of Nagumo's carriers, while a squadron of mostly obsolete fighter planes rose to intercept the inbound planes. As the Japanese neared the atoll, the Marine pilots pounced, scoring a few early kills, but their outmoded planes were no match for the *Zeros*.

With Midway's fighter force batted aside, more than 100 bombers and fighter planes swarmed across the two islands. They bombed and strafed the airfield, oil storage tanks, and seaplane hangars, hitting the base infrastructure and Marine defenses hard. The airstrip suffered minimal damage, though, and with the Midway air group already in flight, Midway remained a viable air base, jeopardizing the planned amphibious landing. The Japanese flight leader radioed Nagumo to recommend a second raid, but the admiral was occupied, his fleet under attack and maneuvering to evade bombs and torpedoes from the Midway-based planes. The inexperienced Army and Marine pilots failed to score a single hit, and nearly half were shot down, but the near misses were enough to convince Nagumo that his air commander was right. A second strike against Midway was needed.

Torpedo-bombers standing by for a possible attack against surface ships had to be re-armed with fragmentation bombs more suitable for land targets. As that painstaking process was underway, one of Nagumo's scout planes spotted the American fleet, causing Nagumo sudden consternation. There was no question enemy aircraft carriers were a far bigger threat to his force than Midway, but the timing of the discovery could not have been worse. While Nagumo had some dive-bombers armed and prepared for a carrier strike, he needed to recover and re-arm the *Zeros* that had fended off the Midway-based planes so the dive-bombers would have a fighter escort. His Midway strike force was also returning and desperately low on fuel; he could not recover those aircraft and launch others at the same time. Unwilling to needlessly sacrifice planes and pilots, Nagumo ordered all to land, with each plane to be refueled and armed for an attack against the American aircraft carriers.

Amid this frenzied activity, more American planes arrived. This time it was the torpedo squadrons from the *Hornet*, *Yorktown*, and *Enterprise*, but their attacks were uncoordinated and lacked fighter protection. The plodding, older-model *Devastator* torpedo planes made easy targets for *Zeros* and anti-aircraft fire, and the three squadrons were nearly annihilated. Just six of the forty-one *Devastators* survived the attack, and, like the Midway planes, none registered a hit on the Japanese fleet.

Despite the misses, the torpedo planes sparked the critical sequence of the battle. Forced to dodge oncoming torpedoes, the

Japanese carriers made a series of sharp turns, preventing the launch of their strike force. Attacking from wavetop level, the *Devastators* had also drawn the protective umbrella of *Zeros* to lower altitudes, and to the southeast. The Japanese pilots splashed most of the torpedo planes, but were oblivious to what was happening far overhead, to the southwest and northeast, where forty-nine *Dauntless* dive-bombers from the *Enterprise* and *Yorktown* were lining up to attack.

As the dive-bombers began their vertical plunges toward the Japanese carriers, curtains of anti-aircraft fire filled the sky. Just before pulling out of their dives, the pilots released their payloads, and powerful bombs began punching through the flight decks of the Japanese aircraft carriers. Aboard the *Kaga* and *Akagi*, the blasts ignited furious explosions in hangar bays filled with combustible planes and ordnance, as bomb hits also tore apart a third carrier, the *Sōryū*. Within mere minutes, all three Japanese aircraft carriers were dead in the water and ablaze from bow to stern.

The *Hiryū*, the only Japanese aircraft carrier spared from the strike, immediately launched a counterattack against the American fleet. It was a modest force and most of the planes were shot down, but not before marring the *Yorktown* with three bomb hits. The crew fought desperately to save the ship, but another attack from the *Hiryū* airmen put two torpedoes in the *Yorktown*'s hull, leaving the storied ship burning and foundering in the sea. The *Hiryū* would not escape a similar fate. Attacked late in the day by two dozen *Dauntless* dive-bombers from the *Enterprise* and *Hornet*, the ship burned for hours before it too, was abandoned and sunk with Japanese torpedoes.

Reeling from the jarring loss of four of his best aircraft carriers, Yamamoto had no choice but to withdraw his remaining forces. There were other minor skirmishes, but by June 6, the Battle of Midway was over.

Aftermath

Six months into the war, Midway was the first clear American victory in the Pacific. The US Navy had lost the *Yorktown* and some 360 sailors, but the Japanese suffered far worse, losing four of the six aircraft carriers that took part in the Pearl Harbor attack, some 250 planes, and more than 3,000 dead. The Japanese ships were irreplaceable, a consequence of material shortages and manufacturing inadequacies at home. For the Americans, Midway spawned a newfound confidence, as widely held apprehensions among sailors and pilots about their adversaries finally began to ebb. The Japanese were no longer unbeatable.

· · · · ·

Chester W. Nimitz

Rear Admiral Chester W. Nimitz (1885–1966) was managing a Naval personnel bureau in Washington when he was selected to be the new commander-in-chief of the Pacific Fleet shortly after the disaster at Pearl Harbor. Having commanded submarines, destroyers, and cruisers throughout his lengthy career, the highly regarded Texas native was ordered to "get the hell out to Pearl and stay there until the war is won."

Early in his tenure, the Pacific Theater was divided into two operational areas. General MacArthur, Nimitz's Army counterpart, was assigned the Southwest Pacific, including Australia and New Guinea, while Nimitz managed a broader area that encompassed many of the island chains US forces would need to claim as they pushed the Japanese back across the Pacific.

Nimitz proved an extraordinarily effective leader and strategist and selected competent and experienced subordinates as his tactical commanders. He developed a mostly cooperative relationship with MacArthur, eschewing the sort of competitive rivalry that often encumbered Allied armies in Europe, and abided by a strategy of engaging the Japanese Army on the ground of his choosing, bypassing and cutting off enemy strongholds where the Allies had little to gain and much to lose. Nimitz followed his orders to stay at Pearl Harbor until the job was finished, though he later moved to a forward headquarters on Guam. He arrived in Tokyo Bay on September 2, 1945, aboard his flagship, the battleship USS *Missouri*, where he accepted the Japanese surrender and served as the official signee for the United States.

After the war, Nimitz was promoted one last time to Chief of Naval Operations, a position he held for two years before accepting later postings with the secretary of the Navy and the United Nations. Never retiring from active duty, he died in 1966.

George Gay

Ensign George Gay piloted a torpedo plane off the USS *Hornet* during the Battle of Midway. Of the fifteen *Devastator* crews in his squadron, the 25-year-old Gay was the lone survivor. Crash landing his damaged plane within sight of several Japanese ships, Gay floated for hours in the sea, hiding under his rubber seat cushion and clinging to an uninflated life raft. He was rescued the next day by a floatplane, and two months later, returned to combat. Gay became a flight instructor for the Navy, and after the war, a commercial pilot for Trans World Airlines. When he died in 1994, the Navy spread his ashes in the Pacific waters where the rest of his squadron had perished.

Radar

Radio Detection and Ranging (radar) was still an experimental technology when World War II began. Designed to pinpoint distant ships and aircraft and track their heading and speed, every US aircraft carrier was equipped with an early system by the time the Japanese attacked Pearl Harbor. The technology continued to progress, resulting in wider use that gave American forces a significant advantage during surface and air battles, including at Midway. The Japanese trailed far behind in the development of such technology, unable to convince their German allies to share technical secrets, leaving the systems they produced inferior, erratic, and of little use.

Codebreakers

Though US intelligence had been able to decrypt intercepted diplomatic cables since 1940, Japanese military communications proved a thornier challenge. A breakthrough came in the early months of the war when Station Hypo—the Navy's radio intelligence center at Pearl Harbor—made significant inroads against a key Japanese naval code, allowing certain intercepts to be deciphered by cryptanalysts and translated by Japanese linguists. The intercepts provided early knowledge of Japanese intentions, timetables for planned operations, and even the composition of forces. With the Japanese unaware their code had been compromised, the decrypted intercepts tilted early battles at Coral Sea and Midway in favor of the US Navy and continued to yield Japanese secrets for the remainder of the war.

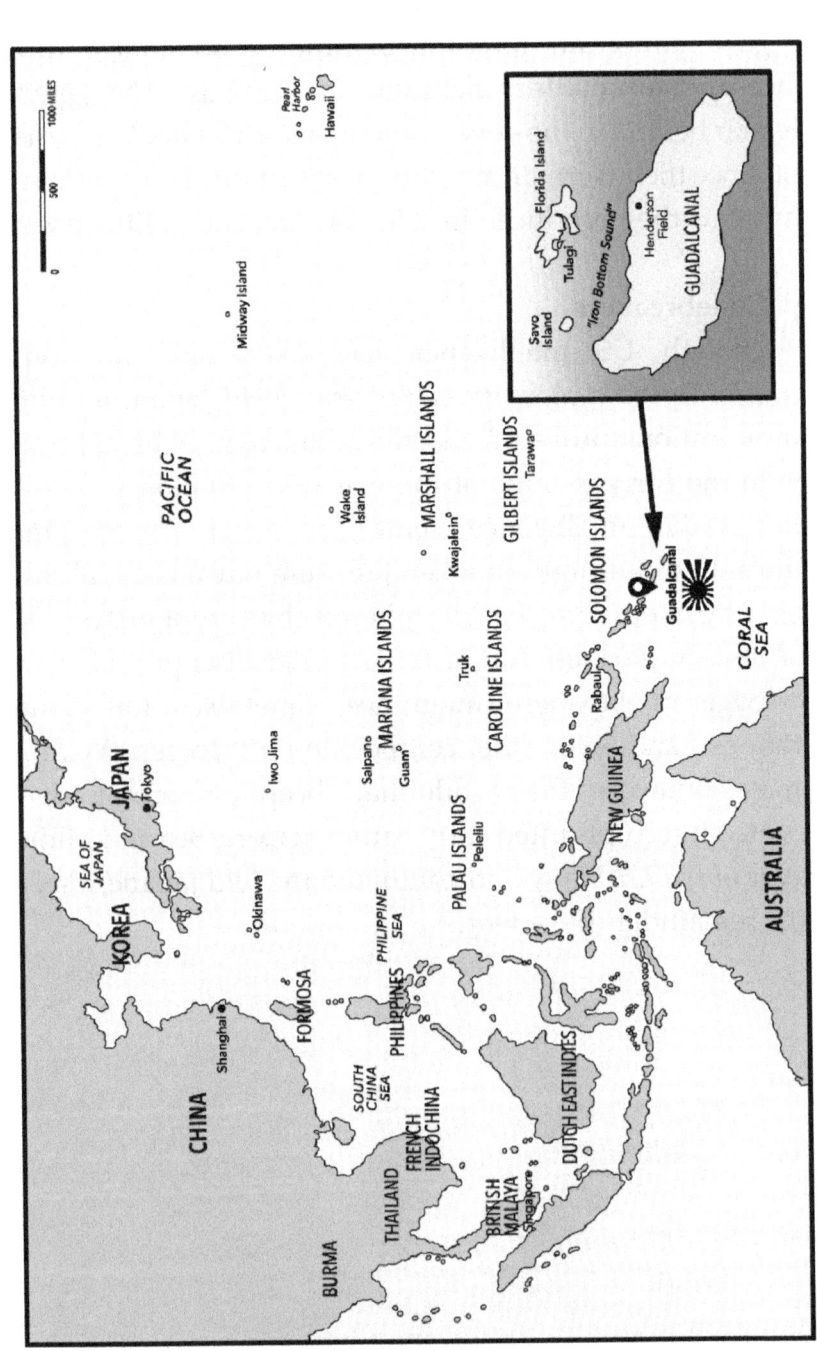

24
GUADALCANAL
AUGUST 1942–FEBRUARY 1943

"These people refuse to surrender. The wounded will wait until men come up to examine them and blow themselves and the other fellow to death with a hand grenade."
–Major General Alexander A. Vandegrift, August 1942

"Nothing can compare to Guadalcanal. That was four months of sheer hell."
–John McCarthy, 18-year-old Marine

As the Navy savored its first meaningful victory of the war at Midway, the War Department continued to manage a historic enterprise at home, scaling up the armed forces to unprecedented levels. Though the conversion of domestic production from consumer to war goods was well underway, months would pass before eagerly awaited quantities of new ships and aircraft arrived in combat theaters. Nor were new divisions of soldiers and Marines fully trained and ready for deployment, despite the induction of hundreds of thousands of enlistees. The men and machinery were desperately needed in the Pacific, where the Japanese still held substantial edges, even after the debacle at Midway.

In early July, a US reconnaissance flight over an obscure South Pacific island spotted Japanese engineers constructing a remote airfield—one that would position long-range bombers within striking distance of the shipping lanes connecting America to close allies Australia and New Zealand. To safeguard those supply and communication lines, a plan was formed to take possession of the airfield before it became operational, as well as the jungle-strewn expanse surrounding it.

The island was called Guadalcanal.

• • • • •

In August 1942, a long column of US naval transports steamed toward the Solomon Island chain in the South Pacific. Just eight months after the attack on Pearl Harbor, the ships carried the lead assault forces for the first large-scale American offensive of the war. The risks were substantial, beginning with the vast distances between the operational area and the nearest Allied bases, and a command structure that lacked experience with complex amphibious landings. With similar campaigns destined to be repeated often across the Pacific, Guadalcanal would serve as an early test of planning and coordination abilities.

Leading the invasion force was the fabled 1st Marine Division, known throughout the Marine Corps as the Old Breed. A mix of pre-war Marines and newer enlistees, the division had orders to capture and hold the unfinished airfield on Lunga Point, some four miles from the landing beaches. Planners expected only moderate resistance, as the Japanese had just a few thousand construction troops and engineers on the island, but the stronghold of Rabaul was just 550 miles away, and vigorous counterattacks were expected. With the transport and supply vessels supporting the Marines particularly vulnerable, Nimitz sent every ship he could spare into the Solomons, including three aircraft carriers and more than thirty cruisers and destroyers. It would not be enough.

THE GROUND ATTACK

On August 7, 1942, the first of 11,000 Marines waded ashore on Guadalcanal, a sprawling island more than ninety-two miles long and thirty-three miles across. The assault troops encountered little opposition along the mostly abandoned coastal area, and as the Marines marched inland toward Lunga Point, they made steady progress across the hilly terrain. The landing zone they left behind, however, would not remain quiet for long. As expected, Japanese bombers and fighter planes arrived from Rabaul, targeting the anchored ships in hopes of choking off support and supplies to the Marines ashore. American naval fighters intercepted the first raids, minimizing their impact, but the aircraft carriers were exceedingly vulnerable in the waters off Guadalcanal and not expected to remain nearby for long.

To the dismay of the Marines, the aircraft carriers and their protective escorts barely lasted a day. They withdrew from the immediate area after citing low fuel among the ships and heavy losses to their fighter groups. Supply ships and a handful of escorts remained nearby, but the Marines ashore were suddenly without air cover, with additional Japanese strikes surely on the way.

The news got worse. In the late-night hours after the aircraft carriers departed, surface fleets collided in the Battle of Savo Island, one of the bleakest chapters in American naval history. The Americans had the advantage of radar, but the Japanese were far more experienced operating their ships in darkness and easily sank four American and Australian cruisers. Stunned by the loss of so much firepower and 1,200 sailors, the remaining supply ships and escorts fled to safer waters, still carrying half of the provisions and ammunition for the Marines.

Cut off from reinforcements and supplies, the abandoned Marines dug in along their tenuous foothold on the island, fortifying a perimeter defense around the captured airfield as they awaited their first clashes with the Imperial Army. Naval construction units labored in blistering heat to complete the landing strip so Marine air squadrons could deploy to the island, but conditions continued to worsen, including dwindling food supplies that forced the men to subsist for days on captured rice and canned fish. The Marines sweltered in the oppressive environment, where a mix of humidity and sporadic rain showers produced infinite mosquitos that feasted on the men, spreading malaria and other diseases.

Determined to wipe out the Marines, the Japanese battered the airfield day and night with naval gunfire and aerial bombardments. The construction crews were resilient, repairing damage after every attack, and on August 20, the airstrip finally became operational. It was given the name Henderson Field after a Marine Corps pilot killed at Midway, and nineteen *Wildcat* fighter planes and twelve *Dauntless* dive-bombers were the first to touch down. Borrowing the code name for Guadalcanal, what came to be known as the Cactus Air Force operated from dawn to dusk, with bleary-eyed Marine pilots and their patched-up planes, joined later by Navy aviators rescued at sea or without carriers to return to, dueling daily with Japanese raiders. Their *Wildcats* were slower and less nimble than the Japanese *Zeros*, but they were also far sturdier, and innovative tactics and maneuvers adopted by the American pilots further evened the odds. Among the "aces" downing at least five enemy aircraft was Marine Captain Joseph Foss, who did not arrive on Guadalcanal until October but shot down more than two dozen enemy planes in just six weeks.

For the Japanese, losses of experienced pilots in the Coral Sea, at Midway, and now in the Solomon Islands were fast becoming a problem, as differences in training between the two sides produced new pilots with sharply contrasting abilities. A distinctive American practice was to rotate veteran pilots into newly formed squadrons to serve as instructors, where they could impart their expertise and experience to new trainees. The Imperial Navy had no such rotational system, and as increasing numbers of experienced pilots were killed in combat, newer airmen were rushed into combat prematurely, with far fewer hours in the cockpit than American trainees and little tutelage from veteran fliers. The disparity in skill became even more pronounced with the arrival of more advanced American fighter planes in 1943.

As opposing ground forces continued brawling on the island, the Marine and Naval pilots also had considerable success chewing up Japanese convoys and slow-moving barges hauling reinforcements and supplies from Rabaul. The Japanese adjusted, shuttling troops and provisions to the island under cover of darkness using their speedier destroyers, a practice dubbed the "Tokyo Express" by the Marines. Though the destroyers had greater success reaching the island, transport capacity was limited, and food stocks eventually became so depleted on Guadalcanal, the Japanese began referring to it as "Starvation Island."

Unable to dislodge the Marines from Henderson Field, the Japanese ordered frenzied charges against the American defenses. Hordes of Imperial Army soldiers, brandishing bayoneted rifles and samurai swords, plunged forward with abandon, shouting battle cries of "banzai," certain they would prevail against those they had been assured were faint-hearted. The Japanese fully expected to push their foes back into the sea, but the Marines remained steadfast, refusing to buckle as they drove back wave after wave of attackers.

As the weeks wore on, neither side could finish off the other. In October, the Japanese landed thousands of fresh troops just as the first US Army soldiers—a regiment of North Dakota National Guardsmen—arrived to reinforce the Marine perimeter. After a ferocious and deafening naval bombardment destroyed much of the Cactus Air Force, the Japanese again attempted to retake the airfield but came under withering fire. By the time the failed offensive ended four days later, close to 3,500 Imperial Army soldiers were dead or missing—more than ten times the number of Americans killed.

THE FIGHT AT SEA

As ground forces slugged it out on Guadalcanal, the two navies continued to battle at sea, filling the adjoining waters with so many sunken wrecks, the area came to be known as Iron Bottom Sound.

Two weeks after their August triumph in the Battle of Savo Island, the Japanese assembled a powerful armada to bombard the Marine defenses around Henderson Field and land additional troops on the island. The American fleet returned and notched a modest victory, sinking an aircraft carrier and preventing the Japanese transports from reaching the shore. The Japanese air groups would soon land their own punches against the American aircraft carriers, sinking the newly arrived *Wasp* and damaging the *Enterprise* and *Saratoga* enough to force their withdrawal. By October, even the *Hornet* – just months removed from ferrying the Doolittle Raiders on their celebrated mission – was on the ocean bottom, blasted apart by bombs and torpedoes.

The competing fleets collided again in November when the Japanese made a final bid to reinforce the island. The two sides lost a combined fifteen battleships, cruisers, and destroyers, and just a fraction of the Japanese troops made it ashore. By December, with the remaining Japanese on Guadalcanal severely weakened by hunger and malaria, and three full divisions of American soldiers and Marines firmly entrenched on the island, leaders in Tokyo finally acknowledged the futility of prolonging the struggle. Emperor Hirohito approved the decision to withdraw, leading to the evacuation of over 13,000 Japanese from the island. By February 9, the fight for Guadalcanal was over.

Aftermath

An astonishing price was paid for control of a single airfield. Neary fifty ships from the two fleets went down in the surrounding waters, and more than 1,200 planes were shot from the sky. The exhausted and disease-ridden men of the 1st Marine Division were relieved in December but would require months to recuperate. Many of the surviving, emaciated Japanese would never recover.

Despite losing half of its remaining aircraft carriers and several cruisers and destroyers, Guadalcanal was a clear win for the United States. Of the 36,000 Imperial Army troops who fought on the island, two out of every three died in battle or from disease. In contrast, of the roughly 60,000 Americans sent ashore, just one in thirty-seven was killed. Perhaps most critical were Japanese losses of planes and experienced pilots, opening the door for American air power to begin dominating the Pacific skies.

The grinding, six-month battle on Guadalcanal was the start of a Japanese retreat that would continue for two and a half years, but the grim fighting also foreshadowed the challenges ahead for American forces. The resolve of the Japanese soldiers, their stubborn refusal to yield ground or surrender to superior forces, and willingness to pay any price to slow their enemy would all become hauntingly familiar to US Marines, soldiers, and sailors in the months ahead on their long, blood-soaked trek across the Pacific.

• • • • •

BUSHIDO

Throughout the Pacific campaign, Japanese officers facing imminent defeat would often order entire companies and regiments to storm fortified American positions with just swords and bayonet-tipped rifles. The irrationality of these banzai charges baffled their American foes, but such sacrifice was the product of a value system foreign to Westerners and deeply rooted in Japanese culture and tradition. For centuries, an ethos known as bushido guided the samurai, Japan's elite warrior class, emphasizing honor and loyalty above all else, including life. As the Imperial Army rose to prominence in the pre-war years, officers embraced this heritage, pledging themselves to the emperor, a deity they considered a living god.

When the Japanese vowed to fight to the end on the emperor's behalf, it was not death they feared in serving him, but dishonor. When defeat loomed, the Japanese devoted themselves to either falling in battle, viewed as an honorable death, or committing seppuku (ritualistic suicide) to atone for battlefield failures. With few willing to surrender—an act considered disgraceful, and under bushido, punishable by death—officers turned to banzai charges instead, convinced bushido and their willingness to sacrifice themselves gave them an edge against Americans consumed with fears of death. Such devotion, however, could not overcome American firepower, and on island after island, failed banzai charges only hastened the collapse of Japanese resistance.

John Basilone

On the evening of October 24, 1942, Marine Sergeant John Basilone was leading a forward section of Marines with two .30-caliber machine guns when nearly 3,000 Japanese attacked his battalion. The 25-year-old led his section in a spirited defense, at one point firing a heavy machine gun while gripping the iron-hot barrel in his bare hands and suffering severe burns. Later awarded the Medal of Honor, Basilone returned home to a hero's welcome, and though he could have stayed stateside, he insisted on returning to combat. Basilone was killed in action on February 19, 1945, leading his men on Iwo Jima.

Seabees

Early in the war, a critical need emerged for specialized units of skilled men capable of building bases, hospitals, airfields, roads, housing, piers and docks, and other needed infrastructure on islands across the Pacific. The Navy began recruiting skilled workers with construction experience, including carpenters, electricians, plumbers, heavy equipment operators, and dozens of other trades, and formed them into Naval Construction Battalions. The initials "CB" produced an instant nickname—Seabees—that stuck.

Because they were forward deployed, the Seabees received combat training and adopted the motto *Construimus Batuimus*, "We Build, We Fight." And fight they did, as Seabees often went ashore with the first waves of assault troops and took up arms when defenses they were preparing fell under enemy attack. On Guadalcanal, the 6th Naval Construction Battalion became the first Seabee unit to serve under combat conditions, patching up Henderson Field again and again as it was bombed and shelled by the Japanese.

Aurelio Tassone embodied the spirit of the Seabees when he was serving with a road-building detachment during an Allied assault in the Treasury Islands. As he and his crew drew heavy fire from a Japanese pillbox, Tassone raised the blade on the bulldozer he was operating and drove it right into the structure, caving it in on top of the occupants and silencing its guns.

More than 325,000 Seabees served in the war, building some 400 island bases. Indispensable to the war effort, they took part in amphibious operations from Normandy to Okinawa, earning thirty-three Silver Stars—including the one awarded to Tassone—and five Navy Crosses for gallantry.

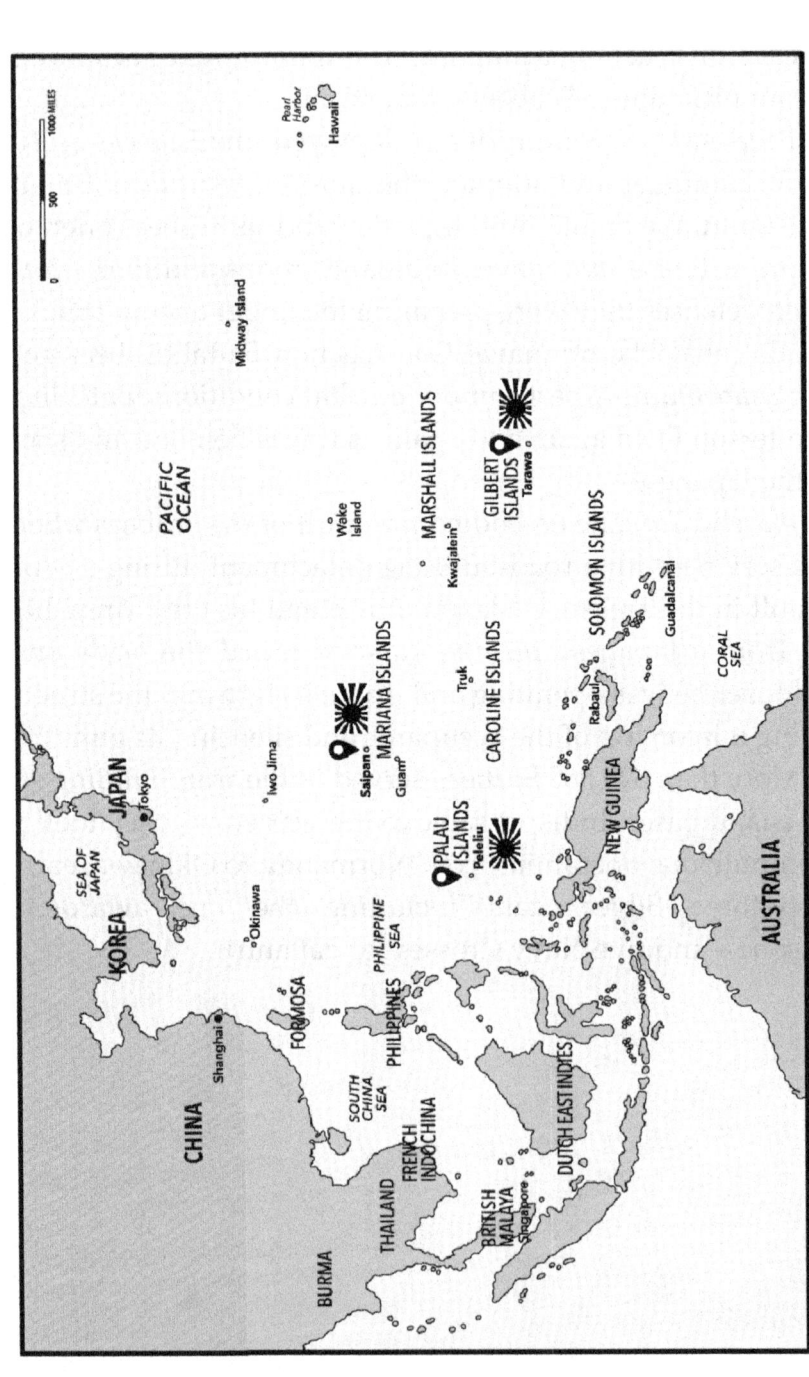

25
ISLAND HOPPING
NOVEMBER 1943–NOVEMBER 1944

"A commander who allows his unit to surrender to the enemy without fighting to the last man or who concedes a strategic area to the enemy shall be punishable by death."
–Imperial Japanese Army Criminal Code

By early 1943, Allied armies were making modest gains in the rain-soaked, disease-infested jungles of New Guinea, a stepping-stone on MacArthur's return path to the Philippines. Their progress was matched in the South Pacific, where Nimitz's forces were completing their sweep across the Solomon Islands.

Important developments were also unfolding in the China-Burma-India Theater. Six years after invading China, the Imperial Japanese Army was still struggling to defeat Chiang Kai-shek's Nationalist forces in the western provinces. In mid-1943, Roosevelt and Churchill agreed to support a counteroffensive in Burma, a former British colony occupied early in the war by the Japanese. With the Chinese army dependent on Allied weapons and ammunition, and the Japanese controlling the only viable supply routes, the Tenth US Air Force stepped in, airlifting supplies from India to China over the treacherous Himalayas. Pilots negotiating the world's tallest mountain range came to dread their flights over what was referred to as the "Hump," where severe winds and navigational challenges led to substantial losses of planes and crewmen. Their sacrifice was not in vain, as Chinese forces managed to tie down more than a million Japanese soldiers on the mainland — troops that could have been shifted to strongholds across the Pacific.

One of those strongholds was Rabaul, the prized Japanese air and naval base on the island of New Britain. Over 100,000 men were garrisoned there, and as American forces edged closer to it, debate stirred in Washington among senior leaders wary of the steep casualties sure to ensue from an invasion. MacArthur and Nimitz ultimately bypassed the base, isolating the forces there and continuing their respective drives toward the Japanese home islands. It marked the beginning of a novel "island hopping" strategy, where US forces leapfrogged well-fortified outposts, cutting them off from resupply and avoiding needless delays and bloodshed. It proved a boon to the Pacific campaign, accelerating progress and leaving enemy garrisons to wither from food shortages and tropical disease.

Not every stronghold could be bypassed. The path to final victory still required crossing a vast ocean, and that meant capturing key bases, anchorages, and airfields, no matter how strongly defended. The prolonged struggle on Guadalcanal was just a preview, and in one amphibious operation after another, US Marines and soldiers were called upon to land on faraway islands, push across rugged terrain and dense jungles in suffocating heat and humidity, and root out dogged Japanese defenders willing to sacrifice their lives rather than give up a single inch of ground.

Tarawa

After nearly two years of war, the US Pacific Fleet began to swell with modern aircraft carriers, battleships, and destroyers delivered from US shipyards. Naval air power also experienced a transformation with the arrival of more powerful and advanced planes, most notably F6F *Hellcat* fighters that outclassed the venerable *Zeros* still flown by their Japanese counterparts. The United States had started the war with severe quantitative and qualitative disadvantages, but domestic industrial production had steadily erased those early deficits, boosting inventories of new ships, planes, and weapons each passing month.

Having concluded the Solomons campaign, Nimitz turned his attention north to Japanese bases and communication centers in the Marshall Islands. As invasion preparations began, planners searched for a nearby launch point for supporting air strikes and reconnaissance missions. They found one on Tarawa, a Japanese-held atoll in the Gilbert Islands, just south of the Marshalls. Anchoring the southwest corner of the atoll was Betio Island, with an airfield thought suitable for larger planes.

The diminutive island—smaller than New York City's Central Park—was well-defended, with nearly 5,000 Japanese squeezed onto a strip of coral and sand less than two miles long and just a half-mile across at its widest point. The garrison was led by Rear Admiral Keiji Shibasaki, and half of it was composed of Special Naval Landing Forces—well-trained equivalents of US Marines. With little ground to defend, Shibasaki entrenched his men in a labyrinth of fortified bunkers and machine-gun pits just behind the beaches. His other advantage came from the large coral reef ringing the island, virtually impassable from the sea when the notoriously unpredictable tides around Tarawa were low. Spearheading the invasion for the Americans would be the 2nd Marine Division, veterans of Guadalcanal but lacking experience with storming contested beaches.

The Tarawa operation began in the early morning hours of November 20, with the first wave of Marines clambering down from their transport ships and into amphibious tractors, the newly designed landing craft capable of navigating both land and water. As the first flotilla of "amtracs" motored toward the coastline, supporting naval gunfire began tapering off. Too soon, many would later argue, as the abbreviated shelling and air strikes made few dents in Shibasaki's fortifications, particularly the hundreds of concrete and earthen bunkers sheltering most of his marines and soldiers.

The morning tide was high, and after successfully scaling the coral reef, the amtracs closed in on the beaches amid a barrage of intensive artillery and machine-gun fire. Most of the amtracs made it ashore, but they could advance little farther, blocked by a stout, five-foot-high seawall the Japanese had erected along the length of the beach. As machine guns sprayed the thin-skinned amtracs, the Marines abandoned them, scurrying behind the seawall, their only cover along the shoreline.

With casualties quickly mounting, reinforcements were called in, but the tides had receded by then, preventing the next wave of amtracs from clearing the reef. Dropping into the water, the Marines waded ashore from hundreds of yards away, slowed by chest-deep swells and raking gunfire. Those who survived stumbled to the seawall, wet and exhausted, where they joined some 1,500 other Marines clinging to the blood-stained beaches. The men attempted to claw forward, but a continuous deluge of enemy fire thwarted any progress. By nightfall, more than 5,000 Marines had been put ashore, a third of those already dead or wounded.

More reinforcements were sent in on the second day, but low tides once again forced the Marines to wade through the surf. Machine-gun and sniper fire tore into their ranks, but on the beaches, handfuls of Marines managed to inch forward and begin clearing enemy trenches and bunkers. A small beachhead was secured, bringing more men, ammunition, fresh water, and artillery ashore, and the Marines gradually fought their way into the island interior. By the third day, Admiral Shibasaki was dead and the garrison nearing collapse, but the remaining Japanese refused to quit. After launching a nighttime counterattack, the two sides grappled for hours in the dark, even fighting with knives and bayonets, but the Marines held their ground, eventually wiping out the last of the resistance.

News of the horrifying carnage on Tarawa, along with stark images sent home by war correspondents trailing the assault forces, staggered the American public and sent shockwaves through the Marine Corps. On Guadalcanal, 1,600 Americans had been killed over a six-month period, but on Tarawa, 1,100 Marines were dead after barely three days. Japanese losses were worse, with Shibasaki's Special Naval Landing Forces even more averse to surrendering than regular Imperial Army troops. Of the more than 4,700 Japanese on the island, just seventeen survived the battle.

Saipan

After scoring quick wins in the lightly defended Marshall Islands, US forces advanced to the next island chain in the Central Pacific, the Marianas. Part of Japan's inner ring of Pacific defenses, the Marianas were coveted for their airfields, from where American bombers could reach the Japanese home islands. Saipan, where the campaign would begin, was 3,500 miles from Pearl Harbor but barely a third of that from Tokyo. Like Tarawa, the island was heavily defended, and though Nimitz's forces were becoming more adept with amphibious landings, the Saipan operation added a new dynamic to island fighting—the presence of a sizable civilian population, many of the inhabitants Japanese colonists.

The invasion began on June 15, 1944, just nine days after Allied forces poured onto the beaches of Normandy, half a globe away. It was led by the 2nd Marine Division—replenished after the mauling months earlier on Tarawa—and the 4th Marine Division, with the Army's 27th Infantry Division in reserve. The 71,000 battle-tested men were considered sufficient for taking on the estimated 15,000 Japanese on Saipan, but intelligence assessments proved grossly inaccurate. The defenders had more than twice that number.

Pre-invasion bombardments from the sea and air again had marginal impact, and as the first waves hit the beaches, a torrent of artillery and mortar shells rained down from the hillsides. Of the 20,000 Marines put ashore that first day, one in ten was killed by Japanese shelling and counterattacks on the beaches. By the second day, the Marines were pushing inland, and to speed their progress, the 27th Infantry Division was ordered ashore. Marine Lieutenant General Holland "Howlin' Mad" Smith, in overall command of the entire operation, later fumed over the Army's sluggish rate of advance. Controversy flared when he relieved its two-star general of command — an extraordinary rebuke that incited a rare bout of rancorous interservice feuding.

Like Guadalcanal, the slugfest on Saipan extended to the sea as well, leading to the largest aircraft carrier battle of the war. Though the Japanese marshaled more than twice as many carriers in the Philippine Sea as they had two years earlier at Midway, US shipyards were delivering new vessels at a torrid pace, giving the Americans a substantial edge in both flattops and aircraft.

The Japanese air groups sought first blood, but with prior defeats robbing the Imperial Navy of most of its best pilots, hundreds of torpedo and dive-bombers were intercepted and cut to pieces by swarms of *Hellcat* fighters. The shellacking became known as the Marianas Turkey Shoot and left the Japanese carriers with fewer than 100 functioning aircraft, far too few to fend off the American submarines and carrier-based planes that began walloping their fleet. By the time the Americans broke off their attacks, the Battle of the Philippine Sea had produced one of the most lopsided outcomes of the Pacific campaign. Without losing a single ship, the Americans sank three Japanese aircraft carriers and destroyed 600 aircraft, wiping out most of the Imperial Navy's remaining air power.

Three weeks after landing on Saipan, US ground forces were closing in on victory when Japanese commanders, refusing to concede and desperate to stave off defeat, ordered the largest banzai charge of the war. In the pre-dawn hours of July 7, thousands of soldiers emerged from their caves and bunkers, led by screaming, sword-waving officers charging ahead into the darkness. Two US Army infantry battalions took the brunt of the assault, firing their heavy weapons into the surging mass, but they could not stop the onslaught. The Japanese poured through the breach in the lines, sweeping into rear areas filled with Marine artillery batteries and command posts. They fought hand-to-hand for hours, and though both sides suffered severe losses, the Marines held, killing more than 4,000 Japanese. The two US Army battalions were ravaged in the attack, with all but 200 of their 1,100 soldiers killed or wounded.

By July 9, the Japanese death count on the island stood at 24,000. Thousands more who refused to abandon their caves and bunkers were later killed with flamethrowers and explosive satchel charges — utterly ghastly means that were necessary to minimize risk among the Americans. US casualties were also high — an estimated 3,500 soldiers and Marines were dead or among the missing, and another 13,000 wounded — but the worst carnage was among the civilians. Terrorized by months of Japanese propaganda characterizing Americans as demons and rapists, many took their own lives by throwing themselves and their children over seaside cliffs and onto jagged rocks hundreds of feet below. Others were prodded to do so by Japanese soldiers forbidding any surrender. By the end of the campaign, more than 22,000 were dead.

Like D-Day in Europe, much would change in the Pacific following Saipan. Prime Minister Tojo was blamed for the failure and ousted from power, and with the later capture of nearby

Guam and Tinian, the US Army Air Forces had ample air bases in the Marianas from which to launch masses of heavy bombers arriving from America. Nearly three years after Japanese bombs fell on Pearl Harbor, dozens of new B-29 *Superfortress* bombers lifted off from the newly acquired airfields, destined for Tokyo to return the favor.

Peleliu

Ten months after Tarawa, and barely nine weeks after the Japanese were defeated on Saipan, Marine amtracs once again plowed through white-capped waves, closing in on yet another remote Pacific island few had ever heard of.

It was September 1944, and they were in the Caroline Islands, a chain stretching for over 1,000 miles across the Central Pacific. At the far western end was the small island of Peleliu, its airfield and garrison of 10,000 men considered a potential threat to MacArthur's pending operations in the Philippines. Picked to lead the attack was the veteran 1st Marine Division, and though they outnumbered the Japanese, some of the most unforgiving terrain in the Pacific Theater awaited.

For three days prior to the invasion, naval gunfire pounded the Japanese defenses, with Marine leaders hoping to avoid a repeat of the bloodbath on the beaches of Tarawa and Saipan. Once again, however, the bombardment had minimal impact on the Japanese, who emerged from their hardened and underground shelters to shower the oncoming landing forces with artillery and mortar fire. The Marines were badly bloodied but managed to advance off the beaches, capturing the island's primary airfield by the second day.

Progress slowed once the Marines began climbing the rugged mass known as Umurbrogol Mountain, a maze of coral ridges, caves, valleys, and ravines. Cloaked by jungle foliage, it was difficult to discern either from sea or the beaches, rendering artillery and air strikes useless and requiring the Marines to root out the embedded defenders, one pocket at a time.

The defense of Peleliu signaled a sharp change in strategy for the Imperial Army. In previous island campaigns, the Japanese had often responded aggressively, ordering counterattacks and banzai charges to overwhelm lightly equipped assault troops. On Peleliu, the defenders chose not to contest the Marines over open ground, burrowing instead into well-fortified bunkers and caves. Their objective was clear — prolong the fighting and make the Americans bleed for every inch — and it turned Peleliu into a frustrating, grinding struggle. Deadly snipers lurked everywhere around the aptly named Bloody Nose Ridge, as temperatures soared to 115 degrees, sapping the Marines' strength amid shortages of drinking water. The 1st Marine Regiment alone suffered so many casualties on the mountain — seventy percent of the men were killed or wounded — it had to be pulled back from the line and replaced with an Army unit.

It took weeks, but Japanese strongpoints were gradually encircled and isolated, and by late October, the worst of the fighting was over. The Army's 81st Infantry Division relieved the battered 1st Marine Division, but mopping up continued until late November, when Peleliu was finally declared secure. The campaign left the Americans with 1,700 dead, but the losses were dwarfed by those of the Japanese. As on Tarawa, most of the 10,000 defenders refused to be taken alive. Just nineteen survived.

Aftermath

From November 1943 to November 1944, American forces engaged in punishing campaigns across the Central Pacific, but the island-hopping strategy paid clear dividends. From newly captured air bases, American heavy bombers began targeting industrial and military facilities inside Japan, just as Japanese naval air power ceased to be a factor in the war. Despite the hard-fought island victories, the intensity of resistance signaled what lay ahead for US forces. As Nimitz and MacArthur drove closer to Japan, the resolve and desperation they found among their adversaries continued to deepen, with the worst still to come.

· · · · ·

In April 1947, nineteen months after the final Japanese surrender, a Japanese lieutenant and twenty-six of his soldiers emerged from hiding on Peleliu, finally convinced the war was over.

Benjamin Salomon

Captain Benjamin Salomon was an Army dentist who volunteered to go ashore on Saipan and replace an injured battalion surgeon. On July 7, 1944, the 29-year-old Salomon was treating wounded men in an aid station when thousands of Japanese began their banzai charge. Salomon used a rifle to fend off several attackers, and with the aid station on the verge of collapse, ordered the wounded and other medical personnel to retreat to safer ground. Salomon remained, covering their withdrawal with a nearby .30-caliber machine gun. He was found days later, his body punctured by dozens of gunshot and bayonet wounds and surrounded by ninety-eight dead Japanese. It would take decades, but Salomon was posthumously awarded the Medal of Honor.

B-29s

First entering service in mid-1944, the ultramodern, four-engine B-29 *Superfortress* was the largest bomber of World War II. With an unsurpassed range of 3,000 miles, it was well-matched for the Pacific, where islands and bases were separated by vast distances. Each B-29 could deliver a ten-ton payload and bristled with machine guns for protection from enemy fighters. They became the centerpiece of a year-long bombing campaign against the Japanese home islands, severely diminishing industrial production and demoralizing the civilian population.

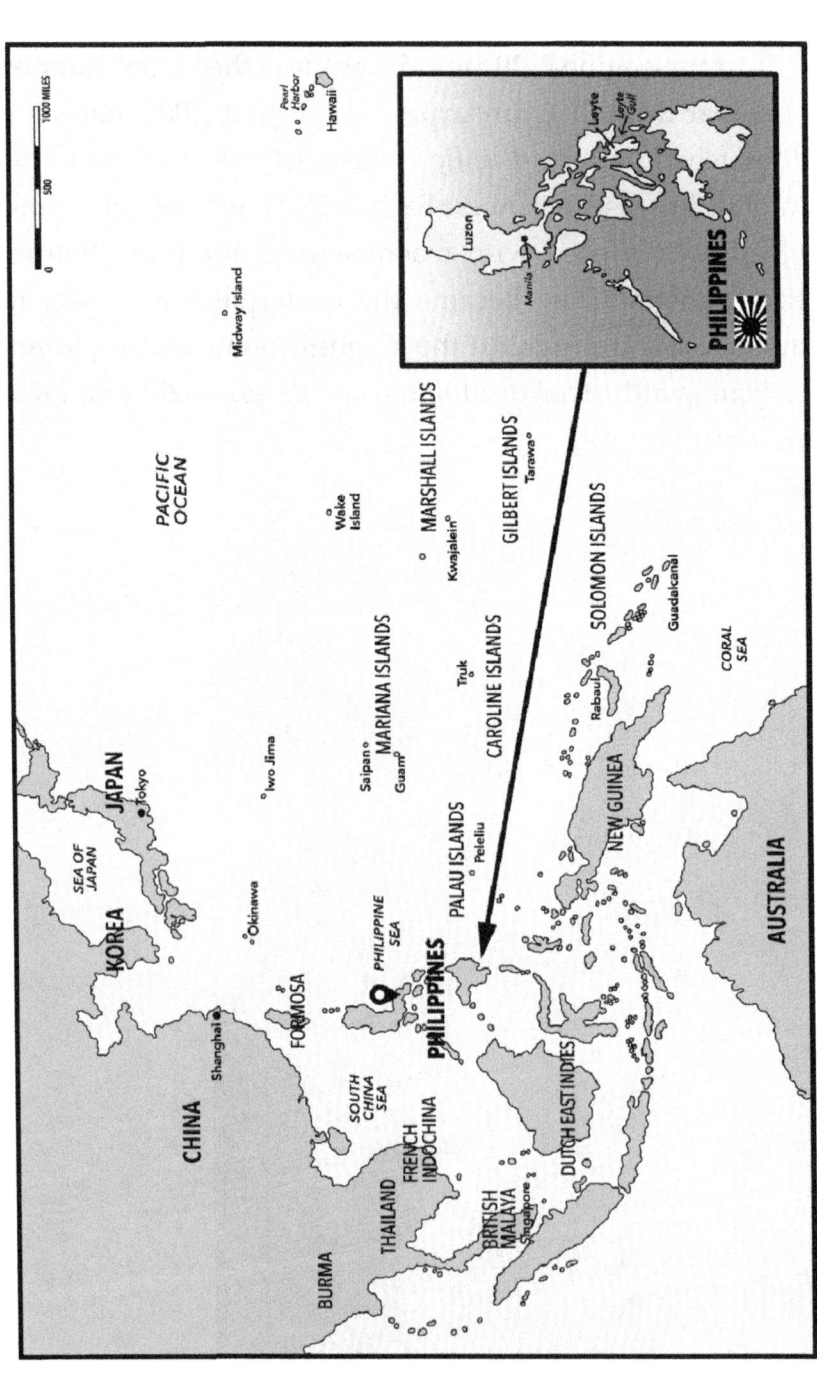

26
THE PHILIPPINES AND LEYTE GULF: MACARTHUR RETURNS OCTOBER 1944

"People of the Philippines, I have returned! By the grace of Almighty God, our forces stand again on Philippine soil."
–**General Douglas MacArthur, October 1944**

As the struggle between the Japanese and Americans on Peleliu reached a crescendo, MacArthur was preparing to embark on his long-awaited reclamation of the Philippines. More than thirty months had passed since the famed general evacuated the islands at President Roosevelt's order, abandoning his beleaguered, disease-stricken forces and the millions of Filipinos he had become so bonded to. His pledge in early 1942 – "I shall return" – was a promise to soldiers and civilians alike they would not be forgotten, and that MacArthur would keep faith with all those left behind, no matter the dark days ahead.

The subsequent undertaking in the Philippines evolved into the largest ground operation of the war in the Pacific. Throughout late 1944 and into 1945, competing armies clashed across the archipelago as naval forces battled offshore in a showdown of historic scale and consequence. In the end, a promise had been kept and a people liberated, but at tremendous human cost, with one of the world's great cities reduced to ruins.

• • • • •

By the eve of his long-planned invasion, MacArthur controlled a wealth of military power. Among the ground, air, and naval components unified under his command was the Sixth US Army, numbering over 200,000 men, and the Fifth US Air Force, brimming with hundreds of bombers and fighter planes. MacArthur had a potent amphibious arm as well, led by Vice Admiral Thomas Kinkaid, whose Seventh Fleet included troop transports, supply ships, protective escorts, and a number of smaller aircraft carriers and older battleships.

Also assigned to Philippine waters, and operating outside MacArthur's control, was Admiral William Halsey's mighty Third Fleet. Halsey commanded the Navy's newest aircraft carriers and battleships, and the air power he brandished was vastly superior to what the Americans had mustered just two years earlier at Midway and Guadalcanal. Kinkaid would preside over the amphibious landings—his air groups and heavy guns were more than adequate for supporting an invasion force—but Halsey was the muscle, responsible for safeguarding nearby waters and controlling the skies above.

The Japanese had positioned a sizeable army on the islands, and with good reason. The survival of their country depended on the continued import and safe passage of food, oil, and other resources from the East Indies and Southeast Asia—a lifeline shielded by bases and airfields throughout the Philippines. In command of the Japanese defenses was Lieutenant General Tomoyuki Yamashita, known as the "Tiger of Malaya" for his skillful rout of British-led forces in Singapore early in the war. Yamashita had a whopping 432,000 men under his command—a force substantially larger than every other garrison the US had faced in the Pacific—as well as supporting armor, artillery, and thousands of planes dispersed across the islands. He also had an iron-clad commitment from Imperial Navy leaders, vowing to throw their remaining weight against any landing forces that dared to enter Philippine waters.

Leyte

Though MacArthur's eventual goal was to capture the main island of Luzon, home to the capital of Manila and the largest concentration of Filipino citizens, the campaign would begin on Leyte. The smaller island was needed as a staging area for later operations, including a future landing on Luzon, where the bulk of Yamashita's forces awaited.

The invasion began on October 20 along Leyte's eastern coast. Four divisions came ashore that morning, encountering little resistance, and by early afternoon, a landing craft carrying MacArthur from his flagship was motoring toward the shoreline. In a carefully choreographed scene captured by news reporters and camera crews in tow, the supreme commander waded through the surf and stepped on Philippine soil for the first time in two and a half years. The liberation had begun.

It was a return the Filipinos had been eagerly anticipating. After the surrender of the islands in early 1942, the Japanese became brutish occupiers, installing a puppet regime of local officials they controlled and issuing a ban on all political opposition. The repressive conditions were enforced with an iron fist, and early resistance among the Filipinos led to a series of violent crackdowns. Tens of thousands fled their communities to form guerilla movements in jungles and rural areas where they were joined by American soldiers who had refused to surrender in 1942. Often supplied with arms and equipment smuggled in by Allied submarines, the guerillas became a disruptive force, ambushing Japanese patrols and raiding camps and supply depots. When the American invasion began, many volunteered as scouts and guides, providing critical intelligence on their hated occupiers.

Aided by local Filipinos, the Sixth Army made steady progress as it battled across Leyte. The Japanese had just 20,000 troops on the island when the invasion began, but Yamashita escalated the fight, reinforcing Leyte with 45,000 men stripped from other island garrisons and ordering air strikes against the support ships anchored offshore. The American amphibious force fended off the air attacks, but a much greater threat loomed outside the Philippines, where remnants of the Imperial Navy were preparing one last strike against the adversaries who had bested them for over two years.

BATTLE OF LEYTE GULF

It was a shrewd, audacious plan, committing most of Japan's remaining naval strength. Losses in the Marianas had left the Imperial Navy with few aircraft carriers and just partial air groups, but the balance of the Japanese surface fleet was still quite formidable, led by two of the mightiest battleships ever put to sea. The Japanese intended to unleash those great guns on the American support ships anchored in the Leyte Gulf, but first had to get by Halsey's armada of aircraft carriers and battleships.

They devised an elaborate ruse, centered around the unthinkable—the sacrifice of their last aircraft carriers. With few remaining planes and pilots, the ships wielded a shadow of their former power and were thus to be used as bait, drawing Halsey's strongest forces away from Leyte. A "Central Force" led by the two super battleships—the *Yamato* and *Musashi*—plus three other battleships, twelve cruisers, and fifteen destroyers, would then ravage the transport and supply ships supporting the American forces ashore. The combined firepower of the Central Force and a smaller "Southern Force" also converging on Leyte was expected to annihilate the weaker ships under Kinkaid's command.

On October 23, the Central Force was detected moving toward Leyte and was soon bushwhacked by American submarines and Halsey's carrier planes. One prize, the massive *Musashi*, absorbed three dozen bombs and torpedoes before sinking with the loss of 1,100 men. The Central Force withdrew, convincing Halsey that Kinkaid's ships were no longer under threat, but it was a fatal miscalculation, as much of the Central Force remained intact, led by the legendary *Yamato*.

The next day, the Japanese aircraft carriers were spotted far to the north of Leyte, and as anticipated, Halsey went for the bait. A task force led by his ten most powerful aircraft carriers and dozens of escort ships hunted down the Japanese flattops, sinking all four shortly after their discovery. The ruse had worked, though, drawing the heart of Halsey's fleet far away from Leyte. The Central Force returned and was soon giving chase to a flotilla of six escort aircraft carriers providing air support on Leyte. The flotilla, known as "Taffy 3," was protected by just three destroyers and four smaller destroyer escorts, none of which could match the heavy guns of the Japanese battleships and cruisers. Nor could the escort carriers—slow, thinly armored, and carrying far fewer aircraft than Halsey's larger fleet carriers—outrun their pursuers. They bolted anyway, launching every available plane to defend themselves while sending out desperate pleas for help.

As the Japanese ships closed the distance on Taffy 3, the three American destroyers fell back, determined to slow and harass their much-larger foes by firing their deck guns and a spread of torpedoes. The four destroyer escorts—lightly armed and built for anti-submarine warfare—also entered the fray, adding their small guns to the fight. The gambit was effective, as the destroyers and destroyer escorts sent the Japanese column into disarray, buying the escort carriers precious time to escape. It came at great cost, though, as three of the smaller American vessels, rocked by the firepower of the Japanese battleships, sank to the ocean bottom.

The Battle of Leyte Gulf raged on, but Halsey's aircraft carriers and battleships soon returned and took their vengeance on the remaining enemy ships. The clash lasted for four days, and though the Americans lost three small aircraft carriers, Japanese losses were catastrophic. In addition to the sinking of four aircraft carriers—including the last surviving aircraft carrier from the Pearl Harbor attack—three battleships and some twenty cruisers and destroyers were also lost. With most of the Imperial Navy on the ocean floor, Leyte Gulf became the last major sea engagement of World War II.

Luzon

By Christmas Day, Leyte was under US control. It had cost MacArthur 3,500 dead and another 12,000 wounded, but the tally was a fraction of the 49,000 men Yamashita had lost. The stand on Leyte had also cost Yamashita more than half his air force, and the transfer of so many troops and supplies to the island weakened his hand for the hardest fighting still to come.

It began in early January, when the first of 175,000 American soldiers landed on the grandest prize in the Philippines—the island of Luzon. With some eight million inhabitants, it was the most populous enclave the Americans would contend with in the Pacific, and the most heavily defended, as Yamashita still had over 250,000 men under his command there. His armor and air power had been badly diminished, though, and by early February, MacArthur's lead elements had battled past the outer line of Japanese defenses and were on the fringes of Manila.

Rather than the celebratory welcome MacArthur expected, the liberation of Manila devolved into a humanitarian disaster. From his command post in northern Luzon, Yamashita conceded the city of some 800,000 people, just as MacArthur once had, directing his troops to sabotage key bridges and other infrastructure before retreating to more defensible ground. But the senior Japanese naval officer in the city defied Yamashita, ordering 16,000 well-armed sailors, soldiers, and marines under his command to remain in Manila and fight to the death instead.

Once the Americans arrived, vicious fighting spilled into the streets, and thousands of city residents became trapped in deadly crossfires. More were killed after the Japanese barricaded themselves in the city center, drawing artillery strikes that leveled entire neighborhoods. Facing defeat, the Japanese rampaged through the city, mercilessly raping, beating, and gunning down Filipinos of all ages while setting large parts of the capital afire. The smoldering, rubble-strewn city was not declared secure until March 3, when the last Japanese were finally killed.

The Sixth Army went on to recapture much of the same ground American forces had surrendered in 1942, including Bataan, Manila Bay, and Corregidor, as Yamashita's forces withdrew into the hillsides and mountains of northern Luzon. Severely weakened by hunger and disease, they were content to play a cat-and-mouse game against an equally sapped Sixth Army, its ranks also depleted by casualties and sickness. The cagey Yamashita held out until the very end of the war, when he finally surrendered with 50,000 of his men. A post-war military tribunal later convicted Yamashita of war crimes against the Filipino population, sentencing the general to death in early 1946.

MacArthur had prevailed in the Philippines but at the cost of more than 46,000 casualties. Japanese losses were far worse, with some 400,000 dead and the Imperial Navy gutted. Among the Filipinos, at least 100,000 were killed in Manila alone, and the picturesque capital, once known as the "Pearl of the Orient," was left utterly devastated and unrecognizable. Retreating Japanese took vengeance on the countryside as well, blowing up bridges and railways, slaughtering livestock and work animals, and destroying schools, government buildings, telephone lines, and other essential infrastructure.

Debate remains whether the strategic gains were worth the price paid for recapturing the Philippines, but two outcomes were undeniable — the most formidable Japanese army outside the home islands and mainland Asia had been soundly defeated, and the Imperial Navy was out of the war.

. . . . .

The combined firepower of the Third and Seventh Fleets during the Philippines campaign was a testament to American shipbuilding might. Midway through the fighting on Guadalcanal, the only operational aircraft carriers remaining in the Pacific were the *Enterprise* and *Saratoga*. Just two years later, Admirals Halsey and Kinkaid employed a combined thirty-five aircraft carriers in Philippine waters alone.

Ernest E. Evans

During the Battle of Leyte Gulf, the destroyer USS *Johnston*, captained by Commander Ernest E. Evans, was at the center of the extraordinary effort to save six American aircraft carriers from almost certain annihilation. While screening the carriers of Taffy 3 from a superior force of Japanese ships, the *Johnston* severely damaged a much larger heavy cruiser before absorbing a flurry of hits from Japanese battleships. It was a barrage one officer later described as "a puppy being smacked by a truck." The *Johnston* later fired a volley of thirty rounds at one of the battleships before Evans steered his wounded ship between the American aircraft carriers and an oncoming column of Japanese warships. The move successfully thwarted the enemy attack, but the Japanese ships took out their fury on the *Johnston*, sinking the destroyer with the loss of more than half the crew, including Commander Evans. He was later awarded the Medal of Honor, posthumously.

Kamikazes

At the height of the Battle of Leyte Gulf, American ships were attacked by six planes from a new "Special-Attack Corps." Carrying just enough fuel to reach the American ships, the pilots were under orders to crash their bomb-laden planes directly into the aircraft carriers. They were thus among the first flights of the war known as kamikaze, a word that translates to "divine wind," alluding to a typhoon that destroyed a Mongol force attempting to invade Japan in the fourteenth century.

In the final months of the war, the Japanese were still manufacturing ample numbers of planes but had few remaining pilots with experience and aerial combat skills. There were, however, enough young airmen—many in their teens with limited flying abilities—willing to die for the emperor, and over time, the kamikazes proved devastatingly effective. At Leyte Gulf, they damaged the escort aircraft carrier, USS *Santee*, and fatally hit another, the USS *St. Lo*, setting off a wave of explosions that sank the ship in under thirty minutes. Through the end of the war, the Japanese launched over 2,500 kamikaze attacks, and though most of the planes were shot down by anti-aircraft fire or combat air patrols, others managed to punch through outer defenses and plunge into their targets. In the final nine months of the war, an estimated 5,000 Japanese pilots sacrificed themselves in kamikaze attacks, sinking thirty-six American ships, mostly destroyers, and damaging forty-three aircraft carriers and battleships.

Kazuo Odachi

Throughout his adolescence, Kazuo Odachi aspired to be a military pilot. In 1943, the 16-year-old was accepted into the Yokaren, a prestigious flight training program for Imperial Navy aviators. The first-ever Yokaren from his village, Odachi received a rousing sendoff on the day he departed for training, with a parade in his honor and over 200 elementary students marching alongside the young cadet.

Odachi entered the elite program with 1,800 other youths from across Japan. He was trained to fly Mitsubishi *Zeros*, and within a few months, Odachi was dueling with F6F *Hellcats*, America's best naval fighter planes. By autumn 1944, Japanese forces were reeling across the Pacific, having suffered enormous losses of ships, aircraft, and experienced pilots. Desperate to slow the American advance, a corps of kamikaze pilots was formed, and the airmen of Odachi's squadron were encouraged to volunteer for the suicide missions. Odachi was among those reluctant to sacrifice their lives so needlessly but unwilling to shame themselves before their comrades for what was considered a high honor. After some goading by their superiors, all raised their hands to volunteer.

They did not assign Odachi to his first kamikaze mission until April 1945. He had long prepared for such a death, but for weeks, poor weather conditions and difficulties finding the American targets thwarted his squadron. On several occasions, American fighter planes intercepted Odachi and his comrades, forcing the *Zeros* to jettison their heavy bombs to flee so they could complete their mission another day.

On August 15, 1945, Odachi was stationed on Formosa when an American fleet was spotted in nearby waters. Odachi was certain his luck had run out, as his squadron was issued strict orders to complete their next mission at all costs, striking any available target. Resigned to their fates, Odachi and others lined their *Zeros* up for takeoff, each with a large bomb wired to its underbelly. The 18-year-old Odachi had his hand on the throttle just as a truck drove onto the airstrip, blocking the planes from lifting off. Japan had surrendered and the war was over, sparing Odachi once again.

There would be some delay before he saw his village and family again. As with many Japanese, Odachi was held for months in China before he could return home in late 1945. In 1947, he joined the Tokyo Metropolitan Police Department, where he served for thirty-six years before retiring to a quieter life. Odachi became a highly respected master of *Kendo*, the Japanese martial art of fencing, and mentored scores of children well into his nineties.

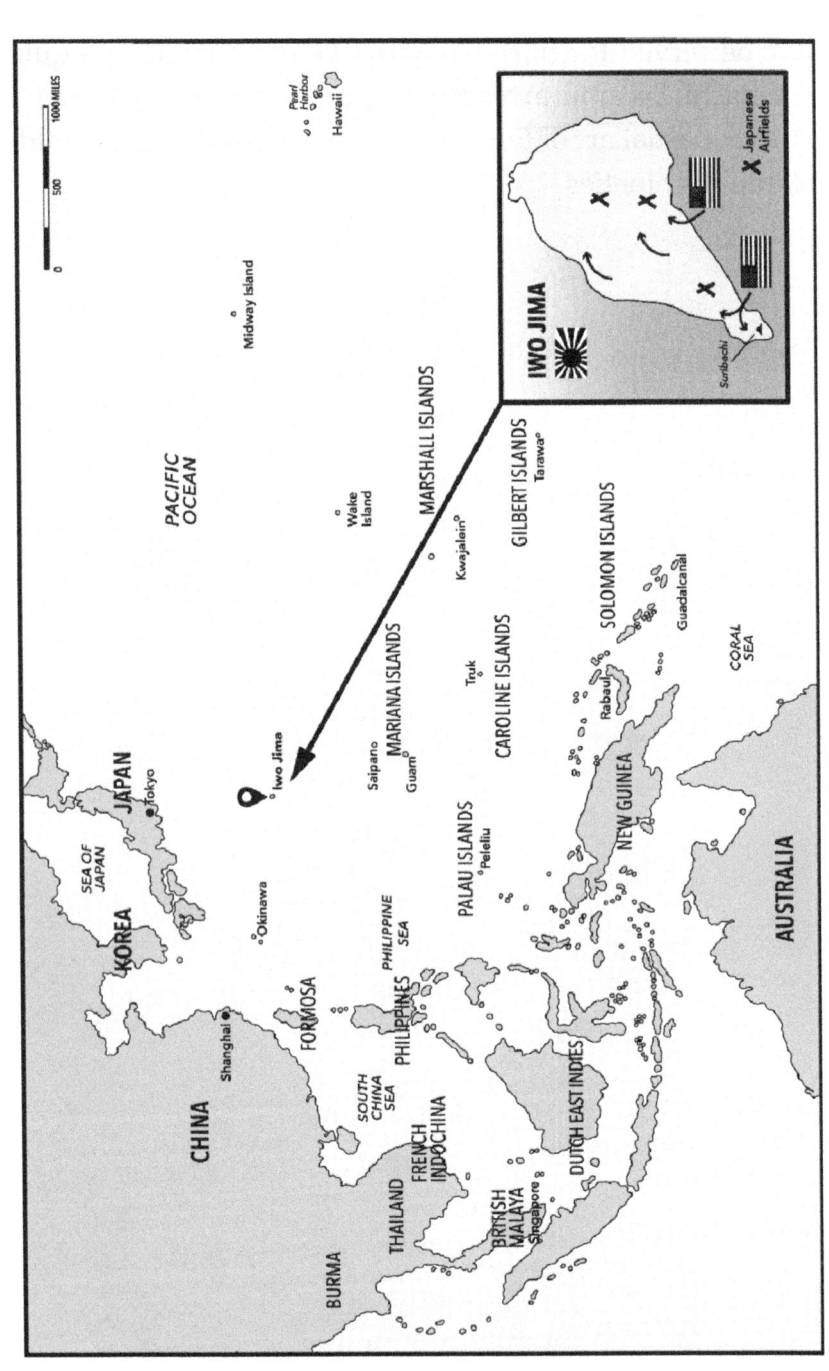

27
IWO JIMA
FEBRUARY–MARCH 1945

"Whenever I land on this island, I thank God and the men who fought for it."
–B-29 bomber pilot

By late 1944, industrial and military targets across Japan were within reach of the growing number of B-29 *Superfortresses* operating from captured airfields in the Mariana Islands. Army leaders were eager to begin a sustained bombing campaign, but danger loomed in the flight path of the B-29s. The tiny island of Iwo Jima, halfway between the Marianas and Japan, was a known base for Japanese *Zeros*. Three Marine divisions were picked to wrestle the island away from their foes, a prize that came with an added benefit – airstrips that could provide emergency refuge to disabled B-29s unable to reach their home bases.

Just four miles long and two miles wide, Iwo Jima was a fraction of the size of Guadalcanal and Saipan, and as the first wave of amtracs approached the shoreline on February 19, 1945, it likely appeared devoid of life. Veterans among the Marines knew better. Though the modest indigenous population had been evacuated, the Japanese garrison was simply out of sight, nestled deep within their caves and tunnels as they waited out the pre-invasion naval and aerial bombardments. Once the first boats began hitting the beaches, unloading thousands of

Marines along the coast, the garrison rushed to their heavy guns, marking the start of another punishing Pacific campaign.

* * * * *

Leading the invasion force was the 4th and 5th Marine Divisions, with the 3rd Marine Division in reserve. Most were battle-hardened veterans with island-fighting experience. They outnumbered their 21,000 adversaries on the island, but the Japanese were superbly led by Lieutenant General Tadamichi Kuribayashi, widely regarded today as the most capable and innovative leader the Americans faced in the entire Pacific Theater. Kuribayashi had long expected an invasion, and his men had labored in the blistering sun for months, transforming Iwo Jima into an island fortress. They built extensive networks of interlocking tunnels and trenches across the island, as well as countless blockhouses and pillboxes made from reinforced concrete, all with narrow firing slits for heavy machine guns.

Aware of the overwhelming American advantages in air power and troop strength, Kuribayashi had no intention of squaring off against the Marines on the beaches. Instead, he allocated most of his troops to the island interior, mirroring the strategy applied so effectively on Peleliu. Though the terrain favored the Japanese, Kuribayashi harbored no illusions of victory. His order for each defender to take as many lives as possible before succumbing was simply intended to prolong their own fateful end while diminishing the strength and resolve of the Americans.

The Assault Begins

For the Marines, Iwo Jima's topography was the most daunting challenge. Anchoring the southern tip was Mount Suribachi, a 550-foot ancient volcano that loomed over the only viable landing beaches, as well as the adjoining plain that held the island's principal airfield. An array of artillery and mortars had been sited across the face of Suribachi, but Kuribayashi embedded most of his army in the north, past the main airfield, where the ground became even more rugged, and the open plain rose to a jagged, uneven plateau.

The Marines landing on Iwo Jima's southern shore had two primary objectives — capturing the airfield just across the beaches and silencing the heavy guns on Suribachi. Once the mountain was secure, the invasion force would drive north to finish off the garrison.

As a parade of landing vessels brought the first assault waves ashore that February morning, the Marines were greeted with the island's notorious fumes, the product of a dormant volcano still emitting noxious gasses. The English translation of Iwo Jima is "Sulphur Island," and it was a fitting description of the barren landscape and rank stench that permeated every square inch. The Marines trudging across the beaches quickly learned another quirk of Iwo Jima; the coarse sand mixed with cinders and volcanic ash was extremely soft, making footing treacherous and running exceedingly difficult.

More than 10,000 men came ashore that morning, and though the landing was unopposed, the quiet reception would not last. Kuribayashi had simply waited until the shoreline had become packed with newly arrived Marines before ordering a murderous artillery and mortar barrage from Suribachi and the northern plateau. The shelling saturated every corner of the beaches with explosions and deadly shrapnel, riddling exposed men unable to find any cover and blasting apart tanks struggling to gain traction in the soft sand. The beaches became a horrifying scene, with scores of wounded men crying out in agony amid a sea of corpses and vehicles reduced to burning hulks.

Desperate to escape the firestorm, the Marines pressed forward, and by sunset, pockets of men had pushed across the narrow southern neck of the island, isolating Suribachi. The modest progress was a testament to their grit and courage, but Kuribayashi's guns had left more than 2,000 men dead or wounded on the beaches.

Clawing to Victory

The assault on Suribachi began the next morning. Many of the estimated 2,000 Japanese defending the mountain were barricaded in concrete bunkers clustered at the base and blocking the approaches. Others were higher up the mountain, behind artillery and machine guns poking out from caves and other concealed positions. As the Marines started scaling Suribachi, high-caliber rounds and exploding mortar shells cut into their ranks, but the men surged ahead, eventually knocking out the bunkers and starting their long climb up the slopes.

Ordered to race ahead and make the final ascent to the top, dozens of men fought their way up the steep incline, killing off snipers and other holdouts before finally reaching the summit and securing the crater. From the rim, they hoisted a small American flag, visible to most of the Marines on the island, who cheered from afar in one of the most stirring and storied moments in Marine Corps history. Hours later, a larger flag was sent forward, where it was lashed to a long piece of pipe and planted in the rocky ground. Photographer Joe Rosenthal, covering the invasion for the *Associated Press*, captured the iconic image, and his Pulitzer Prize-winning photograph was later immortalized in a sixty-foot-high bronze sculpture that became the Marine Corps War Memorial in Arlington, Virginia.

With Suribachi secure, the Marines drove northward, where Kuribayashi held commanding ground, backed by more artillery and mortars. Exploding shells and withering machine-gun fire tore into the Marines, as did landmines and booby traps left behind by the Japanese. It was not until early March that the exhausted men were able to fight through the teeth of Kuribayashi's defenses and take control of key hilltops and a second airfield. Many of the Japanese retreated to tunnels and caves, where the standoffs were ended, once again, with flamethrowers and explosives.

By late March, the Marines controlled most of the island. With Kuribayashi missing and presumed to have taken his own life, the end seemed near, but the Japanese had one last surprise to unveil. On March 26, they launched a deadly nighttime raid far behind the American lines. Hundreds of Imperial Army soldiers charged through rows of tents near the main airfield, hacking at the sleeping airmen with swords and bayonets. The pilots fought back, joined by nearby Seabees and Marines, until every Japanese was killed. The bloodshed was a fitting end to the bitter struggle on the island, with corpses from both sides littering the airfield. Large numbers of Japanese remained in hiding—another 1,600 holdouts were rooted out in the weeks to come—but the battle for Iwo Jima was effectively over.

Aftermath

In operations across the Pacific, Japanese casualties typically far exceeded those of American forces, but not on Iwo Jima. Of the 21,000 men Kuribayashi commanded, all but 216 were killed in the five-week campaign. Among the Marines, 26,000 were dead, wounded, or missing. The 6,140 men killed in action more than doubled combined losses on Guadalcanal and Tarawa.

Despite the bloodshed, there was little question of Iwo Jima's value. It first became evident on March 4 when a B-29 made an emergency landing amid the heaviest fighting on the island, saving the plane and crew. By the end of the war, some 2,400 damaged B-29s carrying 25,000 crewmen had safely touched down on Iwo Jima, with many more undoubtably saved by fighter escorts operating from the island.

Two and a half years had passed since the first Marines landed on Guadalcanal. The United States had blazed a long, blood-soaked path across the Pacific, and both Nimitz and MacArthur were closing in on Japan, with plans for a blockade and eventual invasion already on the drawing board. One final, must-have objective remained—one that conjured more dread among planners than any other operation during the tortuous journey to the Japanese home islands and final victory.

· · · · ·

Code Talkers

During the war, US Army and Naval intelligence devoted considerable resources and personnel to decrypting enemy codes concealing secretive communications. Safeguarding their own sensitive messages from Japanese and German codebreaking efforts was its own challenge, with implications for frontline forces in all theaters.

To assist with encoding communications, the US Army first recruited American Indians in 1940, hoping to use their knowledge of ancient, unwritten languages to transmit secret messages. By the end of World War II, members of at least fifteen American Indian tribes—including Comanche, Chippewa, Oneida, and Navajo—had stepped up to serve in several specialized signals units. In addition to standard combat and communications training, the men were also taught the mechanics of sending and receiving messages encoded in their tribal languages. In some cases, two "code talkers" could simply communicate messages in their shared language via hand-held radios or telephones. With more complicated messages, English words were assigned to each letter of the alphabet, and then substituted with the tribal language equivalent to spell out individual phrases.

Over 45,000 American Indian men and women served in uniform during the war, including hundreds of code talkers who participated in combat missions across the Mediterranean, European, and Pacific Theaters. Navajo code talkers distinguished themselves in several Pacific Island operations, including Iwo Jima, where they were attached to each of the three assault divisions. The 5th Marine Division alone employed six code talker networks during the first two days of the battle, when the men transmitted more than 800 coded messages without error.

None of the unique code talker systems was ever broken by German or Japanese intelligence.

ⓘ Often unheralded during the island fighting were the medical personnel manning the aid stations and field hospitals in combat zones, as well as the unarmed Army medics and Navy corpsmen attached to front-line units who braved the mayhem of battle to care for the wounded. Many of these medics and corpsmen were conscientious objectors who sought to contribute to the war effort without taking the lives of others. Others were pulled from the ranks and selected for these roles, sometimes on the eve of operations, owing to acute shortages of medical personnel and the likelihood of high casualties. Those who wore an armband with a red cross were often targeted during island campaigns, as the Japanese knew other Americans would put themselves in harm's way to protect and save such men. In just five weeks of fighting on Iwo Jima, twenty-three doctors and 827 corpsmen were either killed or wounded.

More Medals of Honor—twenty-seven in total—were awarded for acts of valor on Iwo Jima than any other wartime operation. Fourteen of those medals were awarded posthumously. Many of the recipients sacrificed their own lives to save others, even throwing themselves on top of Japanese hand grenades to smother the blasts and save their nearby comrades.

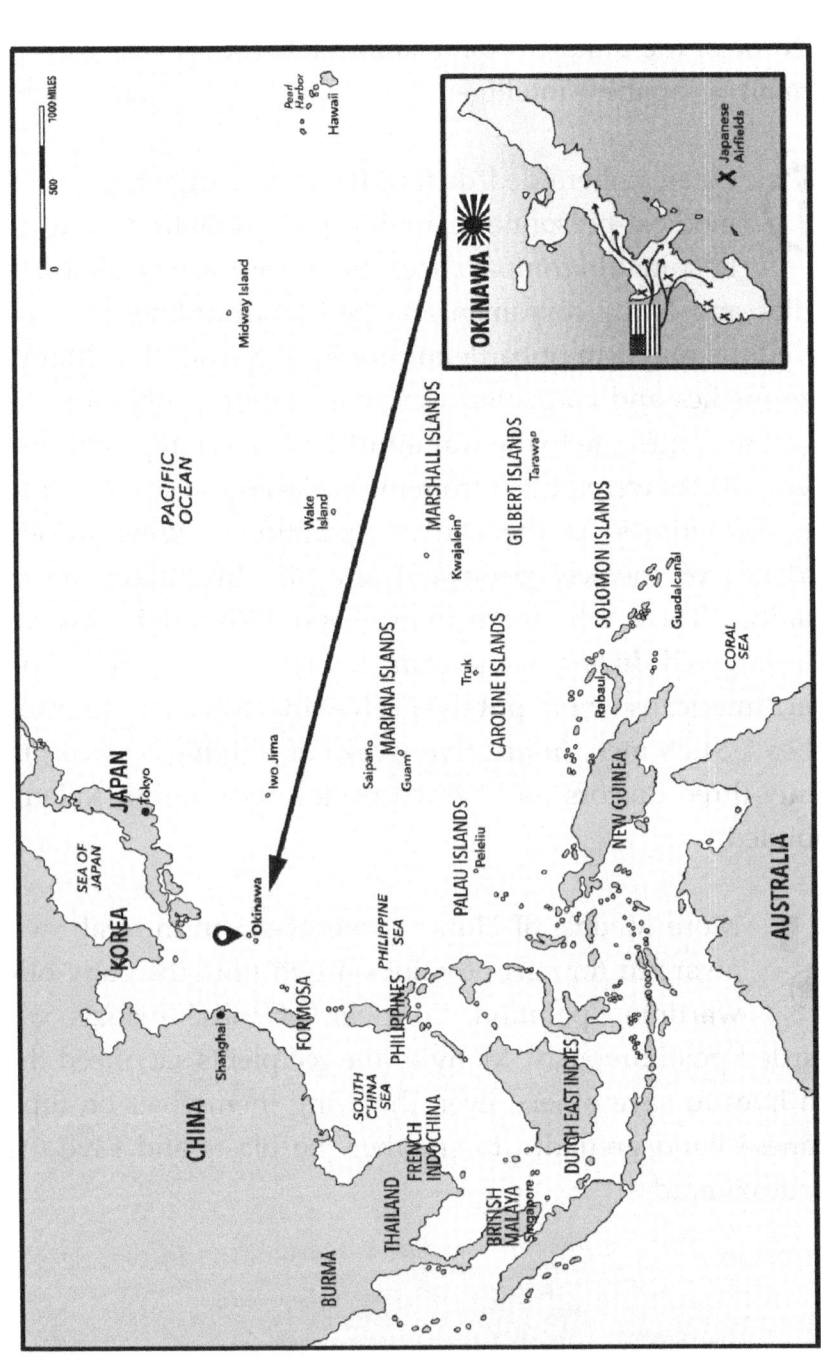

28
OKINAWA
APRIL–JUNE 1945

"One plane for one warship. One boat for one ship. One man for ten enemy or one tank."
–Motto of the Japanese 32nd Army at Okinawa

The loss of Iwo Jima and the Philippines left the Japanese cornered but far from defeated. Their military still numbered in the millions, armed and equipped by a manufacturing base churning out volumes of aircraft, munitions, and other war goods. The Imperial Army had suffered a multitude of defeats across the Pacific, but it remained a fearsome force, holding out with increasing ferocity and desperation the closer American forces drew to Japan.

As planners began sketching out a final invasion of the home islands, a clear need emerged for a staging area and forward operating base to accommodate the immense volume of forces expected to be assembled in the months to come. Okinawa was the obvious choice. A Japanese prefecture since 1879, it was just 350 miles from the home islands, with multiple anchorages and airfields ideally suited to support large-scale naval and air operations.

Capturing the 60-mile-long stronghold, however, was shaping into a potential nightmare. Not only was it defended by a large, seasoned army fighting close to its own soil, there was a sizable civilian population on the island, likely to be caught between the brute power of an invading army and a garrison vowing another fight to the death. Since Guadalcanal, American Marines and soldiers had witnessed the fervent devotion among the honor-bound Japanese to their emperor and warrior code. With those on Okinawa expected to battle equally until their last breath, projected casualty figures were beyond grim.

· · · · ·

In late March, a column of ships carrying 182,000 soldiers and Marines of the Tenth US Army stretched for miles as it crawled across the Western Pacific. The plan called for four divisions to land on Okinawa, with another assigned to a smaller, neighboring island, and two more kept at sea as a floating reserve. With Japanese waters such a short distance away, counterattacks from the sea and air were expected, and thus, an astounding assemblage of naval strength was on hand to protect the amphibious forces and support the ground campaign, including more than 200 aircraft carriers, battleships, cruisers, and destroyers, and 1,400 other auxiliary ships.

Leading the defense of Okinawa was Lieutenant General Mitsuru Ushijima, yet another skilled and accomplished tactician. Along with 77,000 soldiers of his 32nd Army, Ushijima commanded more than 20,000 Okinawan militia and 10,000 Imperial Navy troops. With the distance between Okinawa and Japan the equivalent of New York City to Pittsburgh, Marine and Army officials anticipated another bitter, protracted campaign, akin to a bare-knuckle brawl.

The outcome was worse than expected.

A BITTER STRUGGLE

Consistent with recent doctrine in other island fighting, Ushijima left the beaches mostly undefended. As on Peleliu and Iwo Jima, the nucleus of his army remained farther inland, hidden from American naval gunfire and air strikes in elaborate networks of caves, bunkers, and underground tunnels. They remained there as the American fleet closed in on Okinawa, patiently awaiting the ground advance that would follow an amphibious landing.

The operation began on April 1, 1945, with thousands of soldiers and Marines landing unopposed along Okinawa's western coastline. They seized two nearby airfields with ease before splitting in separate directions. The 1st and 6th Marine Divisions wheeled to the north, where they met little resistance and captured substantial ground, while the Army's 7th and 96th Divisions moved south, marching unwittingly into Ushijima's most formidable defenses. Supporting air and artillery strikes were called in, but it was to little avail, as the Japanese simply retreated to the safety of their shelters until the ground assaults resumed. The defenders then returned to their lines, throwing up curtains of fire that effectively thwarted the Army's progress.

As the skirmishing continued across southern Okinawa, the Americans received jolting news from home—the death of President Roosevelt. The popular 63-year-old, having recently won a record fourth term in a 432-99 Electoral College landslide, suffered a massive cerebral hemorrhage on April 12. When word filtered down from the anchored ships to the front lines, many of the young Americans reacted with tears or stunned silence, as Roosevelt had been the only president most servicemen had ever known. Few had heard of Harry S. Truman, his latest vice president and the man sworn in to replace him.

With the fighting dragging on in the south, reserve elements were sent ashore, joined by Marine divisions no longer engaged in the north. Soaked by torrential downpours, the soldiers and Marines made a concerted push to break through Ushijima's lines, but the Japanese were unyielding, and the challenging terrain added to their struggles. Many of the clashes were in close quarters and became increasingly savage, with the two sides fighting with bayonets, entrenching tools, and even their bare hands.

Amid some of the worst carnage in the Pacific, the soldiers and Marines steadily pushed the Japanese back. Ushijima was achieving his objective, bleeding the Americans for every inch of ground, but it was a war of attrition he could not win. His adversaries had seemingly limitless replacements, food, ammunition, and medicine, while Japanese supply routes from the home islands had been severed long ago. Still, Tokyo had not entirely abandoned Ushijima, ordering suicide attacks against the American fleet operating offshore, hoping to destroy or drive off naval and logistical support and isolate US forces ashore. It was the same gambit attempted at Guadalcanal and Leyte, but this time, the attacks would come from both the air and the sea.

On April 6, the *Yamato*, Japan's largest battleship and longtime jewel of the Imperial Navy, steamed from the safety of its home port with just enough fuel to reach Okinawan waters. Joined by the few escorts that could be spared, the ships had stern orders to blast a path through the American fleet and cripple any offshore amphibious support. After beaching their vessels on the Okinawa shoreline, the crews were instructed to fire their guns until all ammunition had been expended, then move inland and fight as infantry.

It was a foolhardy plan. As the captain of one of the Japanese destroyers later opined, it was "like throwing an egg against a rock." American submarines sighted the flotilla shortly after sailing from Japan, and within hours, hundreds of carrier-based dive-bombers and torpedo planes descended on the doomed ships. The crew of the *Yamato* fought bravely, but without air support it was a one-sided fight, and five bombs and ten torpedoes sealed their fate. In addition to the *Yamato*, US carrier pilots sank a light cruiser and four destroyers, claiming the lives of more than 4,000 Japanese sailors. It cost the Americans just ten planes.

The Japanese had greater success with kamikaze attacks from the air, launching more than 1,400 suicide flights from bases in Formosa and Japan. The kamikazes were relentless, swooping in, day and night, to terrorize the American fleet. Just a fraction of the attacking planes made it past the combat air patrols and anti-aircraft fire, but it was enough. Fitted with large bombs, the kamikazes slammed into the largest ships they could reach, meting out damage and casualties across the fleet.

As the end neared on Okinawa, resistance among the Japanese became even more desperate. They fought with a mix of skill and fanaticism, and though the Americans were accustomed to Japanese aversions to surrendering—the first suicidal banzai charges dated back to Guadalcanal—the degree to which Imperial Army soldiers sacrificed themselves on Okinawa unsettled even the most battle-scarred veterans. Once again, thousands who refused to abandon their bunkers and caves were finished off in the most gruesome manner, with explosives and flamethrowers.

The civilian population fared little better. Some willingly fought alongside Imperial Army forces, but others were used as human shields by the Japanese. Thousands led into deadly crossfires were cut down by hailstorms of bullets and shrapnel, and waves of suicides soon followed. As on Saipan, months of fear-inducing propaganda, depicting Americans as monsters who tortured and raped their enemies, led scores of Okinawans to choose death over capture. Others did so at gunpoint, forced to use army-issued grenades on themselves and their families by Japanese soldiers forbidding any form of surrender.

The battle finally came to a merciful end on June 22. Ushijima had taken his own life, and though few of his men survived, there was little cheering on the American side. Most of the soldiers and Marines emerged from the battle in a stupor, deeply shaken by the weeks of savagery they had experienced. Many would be haunted by the killing and butchery, much of it involving women and children, for the rest of their lives.

Aftermath

For all the horrors experienced from Tarawa to Iwo Jima, the 82-day clash on Okinawa may have been the single most harrowing campaign in the Pacific Theater. Dismay and revulsion over the staggering number of military and civilian deaths reverberated across the globe.

With most Americans aware the war was nearing a conclusion and expecting their sons and fathers to return home soon, the final casualty figures from Okinawa were jarring. More than 50,000 servicemen were dead, wounded, or missing. The Navy suffered its worst losses of the war after kamikazes sank thirty-six ships and damaged hundreds more. The number of sailors lost in the waters off Okinawa more than doubled those killed during the raid on Pearl Harbor. Among the defenders, more than 92,000 Japanese perished on the island, as did an estimated 120,000 Okinawans.

Tremors from the combined human losses rippled across the Pacific Ocean, triggering alarm at the highest levels in Washington. The sheer volume of military and civilian casualties was an arresting preview of the bloodbath almost certain to result from invading Japan, where millions of equally devoted soldiers and civilians were preparing to defend their home soil with their lives. As President Truman weighed every available option for averting another Okinawa-like outcome on the Japanese home islands, an alternative course emerged—one with the potential to minimize American casualties and bring Japan to its knees.

• • • • •

 As the fighting on Okinawa neared its end, Lieutenant General Simon B. Buckner, Jr., commanding the Tenth US Army, was mortally wounded by Japanese artillery

fire, becoming the highest-ranking American officer killed by enemy fire in World War II.

Robert E. Bush

Twenty-four Medals of Honor were awarded to US military personnel for their service on Okinawa, including 18-year-old Robert E. Bush, a US Navy medical corpsman from Tacoma, Washington. Bush was administering blood plasma to a fallen Marine officer when the Japanese counterattacked and charged his position. Holding the plasma bottle in one hand and his pistol in the other, Bush fired into the enemy ranks until he was out of ammunition. Wounded himself, he found a discarded carbine and fired again on the attacking Japanese, killing six more, despite the loss of an eye during the exchange. Bush survived and became the youngest sailor to earn the Medal of Honor during the war.

29
MEETINGHOUSE AND DOWNFALL
MARCH–JUNE 1945

"Killing Japanese didn't bother me very much at the time...I suppose if I had lost the war, I would have been tried as a war criminal."
–Major General Curtis LeMay, architect of the 1945 firebombing of Tokyo

Long before the last holdouts on Okinawa had been subdued, preparations were underway for a final stand on the Japanese home islands. The long succession of defeats and downward spiral could no longer be hidden from the despairing population or masked by hollow propaganda. Hunger pangs, and armadas of B-29s flying overhead, told the true story. An empire that once stretched from mainland China across the Western and Central Pacific was crumbling and in its final throes. Yet there was still no end to the war in sight, as militants in Tokyo remained the dominant voice in government, defiant and refusing to acknowledge Japan's inescapable fate.

Like the Germans, the Japanese still had millions of men in uniform in early 1945. Most were scattered across the map, with half pinned down on the Asian mainland alone. Others were stranded throughout the Pacific and Far East, hundreds or even thousands of miles from the home islands and cut off by naval blockades. Three years earlier, the mighty Imperial Navy was the master of the seas, unequalled among its rivals, but by the last year of the war, it had vanished from sight, virtually every capital ship on the ocean bottom. The few ships still afloat were tethered to home ports by a scarcity of oil, their fuel holds empty.

Conditions in Japan were beyond bleak, and with American naval and air power siphoning off most shipping traffic, food supplies were fast running out. Still, the widening famine and material shortages did little to sway those in power, and resistance among those defending outposts, such as Okinawa, only intensified as American forces drew nearer to Japanese shores. Generals Marshall and MacArthur had long foreseen the necessity of a full invasion, but with casualties from such an operation likely to reach into the hundreds of thousands, officials turned to strategic bombing as a means of concluding the war. By crippling domestic production and raiding population centers, it was hoped civilian and military leaders in Tokyo would be convinced of the futility in prolonging hostilities. The subsequent, months-long bombing campaign delivered the promised destruction, reducing much of the Japanese war economy to ashes, but came with dire humanitarian consequences.

• • • • •

Prior gains in the Mariana Islands had yielded multiple new air bases less than 1,500 miles from Japan, just as long-range B-29s rolling off assembly lines across the United States began arriving in the Pacific Theater. There was much anticipation for their well-hyped destructive power, and with the capability to deliver their payloads from six miles in the sky—safely distant from Japanese air defenses—it was hoped losses of planes and air crews would be far less than what American and British flyers had experienced over Germany. But the high altitudes produced an unexpected drawback, as strong gales and the newly discovered jet stream—a narrow band of powerful winds in the upper atmosphere—blew most of the bombs far off course. Less than ten percent were striking their intended targets.

In January 1945, Major General Curtis LeMay, a leading planner of Allied air raids against German population and industrial centers, took command of bombing operations from the Marianas. Unsatisfied with the middling results from the B-29s, the enterprising LeMay ordered a series of immediate changes. Pilots would approach their targets from far lower altitudes, minimizing wind interference, and missions were moved to nighttime, mitigating the threat from Japanese air defenses. The planes were thus also stripped of their defensive armament, and the weight shed substituted with heftier payloads.

There was one other significant change—a switch from high-explosive to incendiary bombs. Earthshaking blasts from the former had flattened German structures of stone and concrete but had proven less effective against Japanese cities built from wood. Moreover, unlike the Germans, who had clustered their manufacturing in easily identifiable complexes in industrial regions or suburban areas, the Japanese relied on smaller factories dispersed across their cities and tucked into densely populated commercial and residential districts. With such targets impossible to pinpoint from the air, LeMay counted on the incendiaries to produce broader ruin, burning factories and industrial plants of all sizes to the ground. The flames were sure to also consume nearby homes, schools, and hospitals, but LeMay was unmoved by the likely civilian losses and suffering, viewing it all as a necessary consequence.

The first major test of the new strategy came when LeMay ordered a sledgehammer blow against the heart of Japan, known as Operation Meetinghouse. In began in early March, when a force of 279 B-29s departed their bases in the Marianas, destined for Tokyo and packed with bombloads of jelly-like napalm, a highly flammable chemical mixture. Atmospheric conditions over the target area were expected to be ideal for the incendiaries, with ground winds gusting up to sixty-five miles per hour. The lack of any rainfall in weeks had also made the wooden city a tinderbox, ready to ignite.

The B-29s passed over Tokyo shortly after midnight, releasing their bombs over a target zone of less than four square miles. Waves of explosions ripped through the darkness as the area instantly erupted into an inferno, generating a firestorm with temperatures reaching up to 1,800 degrees. The flames swept across the city, incinerating everything in their path and consuming whatever they touched. That included oxygen, asphyxiating those who had not immediately burned to death. Primitive and sparse firefighting equipment further doomed the city, allowing the blaze to rage out of control for days. By the time the fires were extinguished, the center of Tokyo was a scorched landscape, blanketed with the remains of at least 100,000 dead. An estimated 250,000 buildings, houses, and other dwellings were also reduced to cinders, leaving more than one million survivors homeless in the city.

Tokyo was not alone. In subsequent days and weeks, Nagoya, Kobe, and Osaka experienced a similar fate after more firebombs rained down from the B-29s. When his stores of incendiaries were depleted, LeMay resumed the use of conventional explosives, hammering dozens of Japanese cities from the air. The civilian death toll soared, and industrial production fell to new lows, but key officials in Tokyo remained obstinate. No matter the scale of destruction, they continued to dismiss the threat from American air power, wedded to the delusion that no foreign army could ever conquer Japan.

INVASION PREPARATIONS

With the German surrender in May 1945, President Truman faced mounting pressure to end the war in the Pacific. The United States had been fortuitous, avoiding the physical devastation that scarred so many other lands, yet the public was exceedingly war-weary and eager to declare victory. With every battlefield success, Americans sensed the end was near, knowing the Japanese had been badly whipped, but casualties continued to climb, and they longed for their husbands and sons to return home.

Some in Truman's inner circle counseled patience, arguing LeMay's bombs and the naval blockade should be given sufficient time to wear down Tokyo and compel a surrender. Truman, siding with his generals, decided otherwise, convinced an invasion was the only feasible option for toppling the remaining resistance and bringing the war to a rapid conclusion.

The plan under consideration was Operation Downfall, and the prescribed troops, resources, and logistical support for it promised to exceed every other amphibious operation of the war, including Normandy and Okinawa. More than 1.2 million soldiers and Marines would take part in the invasion and later occupation, with many of those already staging in the Philippines. They would soon be joined by veteran divisions transferring to the Pacific from the now-dormant European Theater, all slated for months of training as they prepared for an invasion of unprecedented magnitude.

Under the first phase of the operation, codenamed Olympic, 600,000 soldiers and Marines would land on Kyushu, the southernmost island and home to millions of Japanese. Their objective would be to capture anchorages and airfields needed for a later and much larger landing on the main island of Honshu. More than one million Allied personnel were earmarked for that phase, scheduled for early 1946. Home to Tokyo, the sacred Imperial Palace, and the preponderance of Japanese, the clash on Honshu was expected to be epic.

Centuries had passed since Japan was last threatened by invasion, a legacy the propaganda ministry trumpeted often. American officials, aware how prideful the Japanese people were, with a warrior spirit and passionate attachment to their emperor, expected to face not only a disciplined, determined army, but a secondary force of civilians as well, all pledged to preserving their sacred homeland with their lives. Intelligence estimates counted some two million soldiers among Japanese defensive forces, and with millions of civilian reserves and militia and thousands of kamikaze aircraft also available, casualty forecasts for Olympic were shockingly high.

They were also far too low. The Japanese had predicted a landing on Kyushu, even identifying the likely assault beaches, and by August, more than 900,000 troops had been dispersed along the southern coast, far more than US intelligence was aware of. The remnants of the Imperial Navy also intended to be heard from. Though its world-class armadas had been whittled down to a limited number of submarines and destroyers, 3,000 smaller vessels had been converted to suicide boats and fitted with explosive charges in their bows. Kamikaze attacks typically targeted American aircraft carriers, but for the pending invasion, the suicide boats intended to ram into far more vulnerable targets—the slow, lumbering transports carrying assault troops by the thousands to Japanese shores.

It was the expected last line of Japanese defense, the civilian population, which caused the most angst among planners. Edicts on Kyushu mandated the mobilization of all males between the ages of 15-60, and females between the ages of 17-40. With few available weapons—most were armed with just hand grenades, bamboo spears, and knives—hundreds of thousands would likely be killed in hopeless attacks against American soldiers and Marines. Many more were expected to take their own lives, either willingly or at Japanese bayonet point, as on Saipan and Okinawa, rather than submit to defeat.

Few questioned whether Downfall would ultimately succeed. The United States had a nearly limitless reservoir of resources, and its air, naval, and ground forces brimmed with modern firepower that the Japanese could not possibly withstand. The price of such a victory was another matter. The expected loss of human life on both sides was unfathomable, as was the notion of the war continuing for at least another year. Significant developments in July, however, changed everything.

· · · · ·

Harry S. Truman

Harry S. Truman (1884-1972) was a little-known United States senator from Missouri when he was nominated to serve as President Roosevelt's running mate in what would be FDR's third and final re-election campaign.

Truman had been a captain of field artillery in the First World War, and when his military service ended, he returned to Missouri and worked as a clothing retailer until elected to a county judgeship. The folksy, plainspoken Truman won a US Senate seat in 1934, and was in just his second term in the summer of 1944 when Democrats selected him to join Roosevelt on the national ticket. The pair won a landslide victory that year, and Truman was sworn in as vice president in January 1945.

Three months later, Roosevelt's sudden death thrust the 60-year-old Truman onto center stage, where an array of extraordinary challenges awaited his first year as president. Among his achievements, he joined with other Allied leaders at the 1945 Potsdam Conference in negotiating terms for the occupation of Germany and surrender of Japan, approved the use of two atomic bombs, and navigated post-war tensions with the Soviets in Europe. Domestically, Truman faced several political headwinds, including a Republican Congress and an electorate fatigued by war and loathe to risk further conflict overseas. With his own party badly splintered, Truman was widely expected to lose his 1948 re-election bid, but in one of the great upsets in American political history, he shocked the country by defeating Thomas E. Dewey, the Republican governor of New York.

By necessity, Truman's early focus was on the international realm, and his tenure was marked by a series of high-stakes decisions that propelled and guided America's global rise amid the spread of Soviet influence across post-war Eastern Europe. He committed US military and economic aid to democratic countries resisting Stalin's aggression and championed the Marshall Plan to underwrite reconstruction efforts across Western Europe. In his second term, he managed the developing crisis on the Korean Peninsula and feuded with MacArthur over wartime strategies. Their disagreements and quarreling led to Truman famously relieving the Army legend of command for his insistence on expanding the war against communist China.

With the opposition party controlling Congress, Truman's domestic agenda was more modest, but he made surprising progress on early civil rights reforms, including a landmark desegregation of the armed forces and a prohibition against racial discrimination in the federal workforce. After his first full term in office expired in 1953, Truman stepped away from the presidency. He retired to Independence, Missouri, and died in 1972.

ⓘ The B-25 bombers that took part in the Doolittle Raid in April 1942 dropped approximately thirteen tons of high-explosive bombs on Tokyo and its suburbs, an attack that caused nominal damage to Japanese industry and infrastructure. Three years later, the 279 B-29s that were part of Operation Meetinghouse dropped 1,665 tons of incendiary bombs on Tokyo, annihilating sixteen square miles of the city.

30
FINAL SURRENDER
JULY–AUGUST 1945

"Following are our terms. We will not deviate from them. There are no alternatives. We shall brook no delay...We call upon the government of Japan to proclaim now the unconditional surrender of all Japanese armed forces...The alternative for Japan is prompt and utter destruction."
–Allied Declaration
July 26, 1945

As preparations for Operation Downfall gained steam, a historic milestone was achieved at the secret atomic weapons laboratory in Los Alamos. On July 16, 1945, a plutonium-fueled test device called Trinity was successfully detonated in the New Mexico desert, releasing an explosive force of extraordinary power.

The blast validated the claims of those who had long championed the potential of atomic energy. It also left the Los Alamos lab with enough enriched uranium and plutonium for just two more bombs. As the scientists and technicians scrambled to complete the new weapons, the War Department unveiled updated casualty forecasts for Downfall. One model offered a sobering new estimate, projecting 400,000 to 800,000 soldiers and Marines would be killed in the operation. Expectations of Japanese casualties were equally jaw-dropping, with combined military and civilian deaths likely to reach somewhere between five and ten million.

As the Trinity test was making history, President Truman was overseas, meeting with other Allied leaders in Potsdam,

Germany to discuss strategies for managing the post-war peace in Europe and concluding the war in the Pacific. On July 26, the United States, Britain, and China—the Soviet Union still maintained a neutrality agreement with Japan—issued a joint declaration from Potsdam calling for an immediate, unconditional surrender. Key demands included the removal of Japanese political and military leaders from positions of authority, full disarmament of the military, and a temporary occupation of the home islands. In exchange, the Allies pledged to support and assist Japan with rebuilding its infrastructure, implementing democratic reforms, and revitalizing its industrial sector. Importantly, the leaders also promised self-determination, allowing the Japanese people to choose their own form of government. Intentionally omitted was any sort of explicit pledge that Emperor Hirohito would remain on his throne. His fate would be left in the hands of Japanese voters.

Though war ministers in Tokyo greeted the Potsdam Declaration with the usual bravado and defiance, most civilian leaders grasped the war was over. Hundreds of thousands of Japanese had perished in bombing raids that left cities and infrastructure across Japan in ruin. With millions homeless and the population teetering on the edge of starvation, many quietly favored a negotiated settlement to end the hostilities, but a powerful bloc of military leaders still reigned supreme. They were unwilling to compromise, convinced a potential dismantling of the imperial system was afoot, and their refusal to acknowledge defeat or agree to the Allied terms left the government in deadlock. With Hirohito himself averse to weighing in, the conflict continued, seemingly without end.

• • • • •

The success of Trinity was welcome news at the White House. So closely guarded was the secret of atomic weapons that Truman had only known about the program since succeeding Roosevelt in April. As his inner circle wrestled with how to make use of the new weapons, there were few qualms about targeting Japanese cities. All agreed the Japanese deserved no leniency, having orchestrated a peacetime attack on American soil and widespread atrocities against Allied POWs and civilian populations across Asia and the Pacific. There was no glee at the White House for the suffering the atomic weapons were sure to bring, but there was also no guilt.

Nor was the White House willing to wait the Japanese out, as decoded intercepts of internal Japanese communications offered no sign that Tokyo was any closer to accepting the Allied terms for surrender. Planning for Operation Downfall continued, but the astronomical number of expected Japanese and American dead—counts that would surely surpass every other operation of the war—gave Truman pause about choosing an invasion over the new weapons. The expansive timetable required for an invasion of such scale was also a factor, likely to extend suffering across Asia, including among Allied POWs, for at least another miserable year.

The only remaining question was how to make the best use of the atomic devices and effectuate a final surrender. It was a dilemma that divided Truman's advisors. Some favored a demonstration on an uninhabited atoll to shock the Japanese into capitulation, sparing mass deaths on the home islands, but Truman rejected that approach, unconvinced such an exhibition would change the right minds in Tokyo. Providing advance notice was also a risk, as it might tempt the Japanese to intercept the weapon or transport POWs to the intended target site.

The fate of those POWs weighed heavily with Truman. Hundreds of thousands remained in captivity, and their odds of surviving the war diminished with each passing day. Post-war records bear this out, as ninety-nine percent of American POWs held in German camps came home when the war ended, while the survival rate among Japanese-held prisoners was just over half that number. Those still alive had already endured years of brutality, pressed into hard labor despite their weakened and malnourished condition. They continued to languish in disease-ridden camps where starvation and beatings were routine.

For Truman, time was running out. Public support for the war was waning, and thousands of combatants, prisoners, and civilians were dying every day. Bombs and blockades had diminished but not defeated Japan, and millions of lives were in the balance. With waiting no longer an option, Truman issued the order for the very first use of an atomic weapon.

HIROSHIMA AND NAGASAKI

On the morning of August 6, 1945, a heavily weighted B-29 lifted off from an airfield on the island of Tinian in the Marianas. The bomber, piloted by Colonel Paul Tibbets, was named *Enola Gay* after his mother, and the five-ton atomic bomb it carried, "Little Boy," was so heavy, Tibbets needed two miles of runway to get the plane aloft. His target was Hiroshima, a city with a population of more than a quarter-million people. It was also a military and communications hub, and headquarters for the army responsible for defending Kyushu.

The *Enola Gay* released Little Boy from an altitude of 31,000 feet—a distance of nearly six miles. It fell for forty-three seconds before detonating in midair, a half-mile over the center of Hiroshima. The blast, the equivalent of 15,000 tons of TNT, began with a blinding flash before flattening four square miles of the city. Every structure above ground was eviscerated, as temperatures quickly reached thousands of degrees Fahrenheit, melting even stone and steel. The explosion generated shockwaves that shuddered the fleeing B-29 more than eleven miles away, as a boiling, white cloud billowed upward from the detonation point, pushing outward, and creating the infamous mushroom shape.

The blast killed an estimated 70,000 people, vaporizing many, and injured more than 70,000 others, most suffering severe burns. The victims had nowhere to turn for care after the explosion and ensuing fires destroyed the city's hospitals and claimed the lives of most doctors and nurses. In later days and weeks, thousands who were outside the immediate blast radius and appeared unhurt became sickened by radiation poisoning, with lethal consequences. By the end of the year, the death toll from the atomic bomb exceeded 140,000.

Two days after the explosion in Hiroshima, and with the Nazis already vanquished, Stalin finally fulfilled his pledge at Yalta. He launched a major offensive against Imperial Army forces in Manchuria, where Japan's once-mighty Kwantung Army was no match for the million-plus Soviet invaders. Military leaders in Tokyo were stunned by the twin blows in Hiroshima and Manchuria, but they remained resolute, refusing to believe the Americans had many more of their new weapons. They were right—Truman had just one more atomic bomb available at the moment. It was enough.

On August 9, another B-29 streaked toward the city of Kokura and its large military arsenal. Poor visibility forced the crew to divert to a secondary target, Nagasaki, nestled along the coast of Kyushu. The port city was a major shipbuilding center, with repair facilities, arms factories, and a naval ordnance plant that once produced the torpedoes used at Pearl Harbor.

The B-29 carried a bomb named "Fat Man," and unlike Little Boy, it was plutonium-fueled, similar to the Trinity test device. The bomb exploded over the city with the impact of 21,000 tons of TNT. It was a more powerful device than Little Boy, but the hills and ravines surrounding Nagasaki partially contained the blast, allowing the city to fare slightly better than the flatter Hiroshima. Still, an estimated 40,000 people were killed by the explosion and spread of fires, and another 60,000 injured. Within five years, the death toll in Nagasaki, including those who succumbed to radiation, matched that of Hiroshima.

THE FINISH

The destructive power of the American weapons, coupled with the intervention of a new enemy on the Asian mainland, began to sway the emperor. With the Americans on the cusp of unleashing an invasion army of extraordinary size, one his people could slow but not overcome, and sure to bring further suffering and ruin to his beloved country, Hirohito finally accepted the inevitable outcome.

His six-member war cabinet, however, remained divided. Three officials were willing to acquiesce to the Allied demands in exchange for assurances the imperial system would be preserved, but three others — the military chiefs — remained opposed, refusing to accept any military occupation of Japanese lands or judicial proceedings that would try the emperor and others as war criminals. Throughout his reign, Hirohito simply approved decisions made by his advisors, but with his cabinet in stalemate, the emperor had to end the impasse, overruling his military leaders and voicing his support for surrender. He recorded a message to the Japanese people announcing the final decision, and on August 14, after a last-minute coup d'état attempt by Army radicals was crushed by Imperial Palace troops, the message was broadcast nationwide. For all but a few Japanese, it was the first time they heard their divine emperor speak.

With the terms of surrender agreed upon, the first American occupation troops arrived in Japan in late August. On September 2, the official surrender ceremony was held in Tokyo Bay aboard Admiral Nimitz's flagship, the battleship USS *Missouri*. As Supreme Allied Commander, General MacArthur presided over the ceremony, with Admiral Nimitz serving as the signatory for the United States. Leaders from Britain, Australia, China, the Soviet Union, and other Allied countries joined the Japanese contingent, along with two special guests also in attendance: Lieutenant General Jonathan Wainwright, who surrendered American and Filipino forces on Corregidor in early 1942 and survived three years of harsh imprisonment, and British Lieutenant General Arthur Percival, another longtime prisoner of the Japanese following the defeat of his Commonwealth troops in Singapore. The ceremony was capped off with an awe-inspiring flyover of nearly 2,000 bombers and fighter planes, a fitting tribute to the industrial magic that powered American forces in the Pacific and played such a pivotal role in the Allied march to victory.

After a parade of signatures, World War II was finally over.

For six years, great military powers armed with the most lethal weapons, machinery, and technology ever assembled battled for supremacy, with the future of humanity at stake. In the skies and on the high seas, and across barren deserts, remote islands, and rolling farm fields, they produced a volume of death and destruction unrivaled in history. It would take a generation to recover from the utter devastation levied across much of Asia and Europe, where so many cities, towns, and villages had been battered into ruins, and the lives of untold millions of soldiers and civilians tragically cut short.

To the dismay of many, it was not long before conflict stirred again, in Europe and beyond, as brewing tensions between the Soviet Union and its former allies in the West reached a boiling point. The peace finally achieved in 1945 was followed by a standoff among the most powerful titans on the globe as former allies morphed into antagonists. Their animus and mistrust would persist for decades, transforming the geopolitical landscape for the next half-century and pushing the world once again to the brink of the unthinkable.

* * * * *

When the war ended in September 1945, over eight million American military personnel remained scattered across the world, awaiting their return to the US mainland. For nearly a year, Operation Magic Carpet ferried them home aboard more than 700 ships, including aircraft carriers, converted cargo vessels, battleships that survived the attack on Pearl Harbor, and even the British luxury liner *Queen Mary*. The massive sealift brought an average of 22,000 men and women home to America every day for a year.

CONCLUSION
THE DAWNING OF A NEW ERA

"We can well afford to pay the price of peace. The only alternative is to pay the terrible cost of war."
–President Harry S. Truman

When the assembled dignitaries aboard the USS *Missouri* inked their signatures on the final surrender documents, they closed the chapter on the darkest period in world history. Jubilation erupted across every corner of the globe, but among those who survived and bore witness to the worst horrors, the mood was more somber. The power of innovation and modern technology had exacted an astounding human toll and ravaged two continents with unprecedented devastation. Tens of millions were dead, and millions more carried physical and psychological scars that would never heal.

Generations later, we are still uncertain of just how many lives were lost. Broad estimates from China and the Soviet Union cloud the final tallies, but the number certainly exceeds sixty million. Unlike the previous world war, where killing was confined to the battlefields, civilians accounted for most of the fallen, exceeding military losses. At least twelve million Europeans alone—half of them Jews—died in Nazi concentration camps and killing centers; millions more were massacred in other settings. The human suffering was incalculable, with men, women, and children of all ages subjected to starvation, torture, enslavement, and rape.

The Axis powers were responsible for the savagery and would pay for their sins. More than three million Japanese and six million Germans died in the war, their population centers and industrial bases bombed into heaps of rubble and ash. Yet those who faced the brunt of early Axis aggression fared far worse, beginning with Poland, which lost one-sixth of its pre-war population to the Nazis. Soviet and Chinese casualties were worse, and almost beyond belief. Shouldering a hugely disproportionate share of the losses within the Allied coalition, estimates of their combined deaths are in the tens of millions.

Though casualties were far fewer among the Western powers, they were hardly insignificant. The British lost 384,000 servicemembers, as well as tens of thousands of civilians who perished in bombing raids and rocket attacks on their home soil. France's military losses — 217,000 killed — were topped by their civilian losses, numbering over 350,000, while American military deaths were higher than both France and Britain, with more than 418,000 personnel killed. Geography was America's savior, sparing the country from the human and physical carnage so many others could not escape.

The depravity of the Germans and Japanese would not go unpunished. The Allies convened international military tribunals to hold key figures accountable after late-war discoveries revealed the full breadth of their monstrous deeds. In trials held in Tokyo and Nuremberg, the cross-section of military, political, and industrial leaders charged by the Allies was intentionally broad, showcasing rampant complicity within each country. In Tokyo, twenty-eight defendants, including former Prime Minister Tojo, were brought to trial. Most were found guilty, with seven sentenced to hang and sixteen others to life imprisonment. In Nuremberg, twenty-two Germans were tried; of those, twelve were sentenced to death and others to lengthy prison terms. Thousands of other Japanese and Germans would eventually face justice, including the many Nazis brought before smaller courts across Europe and the Soviet Union. Former concentration camp commandants and guards, Nazi Party officials, municipal leaders, and others who colluded in the atrocities would answer for their crimes, though a substantial number eluded authorities by fleeing to other continents.

In the months following the German and Japanese surrenders, political and economic volatility continued to plague much of Europe and Asia. Living conditions across both continents were abysmal, with millions in squalor, and most infrastructure—road and rail networks, hospitals, schools, power plants, bridges, dams, factories, and farms—either destroyed or severely damaged. As winter neared, scarce housing and heating fuel portended a humanitarian crisis, as did plummeting agricultural production and food supplies that left millions on the brink of starvation. Parts of Europe were rife with disease, lawlessness, and continued ethnic violence long after the war had concluded. Compounding the struggles, barely functioning communities were saddled with an additional burden—the flood of countless war refugees uprooted and displaced from their native lands.

Post-war conditions were most dire in Germany and Japan, where Western leaders were determined to heed the lessons of the prior world war. In 1919, the imposition of vindictive, draconian measures against a beaten enemy had been calamitous, fueling radical nationalism and the birth of the Nazi Party. Fully demilitarized in 1945, the Japanese and Germans (those living within the boundaries of Western occupation authorities) would instead be encouraged to rebuild their broken countries and rejoin the global community.

In Japan, newly arrived American occupation forces expected a hostile reception from defiant worshippers of the emperor resistant to political or cultural reforms, but the Japanese people were surprisingly deferential. In time, they willingly embraced a conversion to democratic rule, and in 1946, a new constitution drafted by occupation authorities was ratified, tilting the balance of political power away from the emperor to an elected legislature and independent judiciary. New laws expanded rights and opportunities for women, and by the time the occupation formally ended in 1952, the country had reconstituted much of its industrial base. Growth and modernization followed, with Japan evolving into a commercial superpower, a beacon of democracy in the Far East, and a stalwart strategic ally of the United States.

The post-war transition in Europe proved far rockier. The fissure between Stalin and his former allies widened each passing month, driven by sharply diverging geopolitical interests. What Churchill coined as an "iron curtain" descended across Europe, splitting Stalin and his communist puppet regimes from neighboring democratic states in the West. The United States took steps to blunt the further spread of Stalinism, beginning in 1947 with the Truman Doctrine, pledging financial and military support to democratic states under threat from authoritarians. That was followed a year later by an ambitious proposal crafted by George C. Marshall, Roosevelt's wartime Army chief of staff and Truman's secretary of state, to revitalize war-torn Western Europe. In pumping more than $13 billion in direct grants and loans into struggling communities and industries, the Marshall Plan proved a success, rebuilding infrastructure, boosting industrial and agricultural production, and opening new markets for American-made goods.

As American economic aid continued to pour into Europe, Stalin eyed every dollar with suspicion. Amid worsening relations between the two powers, a dozen North American and European countries formed NATO, a mutual defense alliance aimed at deterring aggression from the East. Tensions ratcheted up further in 1949, after the Soviets tested their first atomic device. It was remarkably similar to the plutonium bomb dropped on Nagasaki, thanks to a Soviet spy ring operating inside the United States furnishing key design elements. Stalin's acquisition of atomic power sparked a frenetic nuclear arms race between East and West, leading to the production of the deadliest arsenals ever known to humankind. The bad blood persisted for decades, long after Stalin died in 1953, until the anemic Soviet political and economic systems finally collapsed in 1991.

· · · · ·

The Second World War was the defining event of the twentieth century. It was precipitated by those pursuing hate-filled quests for global and racial supremacy, who expropriated and plundered vast lands and resources in the name of self-anointed destinies. They subjugated, persecuted, and murdered those they conquered while imposing utterly barbaric conditions wherever they reigned. Rising in opposition was an extraordinary coalition of Western democracies, Soviet communists, and Chinese nationalists, all forsaking deep-seated political and cultural differences to defeat a shared enemy of humanity. Prevailing after six agonizing years of bloodshed and sacrifice, the post-war peace they achieved was fleeting, as long-simmering tensions among former allies escalated into conflict and crisis again. Ideological battle lines were redrawn, the international order was remade, and onetime compatriots became rival powers, just a single misstep away from a third world war.

Though Europe and the Far East weathered considerable economic and social upheaval during the war years, it was the United States and Soviet Union that experienced the most profound change. The two countries began the war mired in years of domestic strife and regarded by many as second-tier players on the global stage. Both were fundamentally transformed after realizing their military and manufacturing potential and unleashing it on their adversaries. Unstoppable on the battlefield, each evolved into a dominant geopolitical force.

The speed of change inside the United States was breathtaking. After prolonged economic decline, America was clearly unprepared for war of such magnitude, and yet uniquely suited for it, with abundant raw materials, an idling labor force itching to come off the sidelines, and an industrial sector primed for explosive growth. Pearl Harbor became a catalyst, and in a remarkably brief time, the war economy roared to life, delivering jaw-dropping volumes of weapons, munitions, and machinery, pioneering technologies, and the greatest naval and air forces ever assembled. Social change came too, with record job growth, and women and African Americans finally afforded long-overdue opportunities and standing.

In diplomatic circles, Roosevelt joined early with Churchill in assuming the mantle of global leadership. Britain was hampered, though, by wartime losses and a depleted treasury, while America emerged stronger than ever. An expected drawdown of its military forces came in the post-war years, but with flush coffers and atomic power fully harnessed, Truman was well-positioned to lead the West, promoting and defending democratic interests and values wherever they were threatened.

The Soviet Union also vastly improved its fortunes during the war years, much of it due to the remaking of its military. Throughout the 1930s, Stalin had adeptly consolidated his power within Soviet borders but enjoyed little esteem outside them. Though the pre-war Red Army was impressive in size, political purges had crippled its officer corps, diminishing its caliber, and leading to early-war stumbles. As the war progressed, a largely agrarian economy was revolutionized by a manufacturing boom, as thousands of new factories swelled Soviet forces with new tanks, planes, and heavy guns. After triumphing against Hitler, Stalin capitalized on this military might and the national pride and patriotic unity coursing among the Soviet people. He expanded his domain and influence, strong-arming neighboring states and bolstering communist regimes and movements abroad. When the Soviet Union was officially named one of five permanent members on the new United Nations Security Council, placing it on equal footing with the United States, Britain, France, and China, Stalin basked in his newfound prestige. The Soviet ascent was complete.

Less than five years after the surrender ceremony aboard the *Missouri*, a tenuous peace fell apart when a proxy war erupted on the Korean Peninsula. The North Korean communist regime, backed by the Soviet Union and newly formed People's Republic of China, invaded its southern neighbor, the Republic of Korea, eliciting a forceful response from the fledgling United Nations. Refusing to allow such an incursion to go unanswered, the UN authorized a US-led international force to defend South Korean sovereignty, and it was not long before American soldiers and Marines were at war again, this time grappling with North Korean and Chinese communists, from the port city of Inchon to the frigid, forbidding mountains surrounding the Chosin Reservoir.

The vigorous, multilateral response to developments on the Korean Peninsula was due in large part to the lessons of World War II—lessons that continue to shape the world we know today. The new institutions, agreements, and alliances that arose from the ruins of Europe and Asia were intended to ensure such inhumanity and unspeakable atrocities were never again repeated. Much would depend on the capacity of those who aspired to Roosevelt's Four Freedoms to avoid the early paralysis and indecision that emboldened the likes of Adolf Hitler to impose their political and racial doctrines on others. The collective failure in the late 1930s to challenge those who sought to ruthlessly exploit ethnic and religious divisions and animosities for their own fiendish purposes, with little care for the autonomy and welfare of others, produced the most hellish conditions and worst suffering the world has ever known. It is a lesson humanity cannot afford to learn again.

A NOTE ABOUT SOURCES

The three years I labored on this book were a joyful, albeit hand-wringing experience. As I poured myself into the research, fears of blundering some piece or pieces of history persistently gnawed at my conscience. I had confidence in my research skills, but I am not a trained historian, and I was genuinely surprised how much conflicting information is out there on factual matters that are now decades old. In the end, I was as diligent as I could be, relying on the most credible sources, but if there are factual errors or inaccuracies, the responsibility is mine.

I want to acknowledge the extraordinary work of so many historians and writers over the decades who tirelessly sifted through endless records, reports, logs, images, and memoirs from the war. As a result of those efforts, a trove of secondary sources has been produced, and I used more than two hundred of these invaluable works in the course of my research. Among those I relied on the most, I offer my profound gratitude to the authors that penned the following accounts—*The Oxford Guide to World War II* (I.C.B. Dear); *A World at Arms: A Global History of World War II* (Gerhard Weinberg); *A War to Be Won: Fighting the Second World War* (Williamson Murray and Allan Millett); *The Story of World War II* (Donald Miller); *World War II: America at War 1941-1945* (Norman Polmar and Thomas Allan); *The Second World War* (Martin Gilbert); and *Total War: A People's History of the Second World War* (Kate Clements, Paul Cornish, and Vikki Hawkins).

Other sources that were indispensable include the US Army's Center for Military History, a publisher of numerous books and other resources, including *The US Army Campaigns of World War II* series; the Marine Corps Historical Association, and their *Marines in World War II Commemorative Series*, published during the 50th anniversary of the end of the war; and a host of other organizations who have made so many articles, oral histories, images, and documents available on their public web pages. Among the best are sites sponsored by the Naval History and Heritage Command, the United States Holocaust Museum, and the National World War II Museum. In each case, a roster of historians, researchers, writers, web and graphic designers, and more have contributed to a spectacular array of easily accessible, digital materials. For readers who would like to explore any aspect of the war in greater detail, I cannot recommend the aforementioned resources enough.

ACKNOWLEDGMENTS

The complexity and breadth of World War II, perhaps the most consequential event in modern human history, made this project the most challenging I have ever taken on. To borrow a bit from Churchill, never has one person who thought he knew so much discovered how little he actually knew. Though it was truly a joy to dive into the reading and research material, I simply could not have produced a worthy product without a team of superheroes by my side who not only lent their expertise, insights, and critical reviews to this project, but did so willingly and enthusiastically.

Among those who weighed in on early drafts, or made themselves available as sounding boards are Professor Kenneth Waltzer, my favorite instructor from my Michigan State days and one of the country's leading Holocaust scholars; Dr. Nick Mueller, President Emeritus at the National World War II Museum; Professor Louise Young at the University of Wisconsin; Professor David Krugler (also an outstanding novelist!) at the University of Wisconsin-Platteville; Nick Reynolds, former Marine Corps and CIA historian; and David Hatch, historian with the National Security Agency and National Cryptological Museum.

So many profound thanks are also due to my early readers—Neal Duckworth, Julia Gimbel, and Dean Strang—who provided a bounty of suggested fixes, course corrections, and other needed improvements. Among the many others who provided their expertise along the way, or otherwise weighed in with assistance: Roger Meade, Ray Smith, Jay Venables, Alex Kutler, Steve Wheeler, Corina Rogers, Don Mitchell, Eben Carle,

Katie Smith, Anthony Tully, Matthew Leitch, Joris Nieuwint (best battlefield guide in the Netherlands!), Dr. Robert Gaynes, and Lieutenant Commander Anthony Ivester and Lieutenant Ian McConnaughey of the Naval History and Heritage Command. Special recognition to Laura Hatcher, graphic designer extraordinaire and the talent behind the visually appealing maps used in these pages to orient readers in key chapters, and Joyce Mochrie, a truly exceptional editor and wordsmith who prevented me from butchering the King's English and committing assorted gaffes and blunders.

As always, my greatest gratitude is reserved for my family — my wife, children, parents, siblings, and others. They have long been my most faithful and devoted supporters as I continue on a writing journey that has been such a spiritual lift in my midlife years.

Finally, much appreciation to Reagan Rothe, David King, and the entire team at Black Rose Writing – I have so enjoyed working with these pros on my last two books, and I hope to continue this partnership in the future.

INDEX

100th Infantry Battalion (United States) - 215
101st Airborne Division (United States) - 126, 140, 141, 152, 154
106th Infantry Division (United States) - 153
10th Armored Division (United States) - 154
1st Airborne Division (Britain) - 140, 141, 143
1st Infantry Division (United States) - 128
1st Marine Division (United States) - 288, 292, 304, 305
1st Marine Regiment (United States) - 305
1st SS Panzer Division (Germany) - 155
27th Infantry Division (United States) - 301-302
29th Infantry Division (United States) - 128
2nd Marine Division (United States) - 299, 301
32nd Army (Japan) - 329, 330
332nd Fighter Group (United States) - 202
3rd Infantry Division (Britain) - 127
3rd Infantry Division (Canada) - 127
3rd Marine Division (United States) - 322
442nd Regimental Combat Team (United States) – 215-216, 218
477th Bombardment Group (United States) - 201
4th Armored Division (United States) - 155
4th Infantry Division (United States) - 127
4th Marine Division (United States) - 301
50th Infantry Division (Britain) - 127
588th Night Bomber Aviation Regiment - 81
5th Marine Division (United States) - 322, 326
6th Marine Division (United States) - 331
6th Naval Construction Battalion (United States) - 295
761st Tank Battalion (United States) - 201, 207
7th Infantry Division (United States) - 331
81st Infantry Division (United States) - 305
82nd Airborne Division (United States) - 97, 140, 142, 146
92nd Infantry Division (United States) - 200, 215
96th Infantry Division (United States) - 331
99th Infantry Division (United States) - 153, 157
99th Pursuit Squadron (United States) - 202
9th Armored Division (United States) - 160-161
Aachen - 144
Abyssinia - 17
Afrika Korps - 84, 86, 88, 90
Agricultural Adjustment Administration - 62, 171
Air Force (see Army Air Forces)
Akagi - 282
Albania - 165
Aleutian Islands - 278
Alexander, Harold - 93, 94, 95
Algeria - 83, 87, 91
American Indians - 326
Amphibious Tractors (Amtracs) - 299, 300, 304, 321
Angels of Bataan - 267
Anti-Comintern Pact - 235
Antisemitism - 13, 38, 111, 112, 114
Antwerp - 143, 151, 153
Anzio - 98, 99
Ardennes - 36, 37, 150-152, 155-157, 160
Arizona - 212, 213, 243, 248, 250, 251, 252, 253
Armenia - 67
Army (see United States Army)
Army Air Corps - 176, 200, 201
Army Air Forces - 108, 177, 189, 190, 201, 269, 271, 304
Army Corps of Engineers - 220
Army Group A (Germany) - 36-37
Army Group B (Germany) - 36, 124
Army Group C (Germany) - 36
Army Nurse Corps - 187
Arnhem - 137, 139-143
Arnold, Henry "Hap" - 271
Arsenal of Democracy - 175, 176, 237

Asiatic Fleet - 238, 259, 260
Assembly Centers - 212
Associated Press - 324
Athenia - 54
Atlantic Charter - 59
Atlantic Fleet - 238
Atlantic Wall - 124, 127
Atomic Energy - 167, 193, 219-221, 227, 344
Attlee, Clement - 164-165
Auschwitz - 117
Australia - 50, 51, 83, 262, 264, 277, 283, 288, 350
Austria - 3, 9, 18, 19, 25, 112, 114, 193, 201
Auxiliary Territorial Service - 52
Avenger Torpedo Bomber - 180
Azerbaijan - 67
B-17 *Flying Fortress* - 106, 178, 195, 247, 260, 261, 262, 280
B-24 *Liberator* - 106, 178
B-25 *Mitchell* - 270, 272, 273, 275, 343
B-29 *Superfortress* - 195, 304, 307, 321, 325, 336, 337, 338, 339, 343, 347, 348
Babi Yar - 116
Badoglio, Pietro - 96
Banzai - 291, 293, 294, 303, 305, 306, 333
Barbarossa - 65, 67, 68, 74, 75, 79, 113
Basilone, John - 294
Bastogne - 153-155
Bataan - 261, 262, 266, 315
Bataan Death March - 262
Bataan Peninsula - 262
Bath Iron Works - 181
Battle of Leyte Gulf - 312, 314, 316, 317
Battle of Savo Island - 289, 292
Battle of the Bulge - 149, 156, 185
Battle of the Philippine Sea - 302
Battleship Row - 245, 248, 249
Bavaria - 11, 20, 135
Beaulieux, Jules - 33
Beijing - 235
Belgium - 3, 17, 35-38, 40, 101, 134, 137, 144, 150, 152-153, 155, 201
Belzec - 117
Bergen-Belsen - 121
Berlin - 18, 19, 28, 45, 46, 60, 69, 78, 79, 88, 114, 115, 144, 156, 162-166, 176, 179, 235
Bernatitus, Ann - 266-267
Bestebreurtje, Arie - 146-147
Betio Island - 299
Big Three - 123, 159
Birkenau - 117
Bismarck - 57
Bittrich, Wilhelm - 140
Black Panthers (see 761st Tank Battalion)
Black Tuesday - 170
Bletchley Park - 56, 60
Blitz - 45-47, 105

Blitzkrieg - 3, 27, 28, 31, 36, 71, 78, 137
Bloody Nose Ridge - 305
Bocage - 130
Bomber Command - 103, 104, 108
Borneo - 259
Bouck, Lyle L. Jr. - 157
Boulogne - 37
Bremen - 103
Brereton, Louis - 261
British Army - 42, 48, 146, 175
British Expeditionary Force - 37
British Malaya - 4, 258-259
Bronze Star - 157, 202, 207, 216
Brown vs. Board of Education - 198
Buchenwald - 114
Buckner, Simon B. Jr. - 334
Buffalo Division (see 92nd Infantry Division)
Bulgaria - 149, 165
Burma - 50, 263, 297
Bush, Robert E. - 335
Bushido - 293, 294
Cactus Air Force – 290, 291
Caen - 126, 128, 130
Calais - 37, 125, 126, 127, 129
California - 248
Camp Stewart - 208
Campbell, John - 53
Canada - 50, 54, 58
Caroline Islands – 233, 304
Casablanca - 93
Cash-and-Carry - 55-56
Cassino - 98
Caucasus - 67, 69, 75
Cavite Naval Base - 260-261
Celebes - 259
Central Intelligence Agency - 194
Ceylon - 50
Chain, Ernst - 145
Chamberlain, Neville - 25, 26, 49
Chelmno - 116, 117
Cherbourg - 126
China - 4, 56, 172, 173, 175, 229, 230, 231, 233-236, 238-240, 243, 260, 270, 272, 273, 275, 297, 319, 336, 343, 345, 350, 352, 358
China-Burma-India Theater - 297
Chinese Nationalists - 4, 263, 356
Chippewa - 326
Chosin Reservoir - 358
Chrysler - 185
Churchill, Winston - 25, 42, 43, 47-50, 58, 85, 86, 93, 98, 99, 123, 151, 159, 165, 175, 259, 297, 355, 357
Civilian Conservation Corps - 61
Clark, Mark W. - 97-100
Clinton Engineer Works - 222
Cobra - 131

Code Talkers - 326
Cold War - 165, 174
Cologne - 103, 161
Columbia River - 222
Comanche - 326
Commissars - 73
Commonwealth of Nations - 50
Concentration Camps - 7, 15, 19, 27, 113, 115, 116, 121, 161, 162, 201, 211, 213, 352, 354
Congress - 3, 5, 16, 39, 50, 55, 56, 61, 62, 86, 179, 190, 197, 206, 217, 237, 250, 342, 343
Congressional Gold Medal - 195
Conter, Louis - 243
Convoys - 54-57, 60, 84, 138, 180, 238, 291
Coral Sea - 277, 278, 279, 285, 290
Corregidor - 262, 263, 267, 315, 350
Corsair Fighter Plane - 266
Cotentin Peninsula - 126
Crimea - 160
Crimean Peninsula - 159
Czechoslovakia - 3, 18, 19, 25, 26, 40, 112, 165
Dachau - 15, 113, 120
Danzig - 26, 28, 29
Dauntless Dive Bomber - 282, 290
D-Day - 124, 126, 129, 130, 133, 207, 303
De Gaulle, Charles - 40-41
Death's Head Division - 114
Denmark - 3, 34, 40, 57
Detroit - 177, 185, 197, 205, 208
Detroit Tank Arsenal - 185
Devastator Torpedo Plane - 281, 282, 284
Dewey, Thomas E. - 343
DeWitt, John L. - 210
Diet - 240
Distinguished Flying Cross - 202
Distinguished Service Cross - 157, 193, 194, 218
Dodge - 178
Doolittle Raiders - 273, 278, 292, 343
Doolittle, James - 270-274
Double V - 199, 206
Downfall 336, 340, 341, 344, 346
Draft - 86, 174, 191, 200, 214, 237
Dresden - 107
Drumbeat - 57
Dunkirk - 37, 41, 42
Dutch East Indies - 4, 255, 258, 259
Dutch Resistance - 147
East Prussia - 26, 90, 132
Eben-Emael - 36
Egypt - 83-86
Eighth Air Force (United States) - 105
Eighth Army (Britain) - 85, 86, 88, 94-95
Eindhoven - 140
Einsatzgruppen - 30-31, 69, 113, 116

Einstein, Albert - 219
Eisenhower, Dwight D. - 1, 87-89, 94-96, 99, 100-101, 123-126, 135, 138, 149, 150, 152, 155, 156, 159, 161-163
El Alamein - 85-86
Elbe River - 162
Electoral College - 61, 101-102, 331
Elrod, Henry - 265
Elsenborn Ridge - 153
Enabling Act - 15
Endo vs. United States - 217
Endo, Mitsuye - 217
Enigma - 56, 59-60
Enola Gay - 347
Enterprise - 180, 271, 279, 280-282, 292, 316
Escort Aircraft Carriers - 57, 313, 317
Essen - 103, 161
Essex-class - 180
Estonia - 66
Euthanasia - 116
Evans, Ernest E. - 316
Exclusion Zones - 212
Executive Order 8802 - 205
Executive Order 9066 - 212
Executive Order 9981 - 206
F4U (see *Corsair* Fighter Plane)
F4F (see *Wildcat* Fighter Plane)
F6F (see *Hellcat* Fighter Plane)
Factories - 3, 44, 46, 50, 56, 61, 70, 76, 86, 103, 106, 107, 109, 115, 117, 161, 162, 170, 173, 176-177, 182-184, 188, 192, 205, 266, 272, 338, 348, 354, 358
Falaise - 131
Falaise Pocket - 131
Farm Credit Administration - 171
Fat Man - 348
Federal Bureau of Investigation - 211-212
Fermi, Enrico - 221
Fifteenth Air Force (United States) - 105, 108
Fifteenth Army (Germany) - 125
Fifth Air Force (United States) - 310
Fifth Panzer Army (Germany) - 153
Fighter Command - 44-46, 48
Fillmore, Millard - 229
Final Solution - 110, 115
Finland - 67-68, 149
Fireside Chats - 62, 175, 176
First Army (Canada) - 144
First Army (United States) - 126, 144
First Sino-Japanese War - 230
First United States Army Group - 125
First World War (See World War I)
Fission - 219-221
Fleet Aircraft Carriers - 180
Fleming, Alexander - 145
Flight Nurses - 196

Florey, Howard - 145
Flying Fortress (see B-17)
Ford Island - 245
Ford Motor Company - 170, 177
Fore River Shipyard - 182
Formosa - 230, 261, 318, 333
Fort Des Moines - 204
Fort Hood - 207
Foss, Joseph - 290
Four Freedoms - 197, 359
France - 2-3, 6, 17-19, 28, 33-42, 45, 49, 54, 55, 83, 84, 85, 90, 91, 93, 94, 99, 100, 107, 114, 123-124, 130-134, 137-140, 144, 154, 155, 191, 193, 194, 201, 215, 233, 236, 353, 358
Franco, Francisco - 17
Frank, Anne - 120-121
Frantisek, Josef - 51
Fredendall, Lloyd - 88
French Indochina - 238, 239
French Resistance - 39-40, 130, 194
Frigidaire - 178
Frost, John - 141-143
Fuchs, Klaus - 167
Gallipoli - 49
Gallup - 193, 236
Gavin, James - 147
Gay, George - 284
Gela - 95
General Government (Poland) - 29
General Motors - 178
Georgia - 67, 72
Gestapo (Geheime Staatspolizei) - 16, 21, 39, 40, 90, 113, 114, 121, 151, 194
Ghettos - 112-113, 115-116, 121
GI Bill - 206, 209
Gilbert Islands - 299
Gleiwitz - 27
Goebbels, Joseph - 110
Gold Beach - 127
Gomorrah - 105
Göring, Hermann - 43-44, 46, 77, 120, 166
Gothic Line - 99
Great Depression - 3, 14, 61, 62, 170, 172, 173, 179, 226, 232, 235, 241, 252, 266
Great Patriotic War - 71
Great Terror - 66
Great War (see World War I)
Great White Fleet - 170
Greater East Asia Co-Prosperity Sphere - 237
Greece - 40, 67, 95
Grotjan, Genevieve - 241
Groves, Leslie R. - 219, 221-223
Guadalcanal - 287-293, 295, 298, 299, 301, 302, 310, 316, 321, 325, 330, 332, 333
Guam - 263, 268, 284, 304

Guerillas - 39, 71, 311
Gulags - 66
Gustav Line - 98
Halifax Heavy Bomber - 105
Hall, Theodore - 167
Hall, Virginia - 193
Halsey, William Jr. - 271, 272, 279, 310, 312-314, 316
Hamburg - 105, 107
Hanford - 222-224
Hanover - 121
Harris, Sir Arthur - 103-105
Harz Mountains - 134
Hawaii - 4, 190, 212, 214, 215, 218, 231, 236, 244-248, 255, 256, 257, 259, 260, 268, 278, 279
Heck, Alfons - 21-22
Hedgerows - 130-131
Hell's Highway - 141
Hellcat Fighter Plane - 180, 266, 298, 302, 318
Helldiver Dive-Bomber - 180
Henderson Field - 290-292, 295
Higgins Boats - 128
Himmler, Heinrich - 15, 120, 166
Hirohito - 233, 239-240, 272, 292, 345, 349
Hiroshima - 347-349
Hiryū - 282
Hitler Youth - 18, 22, 23, 112, 164
Hitler, Adolf - 2, 3, 6, 11-12, 14-20, 25, 27, 30, 35, 38, 42, 43, 46, 49, 66-69, 71, 73, 75-79, 84, 85, 94, 96, 88-91, 108-112, 120, 125, 129, 131-133, 137, 145, 149-151, 159, 161, 163, 164, 166, 197, 359
Hobby, Oveta Culp - 186
Holcomb, Thomas - 200
Holland - 3, 35, 36, 38, 40, 124, 132, 137, 139, 143, 146, 147, 149, 201, 244
Holodomor - 72
Hong Kong - 263
Honshu - 340
Hood - 57
Hoover, Herbert - 171
Hornet - 271, 272, 279-282, 284, 292
Horses - 74
Houston - 259
Huertgen Forest - 144
Hughes, Langston - 197
Hull, Cordell - 239
Hungary - 9, 68, 117, 165
Hurricane Fighter Plane - 45-46
II Corps (United States) - 88, 89
II Waffen-SS Panzer Corps (Germany) - 140
Imperial Japanese Army - 4, 231, 233-235, 239, 243, 250, 255, 258, 259, 260, 263, 273,

274, 289, 291, 293, 297, 301, 305, 325, 329, 333, 348
Imperial Japanese Navy - 234, 251, 258, 260, 277, 290, 302, 311, 312, 314-317, 330, 332, 336, 341
Imperial Palace - 272, 340, 349
Inchon - 358
India - 50, 83, 98, 114, 297
Indonesia - 259
Inouye, Daniel - 218
International Military Tribunal - 119, 353
Internment Camps - 211
Inukai, Tsuyoshi - 234
Iran - 123
Iron Bottom Sound - 292
Iron Curtain - 355
Island Hopping - 297, 298
Issei - 211, 212, 215, 217
Italy - 3, 5, 11, 17, 18, 19, 68, 84, 93-94, 96-100, 102, 105, 123, 149, 200, 202, 208, 209, 215, 218, 237
Iwo Jima - 294, 321-323, 325-327, 329, 330, 334
Japanese Americans - 62, 210-216
Japanese Combined Fleet - 244, 251
Java - 260
Java Sea - 259, 260
Jedburghs - 146
Jemez Mountain - 223
Jews - 6, 11, 13, 15, 17-22, 30, 38, 39, 62, 67, 69, 79, 110-118, 120-121, 134, 352
Jim Crow - 197, 198
Johnston - 316
Joyce, Richard - 268
Jungvolk - 22
Juno Beach - 126, 127
Kaga - 277, 282
Kaiser Shipyards - 181
Kai-Shek, Chiang - 233, 235, 239, 263, 297
Kamikazes - 185, 267, 317-318, 333, 334, 341
Kasserine Pass - 88-89
Katyn Forest - 30
Kellogg's - 178
Kesselring, Albert - 97-99
Kiev - 116, 162
Killing Centers - 7, 115-119, 162, 352
Kimmel, Husband E. - 245-247
King, Ernest J. - 269
Kinkaid, Thomas - 310, 312, 313, 316
Kleiss, Norman "Dusty" - 277
Kobe - 272, 339
Kokura - 348
Konoe, Fumimaro - 239
Korea - 230, 265, 358
Korean Peninsula - 101, 343, 358
Korematsu vs. United States - 216-217

Korematsu, Fred - 216
Kraków - 117
Kremlin - 68, 72, 73, 269
Kriegsmarine - 43, 54, 57, 127
Krier, Mae - 195
Kristallnacht - 19, 112
Kuribayashi, Tadamichi - 322-325
Kursk - 75, 78-79, 81, 162
Kwantung Army - 348
Kyushu - 340-341, 347, 348
Labor Unions - 205
Lancaster Heavy Bomber - 105
Lanzarath Ridge - 157
Latvia - 66
Lax, Peter - 219
League of Nations - 6, 9, 16, 17, 26, 234
Lebensraum - 12, 67, 79
Legion of Merit - 147, 267
LeMay, Curtis - 336, 338-340
Lend-Lease Act - 56, 71, 177, 179
Lenin, Vladimir - 65
Leningrad - 69, 70, 162
Lexington - 278
Leyte - 311-314, 332
Leyte Gulf - 309, 312, 314, 316, 317
Liberator (see B-24) Heavy Bomber
Liberty Ships - 181
Libya - 83-84, 86
Lightning Fighter Plane - 251, 266
Lincoln, Abraham - 204, 211
Lionel Toy Company - 178
Lithuania - 66
Little Boy - 347, 348
Lodz - 113, 116
Long Lance Torpedoes - 266
Lorraine - 144
Los Alamos - 223-225, 227, 344
Low Countries - 35, 37, 45
Lower Rhine - 139, 143
Luftwaffe - 22, 28, 34, 36, 43-47, 54, 68, 76, 77, 79, 83, 97, 103, 104, 106, 107, 127, 133, 161, 163, 166, 175
Lunga Point - 288, 289
Luxembourg - 35, 36, 144
Luzon - 261, 311, 314-315
MacArthur, Douglas - 100, 260-262, 264-265, 266, 283, 297-298, 304, 306, 309-311, 314-315, 325, 337, 343, 349
Magic Carpet - 351
Maginot Line - 35, 36
Malayan Peninsula - 258
Malaysia - 258
Malmédy - 157
Manchuria - 4, 230, 234, 348
Manhattan Engineer District - 221
Manhattan Project - 219-221, 222, 224-227
Manheim - 135

Manifest Destiny - 231
Manila - 261, 267, 311, 314-315
Manila Bay - 262, 315
Manzanar Relocation Center - 213
Maquis - 39
Mariana Islands - 233, 301, 304, 312, 321, 337, 338, 347
Marianas Turkey Shoot - 302
Marine Corps War Memorial - 324
Market-Garden - 139, 143-144, 146, 154
Marseille - 131
Marshall Islands - 233, 299, 301
Marshall Plan - 343, 355
Marshall, George C. - 337, 355
Marx, Karl - 72
Mason - 203
McAuliffe, Anthony - 155
McCarthy, John - 287
Medal of Honor - 207, 218, 265, 294, 306, 316, 335
Mediterranean - 34, 83-85, 88, 89, 93, 94, 96, 100, 101, 104, 215, 326
Mediterranean Sea - 84
Meetinghouse - 336, 338, 343
Mein Kampf - 12, 18, 33, 65, 67
Merchant Marine - 53, 58, 206
Messerschmitt 109Es - 44
Messerschmitt Me262 - 108
Messina – 94, 95-97
Metz - 144
Meuse (Maas) River - 36, 139, 140, 151, 153, 155, 157
Midway - 277-285, 287, 290, 302, 310, 316
Milice - 38
Military Order of Williams - 147
Miller, Bert - 213
Miller, Doris "Dorie" - 252
Miller, J. Howard - 195
Mincemeat - 95
Missouri - 265, 284, 349, 352, 358
Mitchell (see B-25) Medium Bomber
Model T - 170
Model, Walter - 161
Monte Cassino - 98
Montgomery, Bernard Law - 83, 85-86, 89, 94-97, 130, 135, 138, 143, 145
Morocco - 83, 87, 91, 93
Moscow - 26, 28, 68, 69, 70, 71, 75, 78, 86, 149, 162, 227, 238
Moselle River - 144
Mukden - 234
Munich - 12, 15, 18, 20, 113
Munich Agreement - 3, 18, 25
Musashi - 312-313
Mussolini, Benito - 3, 11, 12, 17, 18, 84, 93, 94, 96, 102
Mustang Fighter Plane - 106, 107, 109, 202

Myanmar - 50, 263
Nagasaki - 347-349, 356
Nagoya - 272, 339
Nagumo, Chūichi – 244-246, 248, 249, 250, 258, 279-281
Nanking - 235, 236, 273
Napalm - 338
National Socialist German Workers' Party (see Nazi Party)
Nationalist Party (China) - 233
Navajo - 326
Naval Construction Battalions (Seabees) - 203, 289, 295
Naval Expansion Act - 179
Navy (see United States Navy)
Navy Cross - 252, 295
Navy Nurse Corps - 187, 266
Nazi Party - 2, 11, 12, 14, 15, 20, 29, 111, 354
Neutrality Acts - 16, 55
Nevada - 249
New Deal - 61, 171-172, 173
New Guinea - 264, 277, 283, 297
New Zealand - 50, 51, 98, 288
Nicholas II - 65
Nigeria - 50
Night of the Long Knives - 16
Night Witches - 81
Nijmegen - 142, 146, 147
Nimitz, Chester W. - 277, 278, 279, 283-284, 288, 297-299, 301, 306, 325, 349-350
Nineteenth Amendment - 186
Nisei - 210, 212, 215
NKVD - 30
Normandy - 39, 90, 99, 101, 107, 125-127, 129-133, 137, 146, 154, 202, 207, 295, 301, 340
North Africa - 83-90, 93, 100, 128, 134, 202, 208
North American Treaty Organization (NATO) - 101, 355
North Korea - 265, 358
North Sea - 34, 160
Norway - 3, 34, 40, 54
Nuremberg Laws - 17
Oahu - 244-249
Oak Ridge - 222-223
Odachi, Kazuo - 317-319
Oder River - 162
Office of Strategic Services - 146, 194
Official Secrets Act - 60
Okinawa - 267, 295, 329-335, 336, 337, 340, 341
Oklahoma - 248, 250
Olympic - 340-341
Olympic Games - 18, 134, 146
Omaha Beach - 123, 126, 128, 129, 207

Oneida - 326
Oosterbeek - 140, 143
Open Door Policy - 234
Oppenheimer, J. Robert - 221, 223, 225
Oradour-sur-Glane - 40
Osaka - 272, 339
Overlord - 123-124, 126, 137
Owens, Jesse - 18
P-38 (see *Lightning*)
P-40 (see *Warhawk*)
P-47 (see *Thunderbolt*)
P-51 (see *Mustang*)
Pacific Fleet - 4, 238, 245, 249-251, 252, 257, 269, 271, 277, 278, 283, 298
Packard Motors - 205
Pact of Steel - 19
Palermo - 95
Panay – 235-236
Panther Tank - 31, 78-79
Patrol, Torpedo (PT) Boat - 262
Patton, George S Jr. - 88, 89, 94-96, 98, 101, 125, 127, 129, 131, 134-135, 138, 144-145, 149, 155-156
Paulus, Friedrich - 76-78
Pearl Harbor - 4, 5, 71, 87, 146, 199, 211, 214, 216, 220, 236, 238, 240, 244, 247, 249-253, 255-258, 260, 261, 263, 268, 269, 271, 274, 278, 279, 280, 283-285, 288, 301, 304, 314, 334, 348, 351, 357
Peiper, Joachim - 155, 157
Peking - 235
Peleliu - 304-306, 309, 322, 330
Penicillin - 145-146
Pentagon - 221
People's Republic of China - 358
Percival, Arthur - 258, 259, 350
Perkins, Frances - 172
Perry, Matthew C. - 229, 230
Pershing, John - 100
Pétain, Henri Phillipe - 38
Petrograd - 65
Philippine Sea - 302
Philippines - 100, 169, 220, 231, 238, 240, 246, 255, 260-264, 266, 268, 269, 297, 304, 309-312, 314-316, 329, 340
Placentia Bay - 59
Plessy vs. Ferguson - 198
Plutonium - 220-222, 224, 225, 227, 344, 348, 355
Pogroms - 110
Poland - 1, 2, 19-20, 25-31, 32, 40, 47, 49, 53, 66, 67, 112, 113, 114, 116, 119, 156, 160, 162, 165, 191, 219, 236, 353
Polish Corridor - 26
Portsmouth Naval Shipyard - 181
Potsdam - 164-166, 342, 344, 345
POWs (see Prisoners of War)

Presidential Unit Citation - 201, 216
Prince of Wales - 258, 260
Prinz Eugen - 57
Prisoners of War (POWs) - 73, 116, 124, 240, 263, 346
Project Y - 221
Proximity Fuse - 184
Puerto Rico - 169
Purple Heart - 207, 216
Purple Heart Battalion (see 100th Infantry Battalion)
Putsch - 12
Pyrenees Mountains - 194
Queen Mary - 351
Rabaul - 288, 289, 291, 298
Radar - 44, 45, 46, 48, 51, 52, 55, 57, 191, 247, 256, 261, 280, 284-285, 289
RAF (see Royal Air Force)
Randolph, A. Philip - 205
Rape of Nanking - 238
Raskova, Marina - 81
Rats of Tobruk - 84
Ravensbrück - 19, 114
Red Air Force - 81
Red Army - 28, 66-71, 73, 75, 76, 78, 123, 149, 156, 162, 163, 357
Red Ball Express - 202
Red Tails - 202
Refugees - 112, 354
Reichstag - 14, 15, 17, 27, 164
Relocation Centers - 213
Remagen - 160-161
Republic of Korea - 358
Repulse - 258, 260
Reynaud, Paul - 37-38
Rhine River - 139, 145, 150, 160, 161, 163
Rhineland - 17, 21, 28, 160
River Rouge - 178
Robinson, Jackie - 207
Rogers, Edith Nourse - 188
Roma - 19, 114, 118
Romania - 68, 76, 77, 149, 165
Rommel, Erwin - 84-91, 124, 125, 127-130, 132, 133, 137
Roosevelt Administration – 56, 198, 204
Roosevelt, Franklin D. - 4, 5, 14, 16, 39, 49, 55, 56, 58, 60-62, 85, 87, 93, 94, 128, 151, 164, 171, 175, 176, 197, 198, 204, 205, 206, 211, 212, 217, 219, 220, 221, 235, 236, 237, 238, 250, 261, 264, 268, 297, 331, 342, 345, 357
Roosevelt, Theodore - 170
Rosenthal, Joe - 324
Rosie the Riveter - 195
Rosie the Riveter National Historic Park - 195

Royal Air Force - 43-46, 48, 50, 51, 55, 83, 103, 104
Royal Navy - 34, 41, 43, 48, 50, 54, 57, 258
Ruhr Pocket - 161
Ruhr Valley - 12, 105, 139, 161
Sachsenhausen - 114
Saint-Lô - 131
Saipan - 301-304, 306, 321, 333, 341
Salerno - 97, 98
Salomon, Benjamin - 306
Samurai - 229, 291, 293
Santee - 317
Saratoga - 180, 257, 292, 316
Savo Island - 289, 292
Scheldt River - 143
Schutzstaffel (SS) - 14
Sea Lion - 43, 46
Sea of Japan - 269
Seabees (see Naval Construction Battalions)
Second Army (Britain) - 126
Sedan - 37
Segregation - 5, 197, 198, 206
Selective Training and Service Act - 174, 237
Seppuku - 294
Seventh Army (Germany) - 125, 127, 131
Seventh Army (United States) - 94, 96, 131
Seventh Fleet (United States) - 310, 316
Shanghai - 234, 235
Sherman Tanks - 31
Shibasaki, Keiji - 299-301
Shipbuilding - 54, 58, 105, 179-181, 316, 348
Short, Walter C. - 245, 246
Sicily - 94-97, 100, 128, 134, 135
Signal Intelligence Service (US Army) - 241
Silver Star - 157, 216, 275, 295
Singapore - 258-259, 310, 350
Sixth Army (United States) - 310, 312, 315
Sixth Army (Germany) - 76, 77, 78
Sixth SS Panzer Army (Germany) - 153, 155
Slave Labor - 7, 29, 69, 115, 134, 231, 263
Slovakia - 68
Smith, Holland - 302
Smith, Nels H. - 213
Smith, Rothacker - 208
Sobibor - 117
Social Security Act - 62, 172
Solomon Islands - 266, 288, 290, 297
Sōryū - 282
South Korea - 265, 358
Soviet-German Nonaggression Pact - 66
Soviet Union - 2, 13, 19, 20, 25, 28, 30, 40, 49, 56, 65, 66-68, 73, 74, 79, 80, 96, 104, 112, 123, 191, 220, 225, 226, 241, 269, 273, 345, 350, 352, 354, 356, 357, 358
Spain - 3, 17, 95, 169, 194
Spanish Civil War - 17
Spanish-American War – 169, 233
Special Naval Landing Forces - 299, 301
Special Operations Executive - 194
Special-Attack Corps - 317
Spitfire Fighter Plane - 45-46, 133
St. Lo - 317
St. Vith - 153
Stalin, Joseph - 12, 49, 65, 66, 68, 69, 71, 72-73, 75, 76, 78, 80, 81, 101, 118, 123, 159, 160, 162, 163, 165, 166, 167, 343, 348, 355, 356, 357, 358
Stalingrad - 75-78, 89, 162
Stalinism - 355
Stark, Harold R.- 239
State Department - 194
Station Hypo - 285
Steel Production - 161, 169
Stimson, Henry - 234
Strategic Bombing - 104, 107, 337
Stratton, Donald - 252-253
Stuka Dive-Bomber - 44, 45
Sturmabteilung (SA) - 11
Sudetenland - 3, 18
Suez Canal - 83
Suicide Boats - 341
Sulphur Island - 323
Sumatra - 259
Superfortress Heavy Bomber (see B-29)
Supreme Headquarters Allied Expeditionary Forces (SHAEF) - 124, 125
Suribachi - 322-324
Sweden - 3, 33, 134
Switzerland - 3, 146
Sword Beach - 126, 127
Szilard, Leo - 219
T-34 Tank - 31, 70, 78, 79
Taffy 3 - 313, 316
Taiwan - 230
Taranto - 97
Tarawa – 298-299, 301, 304, 305, 325, 334
Tassone, Aurelio - 295
Taylor, George - 123
Tehran - 123, 159
Tennessee Valley Authority - 171, 222
Tenth Air Force (United States) - 297
Tenth Army (United States) - 330
Thailand - 258
Third Fleet (United States) – 310, 316
Third Reich - 15, 21, 25, 29, 42, 49, 104, 111, 114, 149, 159, 164, 166
Thunderbolt Fighter Plane - 202
Tibbets, Paul - 347
Tiger Tank - 31, 78, 79

Tinian - 304, 347
Tobruk - 84, 86
Tojo, Hideki - 239, 303, 353
Tokyo - 4, 165, 166, 176, 231, 232, 234, 235, 237, 238, 241, 243, 246, 260, 265, 272, 277, 292, 301, 304, 332, 336, 337, 338, 339, 340, 343, 345, 346, 348, 353
Tokyo Express - 291
Torch - 86-87, 91, 100
Toulon - 131
Trade Embargo - 239
Treasury Islands - 295
Treblinka - 117, 121
Trinidad and Tobago - 50
Trinity - 225, 226, 344, 345, 348
Tripartite Pact - 237
Truman Doctrine - 355
Truman, Harry S. - 164, 166, 206, 226, 265, 331, 334, 339, 340, 342-343, 344, 345, 346, 347, 348, 352, 355, 357
Tsukamoto, Mary - 210
Tunisia - 83, 86-89
Turing, Alan - 60
Turkey - 194
Tuskegee Airmen - 201-202
Two-Ocean Navy Act - 179
U-boats - 53-54, 57, 58, 60, 104, 105, 179
Ukraine - 69, 75
Umurbrogol Mountain - 304
Underwood Typewriter Company - 178
Union of Soviet Socialist Republics (USSR) - 65, 72, 73
United Nations - 59, 160, 265, 284, 358
United Nations Security Council - 358
United States Army - 2, 87, 88, 100, 108, 125, 154, 161, 187, 208, 210, 214, 218, 220, 245, 260, 264, 291, 303, 326
United States Fleet - 236, 238, 269
United States Marine Corps - 181, 188, 189, 200, 203, 204, 206, 256, 265, 266, 278, 288, 290, 301, 324
United States Navy - 61, 182, 191, 229, 235, 238, 244, 252, 266, 277, 283, 285
University of Chicago - 221
University of Hawaii - 215
Uranium – 219-221, 224, 344
Uranium Ore - 220, 224
US Coast Guard Women's Reserve - 189
US Marine Corps Women's Reserve - 189
Ushijima, Mitsuru - 330-333
Utah Beach - 126, 127
V-1 Rocket - 133-134, 185
V-2 Rocket - 133-134, 161
Vancouver - 180
Vandegrift, Alexander A. - 204, 287
Versailles, Treaty of - 9-11, 13, 16, 17, 18, 20, 25, 26, 59, 111, 233

Vichy - 38, 83, 87, 91, 114
Victory Gardens - 177, 184
Victory Ships - 181
Victory Tax - 183
Vietnam - 174, 238
Volga River - 76, 77
Volkssturm - 164
Von Bolfras, Artur - 1
Von Cholitz, Dietrich - 131
Von Hindenburg, Paul - 14-16
Von Rundstedt, Gerd - 137, 138, 149
Von Stauffenberg, Claus - 132
Waal River - 139, 140, 142
Wacht am Rhein - 150
Waffen-SS - 114, 150, 157
Wainwright, Jonathan - 262, 263, 350
Wake Island - 256-257, 265, 268
Wannsee - 115
War Bonds - 183
War Department - 146, 177, 190, 212, 213, 215, 221, 271, 287, 344
War Relocation Authority (WRA) - 212
Ward - 247
Warhawk Fighter Plane - 260, 265
Warsaw - 2, 28, 29, 113, 117
Warsaw Ghetto - 121
Wasp - 292
Wehrmacht - 21, 43, 54, 59, 74, 131, 137, 150, 162, 164
Weimar Republic - 10
West Point - 100, 134, 264
West Virginia - 248, 252
Western Hemisphere - 55, 57, 169
Westerplatte - 28
Westwall - 137, 138, 156
White, Thomas - 275
Wildcat Fighter Plane - 256, 265, 290
Wilhelm II, Kaiser - 10
Wilhelmina Canal - 141
Willow Run - 177
Wilson, Woodrow - 9, 61
Wolf's Lair - 132
Wolfpacks - 55, 56, 60
Women Accepted for Volunteer Emergency Service - 188
Women Airforce Service Pilots - 189-190
Women's Army Auxiliary Corps - 186, 188
Women's Army Corps - 188
Women's Auxiliary Air Force - 51
Women's Auxiliary Ferrying Squadron - 189
Women's Flying Training Detachment - 189
Women's Royal Naval Service - 52
Woodson, Waverly B. Jr. - 207-208
World War I - 2, 44, 55, 88, 100, 172, 179, 260, 264, 268, 270

XXX Corps (Britain) - 139, 141, 143
Yalta - 159-160, 164, 348
Yamamoto, Isoroku - 244, 250, 251, 255, 263, 274, 278, 279, 282
Yamashita, Tomoyuki - 310-312, 314, 315
Yamato - 312, 313, 332
Yangtze River - 235

Yokaren - 317
Yokohama - 272
Yorktown - 278-283
Yugoslavia - 40, 67
Zero Fighter Plane – 265-266, 280, 281, 282, 290, 298, 318, 321
Zyklon-B - 116

ABOUT THE AUTHOR

Andy Kutler is a strategic communications professional and an award-winning writer and author. His books include *Honorable Profession, The Batter's Box,* and *The Other Side of Life,* and he has also written extensively for The *Huffington Post* and The *Milwaukee Journal Sentinel*. Over a 30-year career in government and industry, Andy has worked in the United States Senate, the US Secret Service, and the national security community. A Wisconsin native, Andy lives with his wife and two children in Arlington, Virginia.

OTHER TITLES BY ANDY KUTLER

NOTE FROM ANDY KUTLER

Word-of-mouth is crucial for any author to succeed. If you enjoyed *The Fight of Their Lives,* please leave a review online — anywhere you are able. Even if it's just a sentence or two. It would make all the difference and would be very much appreciated.

Thanks!
Andy Kutler

We hope you enjoyed reading this title from:

www.blackrosewriting.com

Subscribe to our mailing list – *The Rosevine* – and receive **FREE** books, daily deals, and stay current with news about upcoming releases and our hottest authors.
Scan the QR code below to sign up.

Already a subscriber? Please accept a sincere thank you for being a fan of Black Rose Writing authors.

View other Black Rose Writing titles at www.blackrosewriting.com/books and use promo code **PRINT** to receive a **20% discount** when purchasing.

Made in the USA
Middletown, DE
08 June 2024